W9-BZN-171

ACCOUNTING THOUGHT AND PRACTICE THROUGH THE YEARS

Edited by Richard P. Brief

A Garland Series

HF
5625
.E88

ESTIMATING THE ECONOMIC RATE OF RETURN FROM ACCOUNTING DATA

Richard P. Brief, editor

OCT 9 1986

Garland Publishing, Inc.
New York and London
1986

472536

For a complete list of Garland's publications in accounting,
please see the final pages of this volume.

The papers in this volume are reprinted with the permission of the journals, editors, and publishers listed in the table of contents.

Copyright © 1986 by Richard P. Brief

Library of Congress Cataloging-in-Publication Data

Estimating the economic rate of return from accounting data.

(Accounting thought and practice through the years)
Includes index.
1. Accounting. 2. Rate of return. I. Brief, Richard P., 1933– . II. Series.
HF5625.E88 1986 657'.48 86-12004
ISBN 0-8240-7857-8

Design by Bonnie Goldsmith
The volumes in this series are printed on
acid-free, 250-year-life paper.
Printed in the United States of America

CONTENTS

Introduction

INTRODUCTION

The articles and notes reprinted in this book address the problem of using accounting data to estimate the economic rate of return. In all of these papers, which were written over the last twenty years, the economic rate of return is defined as the internal rate of return on a series of cash inflows and outflows. While the economic interpretation of the internal rate of return has been questioned, many economists seem to agree that "the economic rate of return on an investment is . . . that discount rate that equates the present value of its expected net revenue stream to its initial outlay."[1]

Most of this work has sought to determine the conditions under which the accounting rate of return would be a "good" estimate of the economic rate of return. While the detailed models differ, the general idea underlying several of the more influential articles is as follows. The firm is assumed to invest in a project or mix of projects depreciated by a standard method such as straight-line depreciation or sum-of-the-years digits depreciation. The project generates a series of cash flows. The firm is assumed either to reinvest a fixed percentage of its cash flows or to grow at a constant rate. Depending on the specific assumptions made about these variables, a steady-state situation is reached. A comparison is then made of the accounting rate of return with the economic rate of return.

In a sense, all of this research can be traced to the early efforts made by actuaries to find a simple approximation for the yield on an annuity or a bond.[2] However, there is a significant difference between the motivation for finding an approximation to the interest rate and the problem of estimating the economic rate of return from accounting data. In approximating the rate of interest on an annuity or bond, complete information about cash flows is given and the approximation of the interest rate is necessary because of the difficulty of finding a solution to a polynomial equation. Obviously, with modern computers the problem of approximating the interest rate has become obsolete.

On the other hand, most of the articles concerned with the problem of estimating the economic rate of return from accounting data have assumed that information about the firm's cash flows is not available, at least directly. It is the absence of such information that provides the motivation for using accounting data to estimate the economic rate of return.

Ten articles and six notes and comments are reprinted in this volume. Seven of these papers were published in British journals and the rest appeared in U.S. publications. While these writings are available in most libraries, bringing them together in one book should facilitate research on this important subject.

The first article reprinted in this anthology is by Harcourt (1965), who compared the accounting and economic rates of return under a variety of assumed conditions. His final comment was that "any 'man of words' (or 'deeds' for that matter) who compares rates of profit of different industries, or of the same industry in different countries, and draws inferences from their magnitudes as to the relative profitability of investments in different uses or countries, does so at his own peril." Fisher, who overlooked this article in his 1983 study with McGowan, commented in his 1984 reply that "of all the literature, Harcourt's valuable article is perhaps the one most closely related to our own work."[3]

Solomon's 1966 paper is also a classic in the field. He studied the relationship between the accounting rate of return (book yield) and the economic rate of return (true yield) in the no-growth and growth situations under different assumed conditions about the life of a project, capitalization policy, depreciation policy, inflation, and lags in cash flows. The basic conclusion was simply that the accounting rate of return is "not a reliable measure" of the rate of return on investment.

Zeff's comment on Solomon's paper gives a short history of the subject and also sketches a proposed solution to the problem, which seems to suggest that some method of direct calculation of the economic rate of return might be feasible.

Vatter's article is also a comment on Solomon, and in private correspondence[4] Vatter said that he thought this article was "loves labor lost!" Basically, Vatter was critical of the idea that the purpose of calculating a period's accounting rate of return was to estimate the economic rate of return. He showed that the same answer would be obtained by discounting cash flows at the book rate or the internal rate of return: "The book yields for individual years, (which Solomon dismissed as misleading and capricious), will discount the cash receipts to exactly $1,000, just as the 10 per cent average rate did! . . . Evidently, the 'distorted' annual rates of return still have as much validity as the 10 per cent 'true' yield." Peasnell, in his 1982 article reprinted here, proved this result.

Solomon's second article on the subject is an elaboration of his earlier work where he once again points out the hazards of using the accounting rate of return to estimate the economic rate of return. Cautioning against the misuse of "rates of return," Solomon stresses that accounting and economic rates of return are different things, not estimates of the same thing.

The next item in this book is by Livingstone and Salamon. They review and synthesize the earlier work area and then, using examples that assume different cash-flow profiles, project lives, economic rates of return, and the proportion of cash flows reinvested, discuss the relationship between the accounting rate of return and the economic rate of return. Livingstone and Salamon conclude that these variables must be analyzed jointly. They also found that a constant reinvestment rate tends towards a constant rate of growth in gross investment.

The 1971 article by Stauffer extends and qualifies Solomon's results, but his conclusion is basically the same: " the accounting rate of return is generally a very poor proxy for the economic . . . rate of return, which is relevant either for capital budgeting decisions within the firm or for external assessment of the firm/industry's market performance." Stauffer's analysis assumes that the firm invests in a project and reinvests a fixed proportion of cash flows in each period in identical projects. The investment process associated with this assumption is described by a Voltera integral equation of the second kind; the associated mathematics is not easy.[5] Within the framework of this model, Stauffer analyzes the impact of cash-flow time shapes, depreciation methods, capital structure, and income taxes on the relationship between two accounting-based rates of return and the economic rate of return.

Next is an article by Kay, followed by Wright's comment, Kay's reply, and a note on Kay's work by Stark.[6] Kay derived an algorithm that purports to estimate the economic rate of return from accounting data. However, as Wright points out, the algorithm assumes that the accountant's figure for the firm's book values at the beginning and end of the multiperiod time horizon over which the economic rate of return is estimated is equal to the value of the firm at these points of time. Stark then noted that if this assumption is correct, the economic rate of return could be calculated directly by finding the rate of return that equates the firm's initial value with its discounted future cash flows (counting the terminal point value as the final cash flow).

Thus, while Kay's method does not really bring us any closer to finding a solution, it does identify the "terminal value" problem as one of the central issues in attempting to estimate the economic rate of return from accounting data. In other words, the deficiency in Kay's method makes it quite apparent that the problem of estimating the economic rate of return boils down to one issue, namely, estimating the firm's cash flows over its uncertain future.

Whittington's paper takes a slightly different tack. He attempts to "define those uses in which the deficiencies of ARR [accounting rate of return] are relatively unimportant and to identify the specific sources of deficiencies in ARR, so that they can be corrected or allowed for in uses in which they are potentially important." While Whittington agrees that there are dangers inherent in using the accounting data to estimate the economic rate of return, he suggests that "the absence of better information will force him [the user of accounting information] to continue to use ARR, and it is better to define the nature of the peril and draw up safety rules, rather than to forbid the use of ARR." A point in this article is clarified by Whittington and Skerratt in the note that follows.

In the next paper Salamon tries to solve the problem of estimating the economic rate of return by proposing a method that is invariant to accounting methods, thereby avoiding some of the difficulties previous researchers have stressed. His method requires information about the firm's cash recovery rate and also depends on estimates of the time shape of cash flows, the growth rate in gross investment, the rate of inflation, and the life of the projects in which a firm invests. However, Salamon's method is based on a model that, as Brief points out in a note, in effect assumes that the firm's future cash flows grow at a constant rate. Obviously, the external validity of this assumption (which is in doubt) needs to be determined.[7] Nevertheless, Salamon's work is interesting and merits further study.

In many ways Peasnell's article is a synthesis of some of the earlier work, and its contribution is in its emphasis on the basic analytical aspects of accounting rates of return within the framework of the double-entry bookkeeping process. On the assumption of "clean surplus" and the articulation of the balance sheet and income statement, Peasnell presents a number of properties of accounting numbers. Since accounting is in part a statistical discipline, accountants should become better acquainted with these properties.

In addition to the writings reprinted in this volume, there have been a number of other articles, notes, and comments written on the subject, including:

L. A. Gordon, "Accounting Rate of Return vs Economic Rate of Return," *Journal of Business Finance & Accounting* (Autumn 1974), pp. 343–356.

F. K. Wright, "The Ex-Post Internal Rate of Return: Who Needs It?" *Accounting and Finance* (May 1979), pp. 71–79.

F. M. Fisher and J. J. McGowan, "On the Misuse of Accounting Rates of Return to Infer Monopoly Profits," *American Economic Review* (March 1983), pp. 82–97.

Ira Horowitz, "The Misuse of Accounting Rates of Return: Comment," *American Economic Review* (June 1984), pp. 492–493.

William F. Long and David J. Ravenscraft, "The Misuse of Accounting Rates of Return: Comment," *American Economic Review* (June 1984), pp. 494–500.

Stephen Martin, "The Misuse of Accounting Rates of Return: Comment," *American Economic Review* (June 1984), pp. 501–506.

Michael F. van Breda, "The Misuse of Accounting Rates of Return: Comment," *American Economic Review* (June 1984), pp. 507–508.

F. M. Fisher, "The Misuse of Accounting Rates of Return: Reply," *American Economic Review* (June 1984), pp. 509–517.

Peter F. Luckett, "ARR vs. IRR: A Review and Analysis," *Journal of Business Finance & Accounting* (Summer 1984), pp. 213–231.

Gerald L. Salamon, "Accounting Rates of Return," *American Economic Review* (June 1985), pp. 495–504.

Robert N. Anthony, "Accounting Rates of Return: Note," *American Economic Review* (March 1986), pp. 244–246.

Anthony's 1986 note, which is the latest paper written on the subject, claims that "a substantial part of the difference between the measurement of profitability by accountants and by economists can be eliminated by making two changes in accounting principles": (1) require companies to use annuity (economic) depreciation, and (2) recognize the cost of equity capital in financial reports.[8]

This latest proposal does not, of course, solve the problem, because it assumes a situation in which all relevant cash flows are known. As Zeff pointed out in his discussion of Solomon's 1966 paper, economic depreciation is a "weak reed for the very reason that the problem exists: uncertainty."

The search for a solution to the problem of using accounting data to estimate the economic rate of return has been an important episode in the history of accounting thought. The papers reprinted in this book are the foundation of this intellectual effort, which will, undoubtedly, continue in the future.

NOTES

1. F. M. Fisher and J. J. McGowan, "On the Misuse of Accounting Rates of Return to Infer Monopoly Profits," *American Economic Review* (March 1983), p. 83.

2. Gabriel Hawawini and Ashok Vora, eds., *The History of Interest Approximations* (New York: Arno Press, 1982).

3. F. M. Fisher, "The Misuse of Accounting Rates of Return: Reply," *American Economic Review* (June 1984), p. 510.

4. Letter of June 29, 1985.

5. Preinreich's much earlier work employs related methodology. See Gabriel A. D. Preinreich, "Annual Survey of Economic Theory: The Theory of Depreciation," *Econometrica* (July 1938), pp. 219–241; reprinted in R. P. Brief, ed., *Depreciation and Capital Maintenance* (New York: Garland Publishing, 1984). The model developed by Dorfman also has certain similarities to Stauffer's. See Robert Dorfman, "The Meaning of Internal Rates of Return," *Journal of Finance* (December 1981), pp. 1010–1022.

6. Stark's 1982 article actually appears after Whittington's, which is discussed below.

7. In addition, Stark, in a recent note that is forthcoming in the *Journal of Business Finance & Accounting*, has shown that the observed cash recovery rate, on which the estimate of the economic rate of return depends, is a biased estimate of the "true" cash recovery rate in Salamon's when current assets are factored into the analysis. Andrew W. Stark, "On the Observability of the Cash Recovery Rate."

8. The extensive literature on the subject of economic depreciation is directly related to the problem of using accounting data to estimate the economic rate of return. Many of the papers reprinted in this book or mentioned in this introduction cite these references.

ESTIMATING THE ECONOMIC RATE OF RETURN FROM ACCOUNTING DATA

THE ACCOUNTANT IN A GOLDEN AGE[1]

By G. C. HARCOURT

1. In Mrs. Robinson's celebrated article, 'The production function and the theory of capital',[2] it is not made clear whether the 'man of words', whose doings are contrasted with those of the 'man of deeds', is an economist or an accountant. It is assumed in this article that he is an accountant; and it is proposed to examine how accurate is the accountant's measure of the rate of profit under 'Golden Age' conditions where uncertainty is absent, expectations are fulfilled, and the rate of profit has an unambiguous meaning.[3] The following question is asked: would the answer obtained by using the accountant's measure of the rate of profit correspond
2 with what is known, under the assumed conditions, to be the right answer, namely, that the *ex post* rate of return equals the *ex ante* one. This does not seem to be an entirely pointless exercise, since a number of 'men of words', economists this time, have used the accountant's measure in their empirical investigations,[4] and conclusions have been drawn from both the relative and absolute sizes of their estimates. Thus, Minhas used cross-section studies of the rates of return in the same industries in different countries to test his hypothesis about factor-reversals; and Nevin was depressed by the stable, low level of rates of return in British manufacturing in the post-war period. But if it can be shown that the measure is faulty

[1] The writer is especially grateful to Professor H. F. Lydall for suggesting the research project on which this article is based and for his comments and help. He would also like to thank Mr. R. D. Terrell, members of the Departments of Economics and Commerce, University of Adelaide, and members of the Joint D.A.E.–Faculty Seminar, University of Cambridge. Miss J. M. Higgins checked the mathematical results.

[2] *Review of Economic Studies*, 1953–4, pp. 81–106, portion of which is reprinted in her *Collected Economic Papers*, vol. ii (Oxford: Basil Blackwell, 1960), pp. 114–31. All subsequent references are to the second source.

[3] 'To abstract from uncertainty means to postulate that no such (unexpected) events occur, so that the *ex ante* expectations which govern the actions of the man of deeds are never out of gear with the *ex post* experience which governs the actions of the man of words, and to say that equilibrium obtains is to say that no such events have occurred for some time or are thought liable to occur in the future' ('The production function and the theory of capital', p. 120). These conditions are assumed to prevail in this article.

[4] See, for example, Simon Kuznets, 'Long-term changes in the national income of the United States of America since 1870', pp. 78–88, in Simon Kuznets (ed.), *Income and Wealth, Series II* (International Association for Research into Income and Wealth, Cambridge: Bowes and Bowes, 1952); E. H. Phelps Brown and B. Weber, 'Accumulation, productivity and distribution in the British Economy, 1870–1938', *Economic Journal*, June 1955, especially p. 272 and pp. 283–8; T. Barna, 'The replacement cost of fixed assets in British manufacturing industry in 1955', *Journal of the Royal Statistical Society*, Series A (General), 1957, especially p. 25 and p. 30; 'On measuring capital', Chapter 5 of F. A. Lutz and D. C. Hague (eds.), *The Theory of Capital* (London: Macmillan, 1960), pp. 82–85; B. S. Minhas, *An International Comparison of Factor Costs and Factor Use* (Amsterdam: North-Holland Publishing Co., 1963), Chapter 5; E. Nevin, 'The cost structure of British manufacturing, 1948–61', *Economic Journal*, December 1963, especially p. 646.

even in the equilibrium conditions of a 'Golden Age', it is unlikely to prove a realistic measure in real world situations.

2. The article is in six sections. In section I the various cases which are examined and the assumptions of the article are outlined; the following sections deal in detail with each case; and a concluding section draws the findings together. The principal conclusion is that the accountant's measure of the rate of profit is extremely misleading, even under 'Golden Age' conditions. The measure is shown to be influenced by the pattern of the quasi-rents associated with individual machines in a stock of capital, the method of depreciation used, whether or not the stock of capital is growing, and by what assets are included in the stock of capital. What is more, no easy 'rules of thumb' which would allow adjustments for these factors to be made in the estimates emerge from the analysis.

I

1.1. Four main cases, each of which contains further sub-cases, are considered. The first case is that of the rate of profit, as measured by an accountant, in a business which has a balanced stock of identical machines. The second case concerns the rate of profit in a business, the gross investment in machines of which grows at a constant rate each year. Then, following a suggestion by Mr. H. R. Hudson, variants of the two cases are examined: in the balanced stock case, it is assumed that the accumulation of financial assets, which are purchased as a result of allowing for depreciation as the stock of machines builds up but before any replacement expenditure occurs, is included in the capital of the business; in the constant growth case, it is supposed that the accumulation of financial assets, which occurs from the beginning of the firm until the first year of replacement, plus the further accumulation associated with the difference between current depreciation allowances and replacement expenditure of subsequent years (the 'Domar effect'), are included in the capital of the business. The first two cases might be regarded as representative of stationary and growing 'Golden Age' economies respectively, because the capital in them consists entirely of physical assets. The second two cases can be regarded as representative of firms which hold financial assets as well, and which operate in 'Golden Age' economies. (Holdings of financial assets, of course, cancel out for an economy as a whole.)

1.2. For each of the four general cases, four special cases are considered: first, it is assumed that the machines are 'one-hoss shays' and that the expected quasi-rents of each year of operation are equal. This is referred to as the case of the constant q's, where q_i is the expected quasi-rent of year i ($i = 1,\ldots, n$, n being the life of the machine) and $q_1 = q_2 = \ldots = q_n$.

(With the present assumptions, expected and actual quasi-rents always coincide.) Cases (2) and (3) are those of falling and rising q's respectively; for convenience, it is assumed that $q_i = bq_{i-1}$ ($i = 2,..., n$), where $b < 1$ [case (2)], and $q_i = aq_{i-1}$ ($i = 2,..., n$) and $a > 1$ [case (3)]. Case (4) is a combination of cases (2) and (3); it is assumed that up to q_m ($m < n$),

4

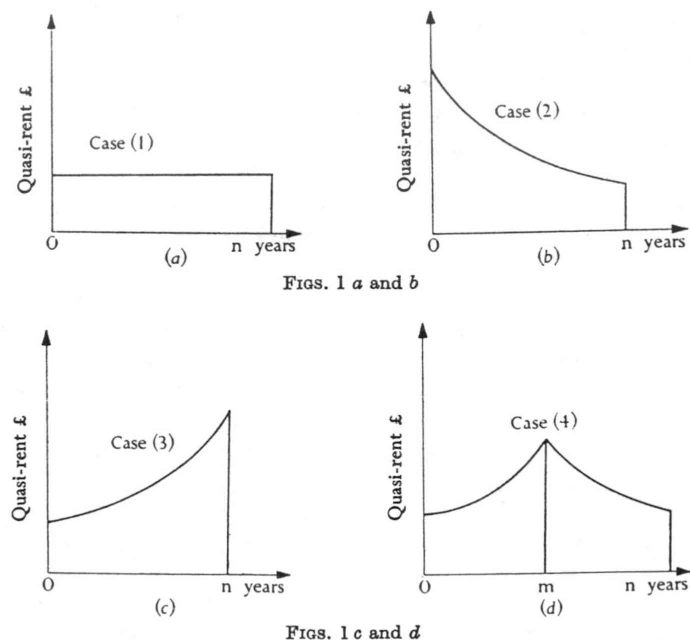

FIGS. 1 *a* and *b*

FIGS. 1 *c* and *d*

$q_i = aq_{i-1}$ ($i = 2,..., m$), $a > 1$; and from q_m on (but not including q_m), $q_j = bq_{j-1}$ ($j = m+1,..., n$), $b < 1$. The patterns of the quasi-rents over the life of a machine are shown for the four cases in Fig. 1. The cases most likely to be met in practice are cases (1), (2), and (4), with $m < \frac{1}{2}n$; perhaps (2) is the most common case. Prices and wages are assumed to remain constant so that the various patterns show the changes in productive efficiency over the lifetimes of the machines.

1.3. Let r be the expected rate of profit of each machine. The expected rate of profit in a 'Golden Age' is the internal rate of return—the rate of discount which makes the present value of the expected quasi-rents equal to the supply price of each machine. Then, because expectations are always realized in a 'Golden Age', and the rate of profit is uniform throughout the whole economy, it is known that each machine, and each business, is in fact earning r. The question which is analysed in this article is whether

the accountant's measure of the rate of profit gives a value of r for each of the four patterns of surpluses for each of the four cases. To answer it, two further sub-cases are introduced, the first assuming that the accountant uses straight-line depreciation when calculating annual accounting profit and the *book* value of capital, the second assuming that he uses reducing-balance depreciation. The accountant's measure of the rate of profit is taken to be the ratio of annual accounting profit to the average of the opening and closing book values of the assets in the business concerned. It is assumed, as is reasonable in a 'Golden Age', that any financial assets owned by a business themselves earn r. Expressions for the accountant's rate of profit for the two sub-cases of the four patterns of surpluses of the four types of businesses are presented in the remaining sections and their values for particular ranges of values of the relevant variables are examined. Where no clear-cut patterns in the accountant's
rate of profit were discernible when, for example, the length of life of 5
machines was varied, the numerical values of the rate of profit were found by running a programme on a computer.[1]

1.4. It is not suggested, of course, that an accountant could actually find employment in a 'Golden Age'. Rather, the article is concerned with what would happen if he were to use his customary box of tools in 'Golden Age' conditions. In non-'Golden Age' situations, the only way of finding out whether expectations concerning rates of profit have been realized is to ask accountants—or use their tools.

II

2.1. The first general case considered is that of a business, the capital of which consists of machines only; it is assumed that it owns a balanced stock of machines, which is already established. The accountant calculates depreciation by the straight-line method.[2] The following notation is used:

L number of machines in any age group and purchased in any year;

n length of life of a machine;

q_i expected quasi-rent in year i;

r expected rate of profit;

S supply price of machine: $S = \sum_{i=1}^{n} \frac{q_i}{(1+r)^i}$;[3]

[1] The writer is indebted to Dr. M. V. Wilkes, Mathematical Laboratory, University of Cambridge, for the use of EDSAC and to Dr. L. J. Slater and her assistants for programming the expressions.

[2] This case was first analysed by Joan Robinson in her paper, 'Depreciation', *Collected Economic Papers*, vol. ii, pp. 216–19.

[3] In a 'Golden Age', the supply prices of machines are always equal to the present values of the expected quasi-rents, the uniform rate of profit being the rate of discount. (See 'The production function and the theory of capital', p. 123.)

S^* $\sum_{i=2}^{n} \frac{q_i}{(1+r)^{i-1}}$;

Q $\sum_{i=1}^{n} q_i$; $Q^* = \sum_{i=2}^{n} q_i$;

K value of capital for the year as a whole;

k book value of capital for the year as a whole (no subscript indicates that straight-line depreciation is used, subscript RB indicates that reducing-balance depreciation is used);

d rate of reducing-balance depreciation; $d = 3/2n$;

A accounting profit (no subscript: straight-line depreciation; subscript RB: reducing-balance depreciation);

R^* accountant's measure of the rate of profit; $R^* = A/k$.

2.2. *If* the accountant were to value capital as the sum of the dis-
6 counted values of the expected quasi-rents, using r as the rate of discount, the value of capital for the year as a whole[1] can be shown to be:

$$K = \frac{L}{2r}[(Q+Q^*)-(S+S^*)].^2$$

The accounting profit for any year is:

$$A = L(Q-S),$$

so that R^*, *in this instance*, is

$$\frac{2r(Q-S)}{[(Q+Q^*)-(S+S^*)]}$$

which is approximately equal to r. That is to say, in this particular instance, if the accountant uses the economist's definition of the value of capital (in a 'Golden Age') and his own measure of accounting profit, the resulting expression for the rate of profit gives approximately the right

[1] Capital is valued for the year as a whole rather than at its beginning or end, because this procedure accords with the accounting practice of averaging the opening and closing values of assets when calculating annual rates of profit.

[2] Suppose that machines are bought at the beginning of each year and that incomes accrue at the end. The value of a balanced stock of capital at the *beginning* of any year (K^*) is:

$$K^* = L\left(\frac{q_n}{(1+r)}\right)+L\left(\frac{q_{n-1}}{(1+r)}+\frac{q_n}{(1+r)^2}\right)+\ldots+L\left(\frac{q_1}{(1+r)}+\ldots+\frac{q_n}{(1+r)^n}\right).$$

By gathering up terms and forming the appropriate geometric progressions,

$$K^* = \frac{L}{r}(Q-S)$$

is obtained.

Similarly, the value of capital at the *end* of any year (K^{**}) can be shown to be:

$$K^{**} = \frac{L}{r}(Q^*-S^*).$$

For the year as a whole, therefore,

$$K = \frac{L}{2r}[(Q+Q^*)-(S+S^*)].$$

answer. Once growth of the capital stock occurs, though, he would also need to use the economist's measure of depreciation (the decline in the value of capital from year to year), not one of his own, in order for this approach to give approximately the right answer.[1]

2.3. However, the accountant is more likely to use the average *book* value of capital for the year as his measure of the value of capital. This can be shown to be $\frac{1}{2}LnS$;[2] and, it follows,

$$R^* = \frac{2(Q-S)}{nS}. \tag{1}$$

In general, this expression is not equal to r. In the 'one-hoss shay' case,

$$R^* = \frac{2}{n}\left\{\frac{nr}{1-\{1/(1+r)\}^n}-1\right\}. \tag{1 a}$$

As $n \to \infty$, $R^* \to 2r$. However, the approach is not monotonic increasing: 7
at $n = 1$, $R^* = 2r$; it then falls to a minimum value, which is always greater than r, at values of n which are related to r itself. For example, when $r = 5$ per cent, the minimum value of R^* occurs between the tenth and twentieth year; when $r = 30$ per cent, it occurs between the fifth and tenth year. That is, in the 'one-hoss shay' case, the accountant's measure of the rate of profit will give different answers for two businesses which are alike in every respect except that the machines of one are longer-lived than those of the other. If, for example, the rate of profit is 30 per cent, the accountant's answer for $n = 5$ years is 42·1 per cent and for $n = 30$ years, 53·1 per cent.

2.4. In passing, it could be mentioned that American studies show that some businessmen estimate rates of return as the ratio of accounting profit

[1] H. R. Hudson discussed this point and gave the formula for 'correct' depreciation in an unpublished paper which was read to the Seminar on Economic Growth, held in the University of Adelaide in August 1960. See, also, H. R. Hudson and Russell Mathews, 'An aspect of depreciation', *Economic Record*, June 1963, pp. 232–6.

[2] At the beginning of any year the *book* value of the machines in the business (k^*) is:

$$k^* = LS+L\left(S-\frac{S}{n}\right)+...+L\left(S-\frac{(n-1)S}{n}\right).$$

By gathering up terms and forming the appropriate arithmetic progressions,

$$k^* = \frac{LS(n+1)}{2}$$

is obtained.

Similarly, the *book* value at the end of any year can be shown to be:

$$k^{**} = \frac{LS(n-1)}{2}.$$

For the year as a whole, therefore, $$k = \frac{LnS}{2}.$$

The remaining expressions in the article may be obtained by following procedures similar to those in this footnote and n. 2, p. 70.

to the *gross* (that is, undepreciated) value of assets. The book value of capital when straight-line depreciation is used is half the gross value. If the investment projects concerned are 'one-hoss shays' and n is large, the accounting rate of profit would approximately equal r. Expression (1 a) may therefore provide a theoretical justification for this business practice.[1]

2.5. The corresponding expressions for cases (2), (3), and (4)—falling; rising; and rising, then falling quasi-rents—are:

$$R^* = \frac{2}{n}\left\{\frac{(1-b^n)(1+r-b)}{(1-b)[1-\{b/(1+r)\}^n]}-1\right\}; \tag{1 b}$$

for case (3) read a (>1) for b; (1 c)

8

$$R^* = \frac{2}{n}\left\{\frac{\dfrac{a^m-1}{a-1}+a^{m-1}\left(\dfrac{b(1-b^{n-m})}{1-b}\right)-\dfrac{1-\{a/(1+r)\}^m}{1+r-a}-a^{m-1}\left\{\dfrac{b[1-\{b/(1+r)\}^{n-m}]}{(1+r-b)(1+r)^m}\right\}}{\dfrac{1-\{a/(1+r)\}^m}{1+r-a}+a^{m-1}\left\{\dfrac{b[1-\{b/(1+r)\}^{n-m}]}{(1+r-b)(1+r)^m}\right\}}\right\}. \tag{1 d}$$

2.6. In case (2), $R^* \to 0$ as $n \to \infty$. There is a value of n where $R^* = r$, as R^* is greater than r for $n = 2$. The rapidity with which this occurs, for certain values of the variables, is shown in Table I.

TABLE I

Values of R^*, case (2) *(balanced stock, physical capital)*
(percentages)

r	n				
	2 *years*	5 *years*	10 *years*	20 *years*	30 *years*
	(non-bracketed figures, $b = 0{\cdot}5$; *bracketed figures,* $b = 0{\cdot}9$)				
5	6·7 [7·4]	3·7 [5·7]	2·0 [4·9]	1·0 [3·8]	0·1 [3·0]
10	13·4 [n.a.]	7·4 [n.a.]	4·0 [n.a.]	2·0 [n.a.]	1·3 [n.a.]
20	n.a. [30·3]	n.a. [24·4]	n.a. [21·4]	n.a. [16·4]	n.a. [12·5]
30	40·8 [46·0]	22·5 [37·9]	12·0 [33·5]	6·0 [25·2]	4·0 [18·9]

Would it be too fanciful to suggest that the low levels of rates of profit which Nevin found in British manufacturing may in part be due to a combination of quasi-rent patterns similar to those of case (2) and rather large n's?

2.7. In case (3), the value of R^* is greater than r (and the values of R^* for cases (1) and (2)) at small values of n, falls slightly as n increases, but then quickly increases, approaching ∞ as $n \to \infty$. With $a = 1{\cdot}1$, $n = 20$ years, and $r = 30$ per cent, R^* is already 108·8 per cent; with $a = 1{\cdot}5$,

[1] The writer is indebted to Mr. F. K. Wright for bringing this practice to his notice.

the corresponding figure is 796 per cent! (R^* is not defined for the case of $1+r = a$.) Case (4) is a combination of cases (2) and (3). For given values of n, the value of R^* lies in between the values of R^* of the two previous cases.[1] As $m \to n$, the case (3) result comes to dominate the expression; as $m \to 0$, the case (2) result comes to dominate. This is illustrated in Table II where certain values of R^* for cases (2), (3), and (4) are shown; r = 10 per cent, $a = 1{\cdot}3$, $b = 0{\cdot}7$, and n = 20 years. Just by a fluke of counterbalancing forces, the accountant's measure could give the right answer in case (4).

TABLE II

Values of R^*, cases (2), (3), and (4), varying values of m (balanced stock, physical capital, straight-line depreciation) (percentages)

9

R^*	m		
	5 *years*	10 *years*	15 *years*
Case (2)	3·3	3·3	3·3
Case (4)	6·3	13·3	24·3
Case (3)	36·3	36·3	36·3

TABLE III

Values of R^*_{RB}, case (1) (balanced stock, physical capital, reducing-balance depreciation) (percentages)

r	n					
	2 *years*	5 *years*	10 *years*	20 *years*	30 *years*	50 *years*
5	10·1	5·2	3·7	3·4	3·4	3 6
10	20·3	10·7	7·9	7·5	7·8	n.a.
30	62·6	35·5	28·1	28·0	28·6	n.a.

2.8. In the article referred to in footnote 1, p. 71, Hudson and Mathews show that if the quasi-rents decline at a particular linear rate, straight-line depreciation is 'correct'. Substituting this pattern in (1) gives $R^* \simeq r$ for moderately large n, say > 10. ($R^* = r$, whatever n, if annual accounting profit is averaged as well as the annual book values of capital.)

2.9. If the accountant calculated annual depreciation by the reducing-balance method, the general expression becomes

$$R^*_{RB} = \frac{Q-S}{S\{\frac{1}{2}(2n-1)-e\}}, \tag{2}$$

[1] There is an exception to this statement when $m \leqslant 1$; but this result can be ignored as it has no economic relevance.

where $$e = \frac{d(n-1)(1-d)-d^2(1-d^{n-1})}{(1-d)^2}.$$

The expressions for cases (1) to (4) are not shown but can be easily derived from expression (2). In case (1) at $n = 2$, $R^*_{RB} > r$; it then quickly drops below r, reaches a minimum and, as $n \to \infty$, $R^*_{RB} \to r$. (See Table III.)

The results for cases (2), (3), and (4) are similar, in the sense that they show the same general patterns for variations of n, to those for the corresponding cases using straight-line depreciation. For $n = 2$, $R^*_{RB} > R^*$; otherwise, for all computed values, $R^*_{RB} < R^*$. Again, there is one particular pattern of decline of the quasi-rents which makes reducing-balance the 'correct' depreciation[1] and for which $R^*_{RB} \simeq r$.

III

3.1. The next main case to be analysed is that of a business, the gross investment of which grows at a constant rate each year. However, it is convenient, first, to comment briefly on the case of a balanced stock where the financial assets which have accumulated over the years 0 to n and which earn r, are included in the capital of the business. By the year n, the value of financial assets (F), in the straight-line depreciation case, is $\frac{1}{2}LnS$, which is the same as the book value of physical assets. Once the year n is reached, the balanced stock is established. Therefore, for all $n+j$ years afterwards ($j = 0$ in year n, then $1, 2, \ldots$), the book value of physical and financial assets in the year $n+j$ is: $k^T_{n+j} = LnS$. Accounting profit in year $n+j$ is:

$$A^T_{n+j} = L\{(Q-S)+\tfrac{1}{2}rnS\},$$

so that $$R^{*T}_{n+j} = \frac{(Q-S)+\frac{1}{2}rnS}{nS},$$

which it is convenient to write as

$$R^{*T}_{n+j} = \frac{(Q-S)}{nS}+\tfrac{1}{2}r. \tag{3}$$

Now, $$\frac{Q-S}{nS} = \frac{1}{2}\left\{\frac{2(Q-S)}{nS}\right\},$$

which is *half* the general expression for the balanced stock, physical capital case (see expression (1)). The accountant's rate of profit in this case, then, is always equal to half its value for the corresponding physical capital case, plus a constant, $\frac{1}{2}r$.

[1] 'An aspect of depreciation', op. cit., pp. 234–5.

3.2. The corresponding general expression if reducing-balance depreciation is used is:

$$R^{*T}_{RB,n+j} = \frac{Q}{nS} - \frac{1}{n} + \frac{r(\frac{1}{2}+e)}{n}. \tag{4}$$

Again, while the values for particular cases show the same pattern of variation around r as n changes, the disparity between the accountant's measure and r is always less. That is to say, in general the influence of financial assets is to reduce the discrepancy between the accountant's measure and r. The explanation is obvious: the accountant's measure now includes in the numerator and denominator elements, namely, financial assets and the income earned on them, which, if expressed as a ratio, equal r. The influence of the inclusion of financial assets in capital on R^* is illustrated in Table IV where the accountant's values for balanced stocks of machines with lives of 10 years and r = 10 per cent are shown.

11

TABLE IV

Values of R^* for n = 10 years, a = 1·5, b = 0·5, and r = 10 per cent (percentages)

	Straight-line depreciation		*Reducing-balance depreciation*	
Case	*Physical capital*	*Total capital*	*Physical capital*	*Total capital*
(1)	12·5	11·3	7·9	8·3
(2)	4·0	7·0	2·5	4·0
(3)	22·7	16·4	14·3	13·4
(4)	10·5†	10·3†	6·6†	7·3†

† m = 5 years

IV

4.1. The next main case considered is that of a business, the gross investment each year of which is the stream: $LS, cLS, \ldots, c^{n-1}LS, \ldots$ $(c > 1)$. It has been argued already (see 2.2 above) that, if the capital stock is growing, the use of conventional accounting methods of reckoning depreciation prevents $R^* \simeq r$, even if capital is valued 'correctly'. If straight-line depreciation is used,

$$R^* = \frac{2(1+r-c)\left[\sum_1^n c^{n-i}q_i - (S/n)\{(c^n-1)/(c-1)\}\right]}{\sum_1^n c^{n-i}q_i + \sum_2^n c^{n+1-i}q_i - c^n(S+S^*)};$$

if reducing-balance depreciation is used,

$$R^*_{RB} = \frac{2(1+r-c)\left[\sum_1^n c^{n-i}q_i - S(x)\right]}{(\alpha)},$$

where $$x = 1-\frac{d(1-d^{n-1})}{1-d}+\frac{cd^n\{1-(c/d)^{n-1}\}}{d-c}$$

and $$\alpha = \sum_1^n c^{n-i}q_i+\sum_2^n c^{n+1-i}q_i-c^n(S+S^*).$$

Neither of these expressions, in general, approximately equals r.

4.2. Expression (5) is the general expression for R^* for the constant growth case in the $(n+j)$th year (that is, after replacement expenditure has

TABLE V

Values of R^*, for $c = 1{\cdot}0$, $1{\cdot}01$, and $1{\cdot}2$, $r = 30$ per cent, $a = 1{\cdot}5$, $b = 0{\cdot}5$, and straight-line depreciation (percentages)

12

		n		
Case	*c*	5 *years*	10 *years*	20 *years*
(1)	1·0	42·1	44·7	50·3
	1·01	41·8	44·0	48·7
	1·20	36·8	34·8	33·5
(2)	1·0	22·5	12·0	6·0
	1·01	23·1	12·9	7·1
	1·20	31·6	26·9	24·6
(3)	1·0	60·9	122·4	796·0
	1·01	59·7	116·7	713·4
	1·20	41·5	49·1	88·0
(4)†	1·0	34·7	39·6	75·9
	1·01	34·7	39·5	74·5
	1·20	35·2	35·0	50·0

† $m = \frac{1}{2}n$

started) when the *book* value of physical capital and straight-line depreciation are used.

$$R^*_{c,n+j} = \frac{2n(c-1)^2\Big\{\sum_1^n c^{n-i}q_i-S(c^n-1)/n(c-1)\Big\}}{S(\beta)} \tag{5}$$

where $$\beta = \{(2n-1)c^{n+1}-(2n+1)c^n+(1+c)\}.$$

This expression is independent of c^j (though the expressions for accounting profit and the book value of capital contain it), but not of c itself. The patterns of behaviour of R^* as n changes appear to be the same, for the four types of machines, as for the balanced-stock cases. However, *in general*, the higher is the rate of growth of the capital stock, the closer, for given n, are the values of the accountant's rate of profit to the correct value. This is illustrated in Table V, where values of R^* are shown for rates of growth between 0 and 20 per cent.

The general expression for the constant growth case when reducing-balance depreciation is used is:

$$R^*_{RB,c,n+j} = \frac{2(1-c)(1-d)(c-d)\left\{\sum_{1}^{n} c^{n-i}q_i - S(x)\right\}}{S(y)} \tag{6}$$

where

$$y = (1-d)(c-d)(1+c-2c^n)-$$
$$-d(1+c)\{(1-d^{n-1})(c-d)-c^n(1-d)(1-(d/c)^{n-1})\}.$$

(Expressions for the four types of machines can be easily derived from expressions (5) and (6).) Except for the case of $n = 2$, R^* for the reducing-balance case is usually less than the corresponding value for the straight-line case. For values of n below twenty years, anyway, the effect of 13
growth is usually to make R^* closer to r than in the corresponding balanced stock case.

V

5.1. To complete the analysis, the case of constant growth where the accumulation of financial assets occurs is briefly examined. The accumulation of financial assets consists of two parts:

(1) the accumulation over the first n years before any replacement expenditure occurs;

(2) the net addition to this fund in subsequent years $(n+j)$ because current depreciation allowances exceed current replacement expenditure.

The summation of the two relevant parts gives the financial capital for the year $n+j$, on which r is earned, and these income-capital ratios combined with expressions (5) and (6) respectively, give the general expressions for $R^{*T}_{c,n+j}$ and $R^{*T}_{RB,c,n+j}$:

$$R^{*T}_{c,n+j} = \frac{2n(c-1)^2\left\{c^j\left(\sum_{1}^{n} c^{n-i}q_i - (S/n)\{(c^n-1)/(c-1)\}\right) + \tfrac{1}{2}rS(g)\right\}}{S(h)} \tag{7}$$

where $$g = \frac{2n(c^n-1)}{c-1} + \frac{c(c^j-1)(c^n-1)}{(c-1)^2} - \frac{(\beta)}{(c-1)^2} - n\left(\frac{c^j-1}{c-1}\right)$$

and

$$h = 2n(c^n-1)(c-1)+c(c^j-1)(c^n-1)+(c^j-1)(\beta)-n(c^j-1)(c-1);$$

$$R^{*T}_{RB,c,n+j} = \frac{2\left\{c^j\left(\sum_{1}^{n} c^{n-i}q_i - S(x)\right) + \tfrac{1}{2}rS[(p)+(t)\{(c^j-1)/(c-1)\}]\right\}}{S(u)} \tag{8}$$

where

$$u = \frac{c^j}{(1-c)(1-d)(c-d)}(y)+(p)+(t)\left(\frac{c^j-1}{c-1}\right),$$

$$p = 1+\frac{d(1+c)}{(1-c)}\left\{\frac{1-d^{n-1}}{1-d}-\frac{c^n(1-(d/c)^{n-1})}{c-d}\right\};$$

and

$$t = d\left(\frac{c^n(1-(d/c)^{n-1}}{c-d}\right)+\frac{c-1}{c}-\frac{d(1-d^{n-1})}{1-d}.$$

5.2. Expressions for the four types of machines can be derived from (7) and (8). These expressions contain a new term, c^j, so that values were computed for a number of values of c^j (the range was: $j = 1\frac{1}{2}n$–$3n$). For the range of values of j examined, though, the values of R^* were hardly affected by variations in j. For example, with $a = 1{\cdot}5$, $b = 0{\cdot}5$, $c = 1{\cdot}01$, $n = 20$, and $r = 5$ per cent, the range was 8·6–8·8 per cent, in the
14 straight-line cases, and 6·96–6·98 per cent in the reducing-balance cases.

Table VI

Values of R^* for $n = 10$ years, $a = 1{\cdot}5$, $b = 0{\cdot}5$, $c = 1{\cdot}1$, $r = 30$ per cent (balanced stock, total capital; constant growth, total capital) (percentages)

Case	*Straight-line depreciation*		*Reducing-balance depreciation*	
	Balanced stock	*Constant growth*	*Balanced stock*	*Constant growth*
(1)	44·7	36·0‡	28·1	30·2‡
(2)	12·0	23·3‡	7·5	18·7‡
(3)	122·4	62·0‡	77·1	53·8‡
(4)	39·6†	35·3†‡	24·9†	29·6†‡

† $m = 5$ years ‡ $j = 30$ years

Again, while the patterns of change of R^* with respect to n have the same general shapes as those of the corresponding constant growth, physical capital cases, the discrepancy between the values of R^* and r, for given n, is usually reduced. Moreover, because the influence of growth is also usually to improve the accountant's measure, the discrepancies between R^* and r, for given n, are least of all of the cases examined. This is illustrated in Table VI where values of R^* for the balanced stock, total capital and constant growth, total capital cases for $n = 10$ years, $a = 1{\cdot}5$, $b = 0{\cdot}5$, $r = 30$ per cent., and $c = 1{\cdot}1$ are compared.

VI

6.1. The article is concluded by briefly summarizing the variations of R^* with respect to n for the various cases examined. The following diagrams illustrate, schematically, the patterns of variation with respect to n.

(I) *Straight-line depreciation, balanced stock, physical capital*

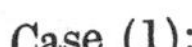

Case (1):

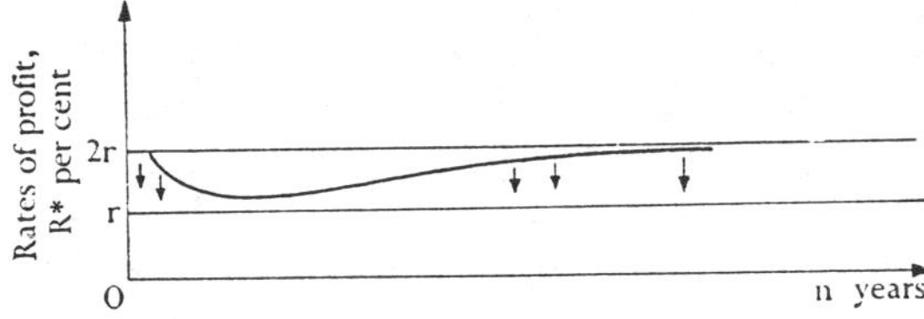

FIG. 2

(The arrows show the influence of growth and financial capital on R^*.)

Case (2):

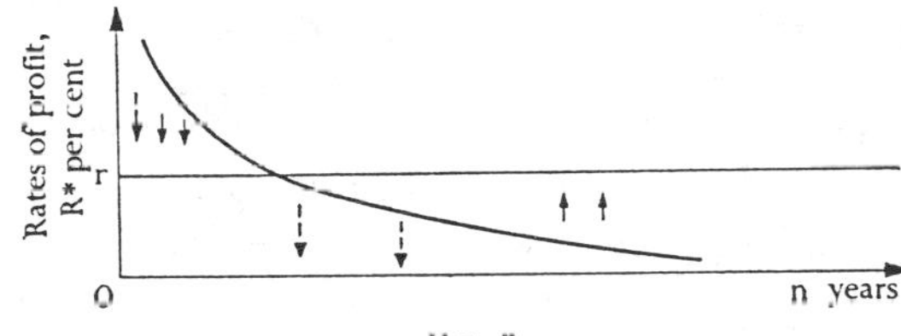

15

FIG. 3

(Dotted arrows show the influence of changes in b—the smaller is the value of b, the faster is the approach to zero.)

Case (3):

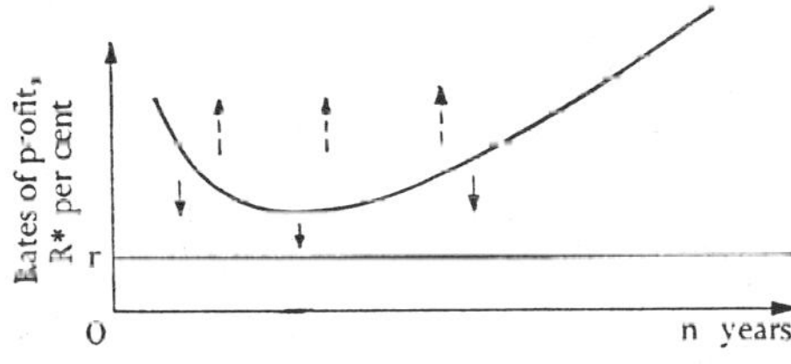

FIG. 4

(Dotted arrows show the influence of changes in a—the greater is the value of a, the faster is the approach to ∞. The function is not defined at $1+r = a$.)

Case (4): This case cannot be shown in a general diagram because it depends on the ratio, m/n. Its value approaches that of (2) as $m\,(< n) \to 0$.

(II) *Reducing-balance depreciation, balanced stock, physical capital*

Case (1):

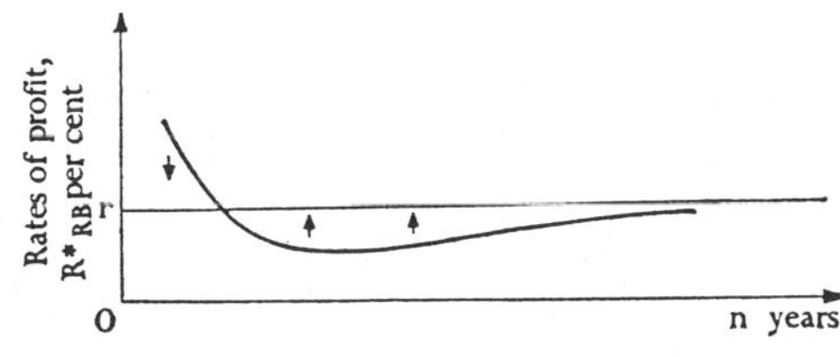

FIG. 5

Cases (2) and (3) are similar to those for straight-line depreciation but, for $n > 2$, $R^*_{RB} < R^*$.

6.2. The implications of the analysis of the article are rather disheartening. It had been hoped that some rough 'rules of thumb' might be developed; and that these would allow accounting rates of profit to be adjusted for the lengths of life of machines, the patterns of quasi-rents, rates of growth, and the method of depreciation used. However, it is obvious from the calculations that the relationships involved are too complicated to allow this. A systematic presentation of the values of R^* for the various cases has not been attempted (though they have been computed). Nevertheless, on the basis of the above analysis, it seems safe to add to the already well-known defects of accounting data on profits and capital,[1] the main conclusion of this article, namely, that as an indication
16 of the realized rate of return the accountant's rate of profit is greatly influenced by irrelevant factors, even under ideal conditions. Any 'man of words' (or 'deeds' for that matter) who compares rates of profit of different industries, or of the same industry in different countries, and draws inferences from their magnitudes as to the relative profitability of investments in different uses or countries, does so at his own peril.

University of Adelaide and
Trinity Hall, Cambridge

[1] See, for example, Russell Mathews, *Accounting for Economists* (Melbourne: F. W. Cheshire, 1962), Chapters 5, 6; Harold Rose, *Disclosure in Company Accounts* (Eaton Paper 1), pp. 31–40.

15

Return on Investment: the Relation of Book-Yield to True Yield

by EZRA SOLOMON
STANFORD UNIVERSITY

18 THIS paper analyses the relationship between the *book-yield* on investment (measured as the ratio of net book income to net book value of assets) and the *true yield* on investment. It examines the effect on this relationship of variation in capitalization policy, depreciation methods, revenue patterns and growth rates. It considers the implications of the potential error in the conventional book-measure of rate of return for managerial evaluation and government regulation of private business.

The rate of return on investment is a key concept which is widely used for a number of significant business and financial purposes. It is of central importance for the evaluation of an individual investment project, the financial evaluation of a company's performance, the evaluation of managerial efficiency for a division or a product-line and finally, as a guide for establishing ceiling prices in the regulated industries.

The most commonly used multi-purpose measure for return on investment is the ratio of net book income, as this is conventionally measured by the accounting process, to net book value of assets employed, similarly measured. The measure has several names such as "the accounting rate of return," "the book rate of return," "the conventional rate of return," but for the purpose of this paper we will refer to it as "book-yield," defined here as follows:

$$a = \frac{F_t - D_t}{K_t} \qquad (1)$$

where

a = book-yield in period t, $t \geq n$
F_t = funds flows from operations, before taxes, in period t
D_t = depreciation charges in period t
K_t = net book value of assets as of the beginning of period t
$F_t - D_t$ = reported before-tax operating profits in period t

One reason for the widespread use of the book-yield as a measure of return on investment is that it ties in directly with the accounting process. A second and even

This article is a development of an earlier paper presented in 1963 at the 38th Annual Meeting of the Society of Petroleum Engineers. I am indebted to two doctoral students, Jaime C. Laya and Robert Carlson, for many of the formulations contained in this essay.

more important reason is that it is the only approach available for measuring the on-going return on investment for a collection of assets which together comprise a division or a company.

In spite of the wide use of the book-yield ratio, surprisingly little work has been done on its validity and accuracy as a measure of rate of return. Does it correctly measure the actual yield on investment? Is it a consistent general yardstick in the sense that it provides comparable measures as between divisions, companies, and industries? These questions have been asked but they have not been answered systematically.

For at least one class of purposes for which return on investment is used, the book-yield measure has been questioned and found wanting. I refer to single investment projects or acquisitions. In this situation the size and timing of all investment outlays and of all net cash receipts flowing from these outlays are available, or can be estimated either retrospectively or prospectively. Given these data, there is an alternative method available for measuring return on investment. This measure is the true or exact yield, i. e., that annual rate of discount at which the present value of investment outlays is just equal to the present value of cash receipts flowing from the invest- 19
ment.

This approach to the measurement of return on investment also has several names. In the financial world, where it is now universally used for the purpose of measuring bond yields, it is called "the effective yield to maturity." Economists have referred to it as "the marginal productivity of capital," "the marginal efficiency of capital," and the "internal rate of return." In the industrial world, where it is being used with increasing frequency to measure the rate of return on single investment projects it has been called, "the discounted cash flow method," the "investor's method," the "scientific method," and the "profitability index." We will refer to it as "true yield."

The nature of the measure does not permit an explicit algebraic definition. However, for a single investment project, in which input takes place at one point of time and output flows occur at annual intervals, the true yield r can be defined implicitly as the rate r which satisfies the following relationship:

$$I_0 = \sum_{t=1}^{n} R_t(1 + r)^{-t} \tag{2}$$

where

I_0 = investment in year zero
R_t = net receipts arising out of project I_0, received in period t
n = length of the investment's productive life.

For the special case in which the investment generates uniform receipts over the life of the project, equation (2) may be restated as:

$$R = I_0\left[\frac{r(1 + r)^n}{(1 + r)^n - 1}\right] \tag{3}$$

For single investment projects it is now well known that project book yield and project true yield may differ, and that the difference between the two measures can be quite large. It is also widely recognized and provable that the answer provided by the true yield method is the correct one and that it is the book-yield measure which is in error. Because of this the financial world long ago abandoned the book-yield measure in favor of the true yield approach as a measure of bond yields. A similar move is now going on in the industrial world as far as single project analysis is concerned.

In contrast to the single project situation, a company or division is a collection of ongoing projects, and we have neither data nor estimates of all cash flows, past and future, associated with this collection of assets. Hence we have no direct way of measuring or estimating the true yield for a company. In contrast, the book-yield is conveniently available.

However, if the book-yield approach produces incorrect results for a single investment outlay it must follow that the book-yield measure for a company is also subject to error. The main purpose of the analysis which follows is to explore the size and nature of the potential error inherent in the book-yield measure.

Methodology

Since it is not possible to get a direct measure of true yield for an ongoing company
20 it is not possible to check directly on the accuracy or error of the observable book-yield measure.

What we can do is to develop hypothetical models of a company using a given true yield on investment and then test the book-yield as it would appear from the *pro forma* income statements and balance sheets of such a company.

This is what is done in the models contained in this paper. All of them assume a hypothetical company that invests in a series of identical projects, each of which has an assumed true yield. The purpose of each test is to establish how the book-yield measure differs from the known true yield when certain basic parameters are changed. The principal parameters are:

1. Length of project life.
2. The timing and configuration of cash inflows relative to the timing of cash outlays.
3. Accounting policy with respect to the capitalization and depreciation of investment outlays.
4. The rate at which outlays grow over time.

It is convenient to divide the overall analysis into two parts: (a) the static or zero-growth situation in which a company's annual investment outlays are constant over time, and (b) the dynamic situation in which the growth rate is something other than zero.

The Basic Zero-Growth Model

Assuming that all projects generate uniform and identical cash inflows per dollar of investment equal to R per period per project, then for any given period subsequent to n (if the investment process starts at period zero), we have:

$$a = \frac{2(nR - D)}{I(n + 1)} \tag{4}$$

nR = the total funds inflows from operations of all n projects operating in period t.
D = total depreciation expense during the period
$I(n+1)\left(\frac{1}{2}\right)$ = net book value as of the beginning of period t:

$$K_t = \frac{I}{n}[n + (n - 1) + \cdots + 2 + 1]$$
$$= \frac{I(n + 1)}{2}$$

For example, consider a company that acquires homogeneous investments each of which requires an outlay of $1,000 in year 0, and generates a cash flow of $229.61 a year for 6 years beginning exactly one year after the outlay is made.

The true yield on each investment is exactly 10 percent per annum. The fact that it is 10 percent and exactly 10 percent can be easily demonstrated by placing a similar amount in a bank which pays 10 percent interest on unwithdrawn balances, and by withdrawing $229.61 each year. The sixth withdrawal will exactly exhaust the balance. (See Table I.)

Assume that the company in question acquires one such investment each year. Since each investment yields 10 percent we know that the company's true yield must also be 10 percent.

What would the book yield be for such a company? This depends of course on the 21
depreciation method used, and on whether we use beginning-of-year, mid-year or end of year net book value.

Using straight line depreciation and beginning-of-year net book values, it is easy to show that the company's net income will grow as it acquires new investments but that net income will settle at $377.66 from year 6 onward. The beginning-of-year net book value of assets will also rise as new investments are acquired, but this will also settle at $3,500 from year 6 onward. Thus from year 6 onward the book-yield will stabilize at $377.66/$3500.00 or 10.79 percent. (See Table II.)

In this particular instance the observable book-yield overstates the true yield by some 8 percent of the true yield, a not insignificant error. The error stems from the fact that, when cash inflows are level, the use of straight-line depreciation reduces net book value at a faster rate than economic value declines.

If the basic characteristics of the model are held constant, i. e., if we continue to assume constant cash flows, no time lag between investment and the flow of benefits, complete capitalization of all investment outlays and zero salvage at the end of

TABLE I

BASIC MODEL: CONSTANT CASH FLOWS

Initial investment outlay, $1,000 (all capitalized)
Constant cash flows for six years
Zero salvage value at the end of the sixth year
KNOWN TRUE YIELD of 10 percent per annum.

Year	*Actual Investment of Year*	*Interest at 10 Percent*	*Balance at End of Year*	*Cash Withdrawal at End of Year*	*Ending Value*
1	$1,000.00	$100.00	$1,100.00	$229.61	$870.39
2	870.39	87.04	957.43	229.61	727.82
3	727.82	72.78	800.61	229.61	571.00
4	571.00	57.10	628.10	229.61	398.50
5	398.50	39.85	438.35	229.61	208.74
6	208.74	20.87	229.61	229.61	—

TABLE II

BASIC MODEL: NET INCOME, NET BOOK VALUE AND BOOK-YIELDS

Project: Single Investment of $1,000

Year	*Cash Flow*	*Depreciation (straight line)*	*Net Income*	*Beginning of the Year Net Book Value*	*Project Book Yield (percent)*
1	$ 229.61	$ 166.66	$ 62.95	$1,000.00	6.30
2	229.61	166.66	62.95	833.33	7.55
3	229.61	166.66	62.95	666.67	9.44
4	229.61	166.66	62.95	500.00	12.59
5	229.61	166.66	62.95	333.33	18.89
6	229.61	166.66	62.95	166.67	37.77

Company: Successive Investment of $1,000 a Year

	Year	*Cash Flow*	*Depreciation*	*Net Income*	*Beginning of the Year Net Book Value*	*Project Book Yield (percent)*
	1	$ 229.61	$ 166.66	$ 62.95	$1,000.00	6.30
22	2	459.22	333.32	125.90	1,833.33	6.82
	3	688.83	500.00	188.83	2,500.00	7.55
	4	918.44	666.67	251.77	3,000.00	8.39
	5	1,148.05	833.33	314.72	3,333.33	9.44
	6	1,377.66	1,000.00	377.66	3,500.00	10.79
	onward	1,377.66	1,000.00	377.66	3,500.00	10.79

Company True Yield—10 percent
Company Book Yield—10.8 percent

each project's life, the error in the book-yield changes with the duration of each underlying project. For example, for a 10 percent true yield project which paid off in 15 installments of $131.50 instead of 6 installments of $229.61, the observable book-yield would be 12.16 percent rather than 10.79 percent. The error in the book-yield

TABLE III

BASIC MODEL: VARIATION OF BOOK YIELD WITH PROJECT DURATION

Initial investment outlay $1,000 (all capitalized)
Constant cash flows
Zero salvage value at end of project life
KNOWN TRUE YIELD at 10 percent per annum
Straight line depreciation

Project Life (years)	*Annual Cash Flow (dollars)*	*Annual Depreciation (dollars)*	*Annual Net Income (dollars)*	*Average Net Book Value (dollars)*	*Average Apparent Rate (per annum)*	*True Yield (per annum)*
6	$229.6	$166.7	$62.9	$583.33	10.8	10.0
10	162.7	100.0	62.7	550.00	11.4	10.0
15	131.5	66.7	64.8	533.33	12.2	10.0
20	117.5	50.9	67.5	525.00	12.9	10.0
25	110.2	40.0	70.2	520.00	13.5	10.0
30	106.1	33.3	72.8	516.67	14.1	10.0
40	102.3	25.0	77.3	512.50	15.1	10.0
50	100.8	20.0	80.8	510.00	15.8	10.0
100	100.0	10.0	90.0	505.00	17.8	10.0
∞	100.0	0	100.0	500.0	20.0	10.0

measure rises as project life is lengthened. At the limit of very long life projects the observable book-yield will approach twice the level of the known true yield. (See Table III.)

Capitalization Policy. A second factor which has a major influence on the difference between the observable book-yield and the true yield is accounting policy with respect to the capitalizing or expensing of initial investment outlays.

If the fraction c of each gross outlay is capitalized on the company's books, with the fraction (1-c) being written off as expense during the current period, then the net book value would be accordingly reduced such that

$$a = \frac{2(nR - I)}{cI(n + 1)} \tag{5}$$

In the no-growth case, total annual deductions from net operating cash inflow nR remains equal to I, thus:

$$D = cI + (1 - c)I$$

where cI = depreciation expense for the period on capitalized investments, and (1-c)I — portion of current investment charged off to expense. 23

For example, if we take the investment assumed in the basic model, i.e., a \$1,000 outlay and \$229.61 cash inflows for 6 periods, but introduce the assumption that \$600 of the outlay is capitalized and \$400 expensed in the first year, we get the following results. True yield (before taxes) remains at 10 percent, but book yield (before taxes) rises to 17.9 percent.

If we take the secondary effect of income taxes into account, the relationship between book-yield and true yield again changes. For example, assuming a 50 percent corporate income tax rate in the model just preceding, the true yield after taxes would be 6 percent, and the book yield after taxes would be 9 percent.

Depreciation Policy. A change in the rate at which book depreciation is taken will also change the relationship between the observable book-yield and the true yield. On a before-tax basis the depreciation rate has no effect on true yield, but it does have a significant effect on observable book-yield.

To illustrate this point, let us return to the basic full capitalization model, and replace the straight-line depreciation used in it with the sum of years' digits depreciation schedule.

Total depreciation expense for each period is the same for both methods. Under the straight-line method we have:

$$D = \frac{I}{n} + \frac{I}{n} + \cdots + \frac{I}{n} = I$$

and under the sum of years' digits method of depreciation, D is also equal to I.

$$D = \frac{nI}{\sum_{t=1}^{n} t} + \frac{(n-1)I}{\sum_{t=1}^{n} t} + \cdots + \frac{I}{\sum_{t=1}^{n} t}$$

$$= \left[\frac{I}{\sum_{t=1}^{n} t}\right]\left[\sum_{t=1}^{n} t\right]$$

In the zero growth case, the real impact of the depreciation method is on the amount reported as net book value. Since relatively larger fractions of initial investment are written off early in a project's life, book values will be lower for more rapid depreciation methods than for the straight-line calculation. For the sum of years' digits method, the net book value of all operating projects will be

$$K_t = \frac{I\sum_{t=1}^{n} t}{\sum_{t=1}^{n} t} + \frac{I\sum_{t=1}^{n-1} t}{\sum_{t=1}^{n} t} + \cdots + \frac{I\sum_{t=1}^{2} t}{\sum_{t=1}^{n} t} + \frac{I}{\sum_{t=1}^{n} t}$$

This reduces to

$$K_t = \frac{I(n + 2)}{3}$$

24 Hence, when the sum of years' digits depreciation is employed, the book-yield is given by:

$$a = \frac{3(nR - I)}{I(n + 2)} \tag{6}$$

A change in the depreciation method used will leave the true yield (before tax) unchanged at 10 percent. Net income will also remain unchanged at $377.66 for year 6 onward. (See Table II.) But the net book value of assets will fall from $3,500 to $2,666.65. Thus the observable pre-tax book-yield will rise from 10.8 percent to 14.2 percent.

Rising Cash Flows. A major variable which influences the size of the book measure relative to the true yield measure is the general timing of cash inflows relative to the timing of investment outlays.

A time-lag between outlays and inflows can take one of three general forms. a) The investment process itself may involve varying amounts of time. For example, the acquisition of a bond or a piece of equipment takes very little time. In contrast the development of a producing oil well could involve a 5-year lag between the inception of initial outlays and the time the project is complete. b) There can be a lag between the completion of a project and the initial inflow of cash from operations. c) The equivalent of a lag may exist when the inflows of cash are distributed over time in a rising pattern so that the bulk of the inflows occur further from the outlay point.

Assuming once again a total outlay of I, the effect of the first type of lag is to require larger cash receipts in order to maintain an effective true yield of 10 percent. If the investment consists of instalments of P dollars per period over a total of $(m+1)$ periods before the project is finally operational, the true yield can be defined as

$$\sum_{t=-m}^{0} P_t(1 + r)^{-t} = \sum_{t=1}^{n} R_t(1 + r)^{-t} \tag{7}$$

It would be acceptable accounting practice to consider the total investment in this project as

$$\sum_{t=-m}^{0} P_t = I.$$

But R would be greater here than was true in the basic model discussed above. For example, if the investment outlay for each project consists of two instalments of \$500, one in year -1 and the other in year 0, the annual receipts required for each project to yield 10 percent would be \$241.09. Using equation (4), the book-yield is seen to be 11.16 percent.

The second kind of lag occurs when, say, an investment made at the beginning of period 1 produces its first cash inflow at the end of period $(1+p)$. In this case, true yield can be defined as:

$$I_0 = \sum_{t=p+1}^{p+n} R_t(1+r)^{-t}$$

$$R = I_0\left[\frac{r(1+r)^{n+p}}{(1+r)^n - 1}\right] \tag{8}$$

if R is uniform over project life. 25

All the other elements required to find book-yield would be the same as in the basic model if we assume, reasonably, that no depreciation is charged off until receipts take place. For example, if there is a lag of 2 years between the year of investment and the year of the first cash inflow (note that lag = 0 when investments produce a first receipt in year 1), book-yield may be seen to be 12.13 percent.

The third type of lag involves the configuration of cash receipts. A cash inflow pattern which rises over time will produce a higher book-yield because the absolute size of dollar inflows generated by a project of given outlay and of given true yield are greater when inflows are delayed in time. If the cash inflows from each project rise logarithmically at the rate h, we have

$$I_0 = A\,\frac{(1+h)}{(1+r)} + A\,\frac{(1+h)^2}{(1+r)^2} + A\,\frac{(1+h)^3}{(1+r)^3} + \cdots + A\,\frac{(1+h)^n}{(1+r)^n}$$

(where A is some constant satisfying the above conditions), and hence we have

$$a = \frac{A\sum_{t=1}^{n}(1+h)^t - I}{K_t} \tag{9}$$

If $r = 10$ percent and $h = 12$ percent, then cash flows from the project would be as follows:

Year	*Cash Inflows*
1	\$ 175.24
2	196.26
3	219.81
4	246.19
5	275.74
6	308.82
	\$1,422.06

After year 6, the total company cash flows will be \$1,422.06. From equations (1) or (9), it may be seen that the book-yield is 12.06 percent.

Conversely, it is possible to envisage an investment project which contains the opposite of this type of time lag, i.e., a project which offers large early returns that decline over time.

An example of such a project with $r = 10$ percent and $h = -12$ percent, would be:

Year	*Cash Inflows*
1	\$ 298.15
2	262.38
3	230.89
4	203.18
5	178.80
6	157.35
	\$1,330.75

The company book-yield would then be 9.45 percent.

26 To summarize, as far as the zero-growth case is concerned, the major findings are 1) the book-yield is not an accurate measure of true yield, 2) the error in the book-yield is neither constant nor consistent. Indeed it is a fairly capricious measure which may sometimes underestimate true yield, but which more generally overstates true yield.

The degree of potential overstatement ranges from slight under certain circumstances to very gross and misleading overstatements in others.

Specifically, the degree to which book-yield overstates true yield is a complex function of four basic factors. These are: a) Length of project life; the longer the project life, the greater the overstatement. b) Capitalization policy; the smaller the fraction of total investment capitalized on the books, the greater will be the overstatement. At the limit for investments which are expensed 100 percent, the observable book-yield will rise toward infinity. c) The rate at which depreciation is taken on the books; depreciation procedures faster than a straight line basis will result in higher book-yields. At the limit the most rapid method of depreciation is, of course, tantamount to 100 percent expensing of outlays and hence leads to the same result. d) The greater the lag between investment outlays and the recoupment of these outlays from cash inflows, the greater the degree of overstatement.

Since no two investments and hence no two companies or industries are likely to hold investments that are identical with respect to all of these variables, it must follow that observable book-yields do not provide a consistent measure of return on investment or even a consistent *ranking* of the underlying true yields actually being earned by such companies or industries.

Growth Situations

We now lift the assumption that the company's growth rate is zero, and we will find that the rate at which a division or a company or an industry acquires new investments is a major variable affecting the size of the error contained in the observable book-yield.

So long as the investments being acquired are homogeneous, i.e., each year's investment produces the same true yield on that investment, it is easy to see that the rate at which investment outlays are made over time has no effect on the true yield being earned by the company as a whole. This will be equal to the true yield on each investment regardless of the rate at which investment outlays grow or decline over time.

However, the book-yield is significantly affected by the pace at which investment outlays are made.

In order to see why this is the case it is useful to return to the basic model. In this model the $1,000 investment in year one produces a cash flow of $229.61 each year for 6 years. Using straight line depreciation, the depreciation allowance is $166.66 a year, leaving net income of $62.95 per year for 6 years.

Although annual net income is constant over the life of each investment, the net book value of assets employed is not constant. Rather, it declines steadily from year 1 until it reaches zero at the end of year 6.

This means that on a year-to-year basis the ratio of net income to net book value for each individual investment rises. In year 1 of the project's life the beginning of year net book value is $1,000 and hence the project book-yield during year 1 is 6.3 percent. (See Table II.)

In the second year of the project's life it has a book-yield of 7.5 percent. By the 27
sixth year, the value of net book assets has fallen to $166, and the project's sixth year book-yield is 37.8 percent.

When a company acquires investments at a constant rate the overall book-yield for the company is simply the weighted average of the year by year project book-yields, with the appropriate net book values used as weights. Thus in Table II the overall book-yield of 10.8 percent is equal to (6.3 percent×1,000 + 7.5 percent×833+ . . . +37.77 percent×166.67)÷3,500.

If, however, a company acquires new investments at a rising pace, the overall company yield in any year will be more heavily weighted with investment projects which are in their early phase of development and for which net book values are high relative to net income. Thus, the observable book-yield for a growing company will be smaller than the observable yield for a non-growing company, even though both hold essentially identical investments.

The opposite is true for a company which commits a smaller amount each year to new investments. For such a company the observable book-yield is more heavily weighted with investment projects which are in their late phase of development and for which net book values are very low relative to net income. For such a company observable book-yield will be higher than for a non-growth company even though both companies hold identical investments.

In general, if the observable book-yield is higher than true yield for a non-growth situation, the introduction of positive growth will tend to lower book-yield relative to true yield. The faster the growth, the more will book-yield decline relative to true yield.

It is necessary to distinguish between two kinds of growth: a) real growth in investment outlays (with no change in prices) and b) money growth in investment outlays due entirely to inflation. Assuming a consistent true yield on each investment and a uniform rate of growth over time in investment outlays, it follows that net book-value, cash receipts, depreciation expense and the reserve for depreciation also grow at the rate at which investment outlays are growing.

Real Growth. When a company's real growth rate is g, book-yield is given by:

$$a = g\left[\frac{(1+g)^n - 1}{1 + (1+g)^n(gn-1)}\right]\left[\frac{1 + (1+r)^n(rn-1)}{(1+r)^n - 1}\right] \tag{10}$$

This is derived from equation (1) and the following relationships; for $t=n$

$$F_n = I_0[1 + (1+g) + (1+g)^2 + \cdots + (1+g)^{n-1}]\left[\frac{r(1+r)^n}{(1+r)^n - 1}\right]$$

$$D_n = I_0\left[\frac{1}{n} + \frac{(1+g)}{n} + \frac{(1+g)^2}{n} + \cdots + \frac{(1+g)^{n-1}}{n}\right]$$

$$K_n = I_0\left[\frac{n}{n}(1+g)^{n-1} + \frac{(n-1)}{n}(1+g)^{n-2} + \cdots + \frac{2}{n}(1+g) + \frac{1}{n}\right]$$

If the book-yield a is higher than the true yield r in the zero-growth case, then as g increases the book-yield falls continuously toward r.

28 In the special situation where the growth rate just equals true yield, the book-yield is also just equal to true yield.

In other words, when $g=r$, a is equal to r. The proof of this fundamental and important equality condition is as follows:

By definition,

$$aK_t = F_t - D_t \tag{11}$$

and

$$gK_t = I_t - D_t \tag{12}$$

Now, the condition $g=r$ exists only when all company receipts are reinvested, i.e., when $F_t = I_t$. In this case

$$aK_t = gK_t.$$

Hence, if $g=r$, $a=g=r$.

It can also be seen directly from equation (10) that $a=r$ if $g=r$, regardless of n. Furthermore, it can be proved that as long as depreciation method, capitalization practice, time lags, and cash flow patterns are consistent over time, the growth rate of all items remains the same as the growth rate in investment, and the $r=g=a$ equality holds.

Inflationary Growth. The existence of inflation in the economy would directly alter the cash flow pattern from individual projects. Assuming for simplicity that inflation has an equal effect on the price level of investment input and cash flow output, we have:

$$I_0 = \sum_{t=1}^{n} \frac{R_t(1+i)^t}{(1+m)^t} \tag{13}$$

where

m = money true yield
i = inflation rate
R = receipts in dollars of period zero.

On the basis of equation (2), equation (13) may be restated as

$$I_0 = \sum_{t=1}^{n} \frac{R_t(1 + i)^t}{(1 + i)^t(1 + r)^t} \tag{14}$$

Thus we have money true yield $m = i + ri + r$.

Another way of looking at the effect of inflation is to say that all real cash receipts are multiplied by $(1+i)^t$ in order to obtain the actual cash inflow in period t. At the same time, actual investment, and hence, depreciation expense and net book value are themselves affected by the inflationary process. The various elements of equation (1) are therefore affected such that

$$F_t = nI_0\left[\frac{r(1 + r)^n(1 + i)^t}{(1 + r)^n - 1}\right]$$

$$D_t = \frac{I_{t-n}}{n}\left[1 + (1 + i) + \cdots + (1 + i)^n\right] = \left[\frac{I_0(1 + i)^{t-n}}{n}\right]\left[\frac{(1 + i)^n - 1}{i}\right]$$

$$K_t = I_{t-n}\left[\frac{n}{n}(1 + i)^{t-1} + \frac{(n - 1)}{n}(1 + i)^{t-2} + \cdots + \frac{1}{n}(1 + i)^{t-n}\right]$$ 29

which simplifies to

$$K_t = I_0\left[\frac{(1 + i)^{t-n}}{ni^2}\right]\left[1 - (1 + i)^n(1 - ni)\right]$$

Thus, the book-yield a may be computed, using equation (1), as follows:

$$a = \left[\frac{nr(1 + r)^n}{(1 + r)^n - 1} - \frac{(1 + i)^n - 1}{ni(1 + i)^n}\right]\left[\frac{ni^2(1 + i)^n}{1 - (1 + i)^n(1 - ni)}\right] \tag{15}$$

Using the above equation, it can be seen that the introduction of a 3 percent inflation rate in the basic model would produce a book yield of 14.7 percent. (See also Table IV.)

Implications

If the findings above are valid, and there is no reason to believe that they are not, they present financial analysis with a serious dilemma. On the one hand, the ratio of net income to net book assets is not a reliable measure of return on investment. On the other hand, analysis definitely requires some measure of return on investment and there appears to be no other way in which this concept can be measured for an ongoing division or company.

The pragmatic answer is that book-yield will continue to be used, but that its use must be tempered by a far greater degree of judgment and adjustment than we have employed in the past, and in extreme cases the measure may have to be abandoned altogether in favor of an alternative measure, such as the ratio of cash flow before depreciation to gross book value.

Adjustments are also required whenever book yields are used for the purpose of making interdivisional, intercompany, or inter-industrial comparisons. While we have as yet no precise basis for making these necessary adjustments, the use of models does

Table IV

Basic Model with Inflation

Real investment outlay, $1,000 (all capitalized)
Constant real cash flows
Zero salvage at end of project life
Known real true yield at 10 percent per annum
Money true yield, 13.30 percent
Inflation rate, 3 percent per annum
Straight line depreciation

Investments Made in Year	*Money Investment*	*Money Inflows in Year 6*	*Annual Depreciation Expense*	*Profits in Year 6*	*Net Book Value in Year 6*
0	$1,000.00	$ 274.18	$ 166.67	$107.51	$ 166.67
1	1,030.00	274.18	171.67	102.51	343.33
2	1,060.90	274.18	176.82	97.36	530.46
3	1,092.73	274.18	182.12	92.06	728.48
4	1,125.51	274.18	185.58	86.60	937.90
5	1,159.27	274.18	193.21	80.97	1,159.27
30	$6,468.41	$1,645.08	$1,078.07	$567.01	$3,866.11

provide an approximate basis for doing so. It is probably better to use adjusted book yields even if the adjustments are imprecise, than to use the unadjusted book yield figures which we know are subject to error.

A final implication is that the conventional rate-base approach commonly used in rate regulation should be amended to take into account the fact that companies and industries differ widely with respect to the basic parameters that affect the accuracy of the book-yield measure. For industry situations in which book yield is equal to true yield, multiplying an intended cost of capital rate by an original cost net book value rate base produces meaningful and intended results. However, for situations in which the book yield is higher than the true yield on invested funds, such a procedure will in fact provide a true yield significantly lower than the cost of capital rate being aimed at.

31

DISCUSSION COMMENTS

by Stephen A. Zeff
TULANE UNIVERSITY

Solomon

In one sense, the essence of Solomon's paper is a reiteration of the arguments of Canning [3] and Alexander [1], but from the point of view of the financial analyst rather than the economist-statistician (Canning) or theoretical economist (Alexander). Solomon implicitly adopts Hicks's thesis that the income of a person should be defined as "the maximum value which he can consume during a week, and still expect to be as well off at the end of the week as he was at the beginning,"[1] though he speaks of the divergence of "book yield" from "true yield."

---

[1] Hicks [5, p. 172].

"The proprietor and those beneficially interested in the proprietorship wish chiefly to know what net changes in power to command future final net income have occurred within a year by reason of the enterprise activities."[2] Both Canning and Alexander recognize "many hindrances to good valuation" (Canning's phrase), though Alexander is less sympathetic to these constraints than is Canning. Says Alexander: "Original cost is advocated as a substitute method of valuation largely because original cost can be objectively measured. In so far as it is objective it is an objective measure of the wrong thing."[3] Canning, by contrast, observes, "[the economist's] work is architecture—not construction."[4]

It is not that accountants have ignored these criticisms. The literature is replete with argumentation. A long line of chapters, articles, and monographs, beginning, perhaps, with Paton and Stevenson's Chapter XX in *Principles of Accounting*,[5] testifies to accountants' concern for the conceptual limitation of conventional procedures.

In a recent group of articles,[6] Coughlan advocates what he calls "industrial accounting," which "incorporates in financial statements the same concept of time
32 preference as is employed in most sophisticated approaches to the problems of capital budgeting."[7] The "industrial accounting" balance sheet shows presently-held cash, prospective net receipts at their discounted value, and the related equities. The "industrial accounting" operating statement is verily a statement of receipts and disbursements, showing a schedule of prospective receipts and disbursements, together with actual receipts for the year and disbursements that have been made for ongoing projects; the excess of project receipts (actual and prospective) over project disbursements is broken down according to realized and unrealized portions.

Arguments for the incorporation into financial statements (in reporting to managers as well as to outsiders) of data that will permit a derivation of "true yield," invariably encounter the rebuttal that it is either impossible or impracticable—for the massive concatenation of ongoing projects that constitutes a business enterprise—to measure true yield. If the computers of the future are capable of storing the entirety of financial data about a firm's ongoing projects, of sensitively classing the outcomes of individual projects according to correct time intervals (with appropriate weightings), and of generating information for particular time intervals or groups of projects, the solution would be attainable. But if more refined approximations of true yield are to be accomplished by today's more crude tools of measurement, many users may agree with Boulding that "If accounts are bound to be untruths anyhow, . . . there is much to be said for the simple untruth as against a complicated untruth, for if the untruth is simple, it seems to me that we have a fair chance of knowing what kind of untruth it is."[8] Even with a computerized accounting system that would generate the needed data in simplified forms, it is not assured that managers would wish to report them all to outsiders.

At base, it seems that Solomon is complaining not so much about the readers'

[2] Canning [3, pp. 169–70]. Author's emphasis has been deleted.
[3] Alexander [1, pp. 59–60].
[4] Canning [3, p. 160].
[5] Paton and Stevenson [7].
[6] See Coughlan [4] for the best statement as well as for references to two other articles.
[7] Coughlan [4, p. 43].
[8] Boulding [2, p. 55].

inability to discover true yield, but about the evident failure of accountants (and the clients who retain them) to seek and utilize measures that would at least facilitate reliable approximations of true yield. Even a cursory examination of the accounting literature would probably reveal that most writers are concerned with this or that reporting procedure, rather than with the entire fabric. It is an open secret, moreover, that accounting procedures are, from time to time, profoundly influenced by such irrelevant factors as the rules prescribed for determining taxable income. LIFO, pooling of interests, methods of accelerated depreciation, and policies for expensing intangible drilling costs and research and development expenditures are among the prominent examples. The earliest influence on accounting procedures was the dividend provisions of state corporation statutes, together with court decisions. Organizations of credit officials have demanded certain kinds of data, and governmental agencies and the New York Stock Exchange have tried to encourage the reporting of others. No articulate and authoritative spokesman for the stockholder, however, has yet emerged. Add to this the probable desire of company managers to determine for themselves what *should* be reported—considering a proper balance between the managers' duplicity and the perspicacity of competitors, governmental departments 33
and agencies, and, it may be supposed, stockholders and their advisors—and one is licensed to conclude that any consistent pattern of relationships between book yield and true yield would be a chance occurrence. Accounting theorists are only now giving attention to the felt needs of users of externally reported accounting data, and it will be the true test of their collective acumen if their investigations can break through the circularity that what readers *really* want to know from published financial statements is no more than they are accustomed to finding in those financial statements. (One may question whether stockholders of non-regulated companies would use the true yield, even if it were available.) It will be most difficult for investigators to induce non-accountant readers of financial statements to conceive ways of reporting that are different from those to which they have become accustomed. The results of one such study on the needs of professional financial analysts for more refined accounting data in periods of changing prices are hardly encouraging.[9]

What solution to the book yield-true yield dilemma may be tried? Surely, the annuity method of depreciation is a weak reed for the very reason that the problem exists: uncertainty. Perhaps it would be feasible to introduce certain synthetic adjustments to the reported results of operations, given some knowledge of the entity's investment behavior. Starting with a comparatively simple operating division within a company, a study might be made of (1) the frequency of major investment decisions, (2) the receipts and disbursements profile of major investment decisions, and (3) the accounting policies for capitalizing and depreciating investment expenditures. From the overall shape of this information, synthetic conversion factors may be developed and applied to conventionally reported accounting data so as to produce a yield that is satisfactorily close to true yield. The division would need to be sufficiently simple to allow the *direct* calculation, as set forth in Solomon's paper, of an approximate true yield. Based on experiments for several successive time periods, relationships between the investment behavior of an entity and a single synthetic conversion factor (of book yield) may be capable of empirical verification. With the use of computers,

---

[9] Horngren [6, p. 577].

synthetic conversion factors may be made applicable to larger and more complex entities. I know of no instances in which this proposal has been attempted or even discussed, but its pursuit may open the door to a solution, albeit partial, of the real problem of which Solomon complains. This proposed solution would not find a home in financial statements prepared for outsiders unless the collective influence of irrelevant criteria in drawing up such reports is somehow neutralized.

Bibliography

[1] Alexander, Sidney S. "Income Measurement in a Dynamic Economy," in *Five Monographs on Business Income.* New York: Study Group on Business Income of the American Institute of Accountants, July 1, 1950; pp. 1–95.

[2] Boulding, K. E. "Economics and Accounting: the Uncongenial Twins," in W. T. Baxter and Sidney Davidson (eds.), *Studies in Accounting Theory.* 2nd Ed.; Homewood, Ill.: Richard D. Irwin, Inc., 1962; pp. 44–55.

[3] Canning, John B. *The Economics of Accountancy.* New York: The Ronald Press Company, 1929.

[4] Coughlan, John W. "Accounting and Capital Budgeting," *The Business Quarterly* [of the University of Western Ontario], XXVII, 4 (Winter, 1962), 39–48.

34 [5] Hicks, J. R. *Value and Capital.* 2nd Ed.; London: Oxford University Press, 1946.

[6] Horngren, Charles T. "Security Analysts and the Price Level," *The Accounting Review,* XXX, 4 (October, 1955), 575–81.

[7] Paton, William Andrew, and Russell Alger Stevenson. *Principles of Accounting.* New York: The Macmillan Company, 1918.

35

Income Models, Book Yield, and the Rate of Return

William J. Vatter

SINCE it is the oldest and most comprehensive of the quantitative models in business, accounting—along with its related measurement procedures—has received its full share of critical comment and review. From the viewpoint of progressive development, this is a good thing; for many significant advances in accounting thought have been given impetus by the efforts of those who can make clear the deficiencies of extant procedures. Refinements of costing procedure which improve the relevance of cost data for managerial decision making are in large measure the consequences of critical comments of managers and economists. The currently growing use of fund statements in annual reports, for example, arose from a need for clearer exposition of financing transactions not reported by earnings-statement procedures. Pressure for better comparability and more adequate disclosure have made American corporate reports the best in the world; yet even now there are demands for extension and improvements in reporting —some of which will no doubt have an effect on practice within the foreseeable future. But the best—if not the only—way in which accounting can be improved is by analysis of those problems with which accounting must deal.

Some issues related to the scope and validity of accounting measurements are unsettled—current discussions are evidence of this. One of these issues is the use of accounting figures in connection with rates of return, especially as this may relate to evaluating the effectiveness of projects, processes, or organizational units. This is in part precipitated and emphasized by capital budgeting techniques such as the discounted flow pattern, in which the rate of return plays an important part for selection of new investments from a group of proposed alternatives. As a short-cut way to express concisely the financial efficiency or desirability of projects or operations, the rate of return is a most appealing meaurement device. Here, compressed into a single fraction, are all of the aspects of income production, put into the context of funds committed to the operation, and neatly related to specified time periods. It is an appealing nutshell of financial numeration, which can be made a powerful tool for managerial or investor analysis and interpretation; this single number can portray a vast collection of operations, conditions, risks, and results in a simple and effective way. Thus, it is

William J. Vatter is Professor of Business Administration, in the School of Business Administration, University of California, Berkeley.

sought after and used in many different situations.

However, the fact that the rate of return is so all-encompassing and concise may be a cogent reason for exercising much care in using it. The amount of income attributable to a given period is not always easy to establish with certainty, and the level of precision is even further reduced when we ascribe income to a part of an enterprise such as a department or a specific project. In order to separate income for a period from the over-all streams of revenues and costs we must break out a piece of the structure of financial activity, severing connections that cannot be
36 severed except by artifice and estimate; but to break out a department or organizational unit or a given activity or equipment item from the organism of which it is a living part is an even harder task. How much investment is actually involved in a division or a project is as difficult to establish with certainty as how much blood is required to nourish and maintain a finger! But the use of concepts is not always closely related to their imperfections; our ingenuity often devises ways to apply concepts in sophisticated ways that cover up the nature of the problems we try to solve.

Accounting measurements are, at this writing, the only basic sources of data which establish (however imperfectly) the income for a period, the amount of investment, and the bases of classification and matching which establish the rate of return currently being realized by operations or projects in which we are interested. The way in which such data are collected and handled is of importance; there should be good reason to raise questions concerning the problems encountered when those measurements are made. Sometimes the discussion of such questions can produce rather striking conclusions. A recent paper advances the suggestion that

> [the use of book yield] must be tempered by a far greater degree of judgment and adjustment than we have employed in the past, and in extreme cases the measure may have to be abandoned altogether in favor of an alternative measure, such as the ratio of cash flow before depreciation to gross book value.[1]

A statement such as this is extremely disconcerting. The author has not only charged that accounting measurements of income are inadequate, but he has also suggested that amortized cost balances ought to be abandoned in favor of gross acquisition cost. One must be really disenchanted with accounting measurements to take such a position!

To establish his conclusions, the author has presented a number of illustrations in his paper to support the contention that book yield (accounting income divided by depreciated investment balances) is inaccurate, untrustworthy, and capricious. He is not so much concerned with the weaknesses of real-world measurements of data as with the differences between the book yields developed from conventional accounting approaches and the pattern of calculation used in the compound-interest model under the abstract conditions of complete certainty.

The case is built by assuming a specific investment situation—a $1,000 project with cash receipts of $229.61 at the end of

[1] Ezra Solomon, "Return on Investment: the Relation of Book Yield to True Yield," in *Research in Accounting Measurement* (American Accounting Association, Collected Papers, 1966), p. 243.

"Cash flow"—[the words "before depreciation" are redundant]—is a derived measure used by some to describe business performance, as an extension or substitute for accounting income. It amounts to "accrual-income after income-taxes-but-without-recognition-of-related-depreciation-or-other-long-term amortizations." Since it is that figure which results from adding back long term amortizations to income, it is an approximation of "funds arising from operations" in the conventional funds statement; but it is not a cash measurement except in a limited sense. It is, of course, a measure of income in only a distorted and incomplete sense, since it omits essential costs related to any determination of income. See Perry Mason, "Cash Flow Analysis and the Funds Statement," *Research Study No. 2* (American Institute of CPA's, 1961).

each of six years to cover income and capital recovery. This project has what he calls a "known true yield" of 10 per cent —which can, of course, be substantiated by any interest table: $229.61 is the annual rent of an annuity which would be purchased by $1,000 when "money is worth" 10 per cent per year.

Having presented this example of the compound-interest model, the author then points out that conventional accounting would report an income of $62.95 per year from this investment. The proceeds of $229.61 would be reduced by depreciation of $166.67 each year (1/6 of $1,000—straight-line amortization). Then, computing the beginning of year book values ($1,000; $833.33; $666.67; $500; $333.33; $166.67), he derives yield rates for each of the six years: 6.29, 7.55, 9.44, 12.59, 18.89, and 37.76 per cent. Thus he has set up his initial argument: If the ***true*** rate of return is 10 per cent per year, a computation that shows an increasing range of annual returns from 6.29 to 37.76 per cent must be grossly in error. The author says:

> For single investment projects it is now well known that project book yield and project true yield may differ, and that the difference between the two measures can be quite large. It is also widely recognized and provable that the answer provided by the true yield method is the correct one and that it is the book-yield measure which is in error. Because of this the financial world long ago abandoned the book-yield measure in favor of the true yield approach as a measure of bond yields. A similar move is now going on in the industrial world as far as single project analysis is concerned.[2]

The case thus stated is carried further. Should one of these investments be acquired each year, the portfolio pattern will stabilize, after six years, with six of these investments being carried on which the calculated book yield will be 10.79 per cent. This is, in the author's words, "an overstatement of the true yield by some 8 per cent of the true yield—a not insignificant error." He does not indicate why this is so; he appears to be concerned only with building the case against book yield, in favor of the compound interest model. But it is shown that as the term is lengthened, the "error" in the book yield rises. He says, "At the limit of extremely long-life projects, the book-yield will approach twice the level of the known true yield." We shall be concerned with this a bit later in this paper.

To show the effect of another kind of depreciation computation in this model, it is noted that the use of different capitalization patterns will alter the book yield, while the true yield will be unaffected. Also, the use of accelerated depreciation by the sum-of-years digits method

> will leave the true yield (before tax) unchanged at 10 per cent. Net income will also remain unchanged at $377.66 for year 6 onward. . . . But the net book value of assets will fall from $3,500 to $2,666.65. The observable pre-tax book-yield will rise from 10.8 per cent to 14.2 per cent.[3]

Some of this appears to be entirely reasonable; of course the average investment will fall with SYD depreciation, and the average investment being less, the indicated return on that investment would obviously be greater. Still, there is something here that does not quite meet the eye; what is there about this "true yield" that keeps it constant when average investment changes?

Other examples are presented to build the case that,

> as far as the zero-growth case is concerned, the major findings are 1) the book-yield is not an accurate measure of true yield, 2) the error in the

[2] Ibid., pp. 233–4. The difference between a bond investment with capital recovery at the *end* of a period and the project providing for capital recovery *within* the term is apparently of no consequence for Solomon's analysis. However, the reason for this really lies in what is assumed about reinvestment.

[3] Page 238. Actually, the compound-interest model is unaffected by the choice of depreciation method, because it has its own built-in capital recovery pattern (of a quite different character). The "true yield" does not change, because it cannot be adjusted away from its own built-in capital recovery formula.

> book-yield is neither constant nor consistent. Indeed it is a fairly capricious measure which may sometimes underestimate true yield, but which more generally overstates true yield. The degree of potential overstatement ranges from slight under certain circumstances to very gross and misleading overstatements in others.[4]

The growth situation, in which investments are acquired at a rising pace, is used to suggest that

> the observable book-yield for a growing company will be smaller than the observable yield for a non-growing company, even though both hold substantially identical investments. . . . In general, if the observable book-yield is higher than true yield for a non-growth situation, the introduction of positive growth will tend to lower book-yield relative to true yield. The faster the growth, the more will book-yield decline relative to true yield.[5]

In his final illustration, the author brings inflation into the picture—using the basic six year $1,000 ten per cent investment, but having its price increase at the rate of 3 per cent annually. Conventional procedures would make no adjustments for the price level shift except to record the higher purchase prices as they occurred; this would presumably result in lower rates of return. But when one investment has been acquired at increasing prices in each of six years, the book yield on the portfolio of six investments works out to a $14\frac{2}{3}$ per cent rate of return in that sixth year. Rates of return on the individual investments would run in that year from 6.98 per cent per year for the most recently acquired item to 64.5 per cent per year for the oldest one.

This extensive collection of examples presumably demonstrates the undependability and bias of book yield, as compared with what the author calls "true yield." He is convinced that book yields ought not to be used in making comparisons:

> Adjustments are also required whenever book yields are used for the purpose of making inter-divisional, intercompany, or inter-industrial comparisons. While we have as yet no precise basis for making these necessary adjustments, the use of models does provide an approximate basis for doing so. It is probably better to use the adjusted book yields even if the adjustments are imprecise, than to use the unadjusted book yield figures which we know are subject to error.[6]

It is difficult to review this material without beginning to wonder what the basic trouble is—what there is about the accounting measure of book yield that makes it so capricious, what the bias is that creates these "errors." This, however, does not concern the quoted author, for he has proved to his own satisfaction what he set out to prove—that book yield is bad!

In any attempt to deal with problems of this kind, it should be noted that a mere comparison of two calculations does not establish the inaccuracy or incompetence of one of them. Starting from the premise that the right answer is known does not necessarily imply that anything else is ipso facto wrong. There are reasons for differences—else there is no logic in the comparison. But if we want the reasons for the phenomena of which the author complains, we shall have to seek them ourselves. The search is interesting and profitable—one can learn some useful things about the compound-interest model by trying to *ex*plain rather than *com*plain. The remainder of this paper is devoted to that end.

The Compound Interest Model

The most striking thing in Ezra Solomon's presentation is that the "true" yield never varies. No matter what kind of a situation is brought to attention, the compound-interest model shows no variation whatever. This may be because "truth" is immutable; but the inquirer may properly ask what it is about these calculations that

[4] Page 240.
[5] Page 241.
[6] Pages 243–4.

keeps them from being affected by the kind of factors which do affect the book-yield model. To be specific, the author's compound-interest model shows no effect on yield as the investment term is shortened or lengthened; it is not affected by the departure from an equal annual contribution to those which increase or decrease over the investment term. The compound-interest model is, apparently, not affected by differences in capitalizing expenditures, by changes in the rates or methods of establishing depreciation, by the forces of inflation; it is peculiarly impervious to all of the factors and forces that have shown themselves to the disadvantage of the accounting book yield! This "true yield" must be a jewel of basic consistency, of logical analysis and economic interpretation, to be able to maintain its aloofness from the onslaught of such various forces!

This vaunted perfection is but an illusion. The only reason for the apparently unchangeable yield is that it is figured that way. The rate of discount which solves the project equation for the yield is taken ipso facto to be the correct measure of "what money is worth." Every calculation in the model is based on the assumption that the internal average project rate is the only relevant interest factor. The cost of capital is not recognized, and nowhere is there any provision for different rates of return in the separate years. The rate of return is set up as a constant, and a constant it remains, because the model is built thus. This is convenient, because compound-interest tables are set up with separate columns for each rate of interest, and they are used that way; crossing over to another column would completely upset the calculations. This may be seen in better perspective if we consider the way in which interest rates are related to conversion periods and the project term—especially in terms of how proposals are analyzed.

Conversion Periods and the Project Term

The method for establishing a project rate of return has been explained often and at length with reference to "discounted cash flow" procedures, and it will not be repeated here. But it should be observed that the "rate of return" thus established is that single rate which will discount expected receipts to a present worth that is equal to the initial investment. The rate is an annual rate only because we choose to state it that way; it really applies to the entire term.

Although the rate of interest is conventionally stated as an annual figure, it may apply to any desired interval. We may have semi-annual or monthly rates, and in some situations it is possible to compound interest per day or even "continuously." On the other hand, there are nominal rates such as 4 per cent compounded annually; this is merely another way of saying "two per cent each six months." We often use "effective" rates for purposes of computation, since interest tables are not prepared for annual rates like 4.04 or 6.09 per cent. However, there is an assumption involved in this that should be recognized; the rates used are mathematically equivalent; but it is assumed that nothing affects the situation except the length of the conversion period. Actually, interest rates do change for various reasons, and the assumption may not hold for *practical* project analysis.

There is a practical advantage in stating the project rate of return in annual equivalents; most people think of interest as a "rate per year." But in strict logic, the conversion period for a project is its *term*, and the rate is established by all the events over the term, even though it may be expressed as an annual equivalent. In the given case, \$229.61 to be received annually for six years represents a 10% yield on a present investment of \$1,000, because that rate fits the equation:

$$\$229.61 \frac{1 - (1 + x)^{-6}}{x} = \$1,000.$$

Once established, the 10% rate also implies the validity of at least two other expressions which describe the terminal value of the project: $\$1,000\ (1.10)^6 = \$1,771.60$, and

$$\$229.61 \frac{(1.10)^6 - 1}{.10} = \$1,771.60.$$

The data in a project analysis necessarily apply to the whole term, as embodied in the project definition. All that is necessary for one to see this is to apply the same discount rate with one additional receipt, or any other change of amount or timing anywhere in the problem: the rate will equate present worth of receipts to the initial outlay only with all of the amounts and times given. Change any item, and you change the rate of return!

Recognizing that the project rate really applies to the entire term is perhaps not of much consequence in the typical case, for a rate of interest compounded sexennially would not be particularly meaningful to people who think of interest and rates of return in terms of per cent per year. But what we really do is to use that nominal rate per year "equivalent" to the project rate per term, and forget that in the process we have converted the effective rate of return on the project to an annual basis. The rates of return indicated by book yields *could* be the real rates of return that are averaged by the process just described.

Principal

The rate of return is a fraction or ratio, and its meaning depends in part upon what is set up as the denominator of that fraction, the "principal" sum. When the investment is made in a single lump sum, and there is no foreseeable possibility of future capital outlays (e.g., purchase of securities), the measurement of principal is easy. But the capital outlay is not always made in a lump sum. When there are a number of related expenditures, it is necessary to establish which are in fact capitalizable and which are not. This will affect compound-interest models as well as the accounting model. For instance, if an outlay in period 1 is actually chargeable to the activities of periods 1, 2, and 3, it is not correct to treat it as a cost only of period 1 if we are at all concerned with the results within individual periods. The project model, however, is not concerned with individual periods but with the project as a whole. With this purpose in mind, it is correct to ignore proration of capital cost. Even if such prorations were attempted, they would be without material effect. To defer a \$500 capital outlay over two years would entail interest accumulations; the first year end would call for a charge of $\$250\ (1+i)$, and the charge at the end of the second year would be $\$250\ (1+i)^2$. In the process of working out the project rate of return these accumulations would cancel out; the result would be the same as if the prorations had not been made. If the prorations had been made using a "cost of capital" rate which was different from the project yield, some residual effect would remain. But this would hardly be large enough to matter.

Nevertheless, if we are concerned with any period less than the full term, proration of capital cost is not only relevant but essential. At the end of three years, for instance, three \$229.61 receipts (total \$688.83) cannot be discounted to equal the initial outlay of \$1,000 by any positive rate of interest. Some evaluation of unexpired service-potentials must be made.

This may appear to be a quibble over an abstraction. It really is not; in the most practical sense, there are a number of capital expenditures that are made in the periods during which an asset serves its purpose. A motor truck requires replacement of various parts—engine, transmission, brakes and bearings to name a few items—at various times over its service-life. These are replacements; and if they are applicable to the services rendered for longer than one fiscal period, they too should be capitalized, and then expensed by amortization. Such expenditures are commonplace in handling most business assets. The only reasons why these outlays can be treated as current expenses are (1) they are relatively small in amount; (2) they do not benefit many fiscal periods; and (3) they tend to offset (by distribution) their effect upon any one period's relative results. But it is not the time of disbursement that determines their significance for income determination; it is the period benefited by their use. Project analysis using the compound-interest model does not concern itself with results for individual periods, and it concentrates on disbursements rather than costs and benefits. This is presumably because only cash transactions are important in project decisions; whereas the measurement of business activity generally must trace cash receipts and expenditures to their usage, transfer, or exchange. One cannot establish the cost of goods sold by reference to one or even a number of cancelled checks. The project decision, as quantified by the compound-interest model, involves issues and objectives that are different from the aims of income determination, and this would permit their being somewhat different in content and method. But there are other factors of importance in this problem.

Capital Recovery and Average Investment

There are but few investments which do not involve capital recovery in one way or another. Some, like the corporate bond, include capital recovery as a lump-sum repayment of principal at the end of the investment term. But the great majority of business projects involve assets that eventually become worthless; most physical assets eventually find their way to some kind of a junkpile. The cost of such investments is recoverable "out of" revenues—which is to say that somehow, their costs are expected to be returned over the term. However, unless the capital recovery process is specified, there is no single way to measure the annual productivity of the investment. In most income measurements—especially those made by accounting procedures—the capital cost is carried into the determination of periodic results by amortization, which serves to allow for capital deterioration in computing periodic income. This amortization may take vari- 41
ous forms—the most common of which is the straight-line method, which assigns asset cost to periods on the basis of time. Other methods assign asset cost to operations on the basis of physical use, which may be more realistic where wide fluctuations in the rate of activity exist. Recent developments have tended to bring into emphasis the "declining charge" methods such as the "constant per cent of declining balance" and the "sum-of-years-digits" methods. There are arguments in favor of declining-charge procedures besides their obvious tax advantages; many assets obviously decline in productivity as they become older, as technological, economic forces erode the advantages of novelty or reduce the level of efficiency which new assets may be expected to have. But there has been little acceptance of amortizations which produce increasing charges as the asset becomes older and usually less desirable. The annuity or sinking fund methods of amortization do provide an increasing charge pattern,—one with the special feature that the charges increase at an increasing rate until the end of the term. Seldom does a business asset show such a pattern of productivity—in which service potentials are released at an increasing rate

TABLE 1

COMPARISON OF INVESTMENT BALANCES—STRAIGHTLINE AND COMPOUND INTEREST AMORTIZATION
BASIC $1,000, SIX YEAR INVESTMENT, ANNUAL RECEIPTS $229.61

Yr.	*Straight Line Procedure*			*Compound Interest Procedure*		
	Beginning of Yr. Investment	*Amortization* 166.66 *each figure*	*Income* 62.95 *each figure*	*Beginning of Yr. Investment*	*Income*	*Amortization*
1	$1,000.00	$ 166.66	$ 62.95	$1,000.00	$100.00	$ 129.61
2	833.33	166.66	62.95	870.39	87.04	142.57
3	666.67	166.66	62.95	727.82	72.78	156.83
4	500.00	166.66	62.95	571.00	57.10	172.51
5	333.33	166.66	62.95	398.50	39.85	189.76
6	166.67	166.66	62.95	208.74	20.87	208.74
Totals	$3,500.03	$1,000.03	$377.64	$3,776.40	$377.64	$1,000.02
Average	583.33	166.66	62.95	629.40	62.94	166.67

that accelerates to a maximum just before the asset is discarded. Even when the output grows in volume and in unit value during the early part of the term, there is almost always a break and a reversal of this, a good while before the end of the use-life. Thus, compound-interest amortizations do not fit many real-world situations.[7]

Capital recovery or amortization is not easily established for any one year of an investment term. Usually, it is determinable only for the project as a whole, and any attempt to establish it for a short period is a matter of systematic rather than empirical measurement, simply because there are no data to do otherwise. But the kind of a systematic calculation used will determine the income for each one of the years or fiscal periods in the term, even though the final total income will be the same regardless of amortization procedure. This may be clearly seen in the comparison that Ezra Solomon made in his original example, here restated in Table 1.[8]

Perhaps the first observation to be made about the presentation in Table 1 is that the compound-interest "mathematics" do not show up therein. In each case, interest is figured for only one period, and the investment balance is a mere carryforward of the unamortized principal. Average investment is merely the sum of the investment balances divided by their number; the other averages are exactly the same in nature. This is because in the compound-interest model nothing happens *within* any conversion period; the interest is figured at the end of each conversion interval when payments are received, and this calculation takes into account the whole force of interest for that interval, including the carryovers of unamortized principal.[9] It will be seen that the average investment of the book-yield calculation is lower than that of the compound interest pattern; but the total income, the total

[7] Compound-interest amortizations assume that the charge for asset use should include both the interest cost of capital and capital recovery, and that their sum should be the same amount in each year. In theory, charging interest on investment is a recognition of the time value of capital, and it may thus be justified. But since in the actual case this "interest" is an imputed rather than a financial cost, it cannot be more than an internal transfer. What is left as a net charge to operations is the difference between the assumed level annual charge and the imputed interest on the declining investment balance.

In passing it may be noted that the "interest" rate in compound-interest depreciation is the *cost of capital*, not the project rate of return.

[8] Pages 235-6.

[9] Theoretically, it is possible to make the conversion period so short as to be practically equivalent to continuous compounding; but for any finite period interest is computed only for one conversion period as a whole at the end of that period.

capital recovery or depreciation, and the total receipts are the same.

The basic differences in the two procedures illustrated in Table 1 is that in the straight-line case, depreciation is computed and deducted in calculating the annual income while the compound-interest model reverses the process—first computing income, which when subtracted from cash revenue, yields the amortization figure.[10] It is this feature of the compound interest model that makes it possible to have a level rate of interest and a declining principal; with constant annual receipts, there is no way to achieve a level rate of return unless the amortization of principal is set up on an increasing charge basis in the "annuity depreciation" calculation. This works out to a higher average investment in the compound-interest model, because the reduction in principal in the early years is small, even though the amount written off in the last years is large enough to produce the same average depreciation over the term, the timing of the larger amounts is so late as to have less effect on the average investment.

If the features of the compound-interest model are understood and their implications are followed through the calculations of Table 1, it is easier to see that the "project" rate of return is indeed an average, not a "true" rate. The case under consideration involves a declining principal, since capital is to be recovered over the term; the decline in investment balance along with constant annual receipts would of necessity cause the rate of return to increase over the successive years, unless the receipts were adjusted to produce the same rate each year. This adjustment is accomplished by "annuity depreciation." Annuity depreciation would not alter the total income over the term, but it would change the annual income figures.

But it is this very kind of depreciation calculation that is necessary to establish a constant rate of return in every year for an investment with constant annual returns. For, with capital recovery that has has to be spaced over the term. It is clear that the investment-balance will decline from year to year; while there may be any number of patterns which this decline will take, the initial balance must eventually be written off; unless is it amortized at an increasing rate, there is no possibility of a constant annual rate of return. There are any number of combinations of annual income and amortization figures that could be set up for any given year, and the rate of return could therefore fluctuate widely. With $229.61 of annual receipts, a division of $20 to income and 209.61 to amortization, or $1 to amortization and $228.61 to income would yield exactly the same over-all rate of return for the project as a whole. The only constraints are (1) that income plus amortization of principal in any one year must together equal the cash receipts for that year and (2) that amortization for the entire term must equal the initial investment to be recovered. Just as one can set up an amortization table to support a 10 per cent return on the investment balance, one might set up a similar amortization to yield a different rate of return in each year that would still have an over-all project rate of return of 10 per cent. Such a table is set up in Table 2.

In Table 2, the individual-year rates range from 1 per cent to 16.8 per cent but average 10 per cent over the term, as given by average income divided by average investment. In no year is the current rate anywhere near 10 per cent, even though the cash receipts may be discounted to $1,000, by applying the 10 per cent per annum rate over the entire term. Thus it

[10] Solomon's original presentation did not show the amortization amounts in this way; the investment balance at the beginning of a year was determined as $I_{t+1}=I_t(1+r)-R$; the principal was accumulated at the compound interest rate, and the receipts deducted without separating the amortization element.

TABLE 2

AN INVESTMENT WITH VARYING ANNUAL RATES OF RETURN AVERAGING "10 PER CENT PER ANNUM" FOR THE TERM

Years	*(1) Investment Beginning of Year*	*(2) Current Year Rate of Return*	*(3) Current Year Income*	*(4) Cash Receipts*	*(5) Amortization (4)-(3)*
1	$1,000.00	14%	$140.00	$ 229.61	$ 89.61
2	910.39	1%	9,10	229.61	220.51
3	689.88	14.9%	102.79	229.61	126.82
4	563.06	15%	84.45	229.61	145.16
5	417.90	2%	8.36	229.61	221.25
6	196.65	16.8%	32.94	229.61	196.67
Totals	$3,777.88		$377.64	$1,377.64	$1,000.02
Averages	$ 729.65	10.0%	$ 62.94	$ 229.61	$ 166.67

is seen that the rates in individual years could be widely different from that which was imputed to the cash flow; any number of varying rate patterns might average out to the average-internal-project rate. Since the compound interest (over-all internal project rate) is established from cash flow, any division of those cash receipts as between capital recovery and income would not alter the compound interest rate of return. If the indicated rates for the specific years were used to discount the receipts, they would be applied in "chain" fashion, working back from the end of the term:

$229.61 ./. 1.168 = $196.58

$196.58 + $229.61 ./. 1.02 = $417.83

$417.83 + $229.61 ./. 1.15 = $563.00

$563.00 + $229.61 ./. 1.149 = $689.87

$689.87 + $229.61 ./. 1.01 = $910.38

$910.38 + $228.61 ./. 1.14 = $999.91

Discounting in each year is accomplished by dividing the balance at end of the year by 1+i (that year's conversion factor).

These conversion factors correspond to the annual rates in Table 2.

Thus the use of the individual rates would still equate future cash receipts to initial investments; those rates are just as "true" as the 10 per cent average rate.

What has been said in general terms may be applied to the straight-line book-yield example. The book yields for individual years, (which Solomon dismissed as misleading and capricious), will discount the cash receipts to exactly $1,000, just as the 10 per cent average rate did! The calculations are in Table 3. Evidently the "distorted" annual rates of return still have as much validity as the 10 per cent "true" yield.

REINVESTMENT

The question is sometimes raised as to whether the compound-interest model does or does not assume reinvestment of the principal as it is recovered. In the present case, it would seem that reinvestment is ignored, for the total income is reported as $337.64, which is 10 per cent of only the average investment. Income from reinvestment does not appear in the figures. The capital recoveries are apparently dropped from the computation, for no disposition is made of the amounts shown. What is really involved may be more clearly seen, however, if we compare the example ($229.61 for six years to recover capital and 10 per cent interest) with a simple accumulation of $1,000 at 10 per cent for six years. Each of these investments has the same accumulated amount ($1,771.58) at the end of six years. Evi-

TABLE 3

SUCCESSIVE DISCOUNTING AT ANNUAL RATES
CASH RECEIPTS FROM $1,000, 6 YEAR INVESTMENT

Year	(1) Carried Down	(2) Current Receipts	(3) Yr.-end Balance (1)+(2)	(4) Interest* Factor	(5) Amount at Beginning of Year (3)÷(4)
6	0	$229.61	$229.61	1.3776	166.67
5	$166.67	229.61	396.28	1.1889	333.32
4	333.32	229.61	562.93	1.1259	499.98
3	499.98	229.61	729.59	1.0944	666.58
2	666.58	229.61	896.19	1.0755	833.28
1	833.28	229.61	1,062.89	1.0629	1,000.00

* Shows book-yield expressed as a conversion factor (1+i).

dently it makes no difference whether the capital is returned along the way, or left until the end of the term!

The reason for this is that in a compound interest-model the rate of interest *is* the "value" of money; that is, any sum is the present worth of a perpetuity of interest payments at the given rate. Thus, when $129.61 is set aside as a recovery of capital in the first year, it is in effect assumed to be "worth" 10 per cent per year forever. The rate of interest is not a rate of return on a given set of activities, but it is "what money is worth"; and in that sense every dollar in existence is inevitably and automatically earning the rate of interest that has been set.

This conception is useful theoretically, but it does not always fit the real-world case. There are various kinds of investment, each of which has a potentially different rate of return; there is also such a thing as purchasing power that is not invested. The project rate of return cannot possibly cover all the ways in which capital recovery funds or income may be employed. Further, it is not always possible to reinvest at the desired or imputed project rate, if the amounts available do not match up to available investment opportunities, or if the time of investment opportunity does not agree with the time when funds are made available from capital recovery or income. Further, when we consider the given project and establish its rate of return, we are presumably considering others; the ones we do not select would be those with a lower rate of return. Hence, recovered funds may have to be invested in "second choices," with lower rates of return than the project from which those funds are produced. There is really no assurance that the rate of return established *ex ante* is applicable to any other project, or that capital recovery or income can be reinvested at the same rate. The rate of return for the compound-interest model assumed that reinvestment could be ignored because it does not affect the rate of return. This may be rationalized by saying that it assumes reinvestment at the project rate, but the real significance of the procedure is that the reinvestment is treated as irrelevant.

The book-yield computation, on the other hand, does *not* assume reinvestment; it drops out the figures for capital recovery and income, but the rate of return is stated only for *that* year, without implication of reinvestment. Inherently the book-yield and the project rate of return are directed at different purposes; the project rate of return should really include the computation of reinvestment results to be correct and meaningful; the book yield does not need to include reinvestment,

TABLE 4

EFFECT OF REINVESTMENT ON INVESTMENT RETURN

Year	*Without Reinvestment*			*Reinvestment at 10% per year*			*Reinvestment at 4% per year*		
	Beginning Investment	*Income*	*Amortization*	*Cash for Reinvestment*	*Income from Reinvestment*	*Reinvestment Fund Balance*	*Cash for Reinvestment*	*Income from Reinvestment*	*Reinvestment Fund Balance*
1	$1,000.00	$100.00	$ 129.61	$ 229.61	$ —	$ 229.61	$ 229.61	$ —	$ 229.61
2	870.39	87.04	142.57	229.61	22.96	482.18	229.61	9.18	468.40
3	727.82	72.78	156.83	229.61	48.22	760.01	229.61	18.74	716.75
4	570.99	57.10	172.51	229.61	76.00	1,065.62	229.61	28.67	975.03
5	398.48	39.85	189.76	229.61	106.56	1,401.79	229.61	39.00	1,243.64
6	208.72	20.87	208.74	229.61	140.18	1,771.58	229.61	49.75	1,523.00
Totals	$3,776.40	$377.64	$1,000.02	$1,377.66	$393.92		$1,377.66	$145.34	

because it is used to measure the return for only a single year.

To see what difference the reinvestment pattern makes in the case we have been discussing, Table 4 shows a comparison of
46 the basic investment example (a) with reinvestment at 10 per cent and (b) with reinvestment at 4 per cent. Reinvestment at 10 per cent per annum produces a final result of $1,771.58 from reinvestment of capital recovery and income, which is the accumulated sum of $1,000 invested at 6 years at 10 per cent. Thus by reinvestment, the project rate is achieved. The total income which arises directly from the project is (as was computed earlier) $377.64 over the term. Thus $377.64 is earned within the project, and $393.94 from reinvestment of proceeds; less than half of the income to make a 10 per cent return comes directly from the project. When the funds are reinvested at 4 per cent, the total fund accumulation is $1,523.00, and the over-all rate of return drops to about 7¼ per cent. This rate is near but not equal to the simple average of rates—$(10\%+4\%)/2=7.0\%$—because the compounding effect of the larger rate is stronger than that of the lower one.

The implication of this is that unless the reinvestment rate is exactly the same as that imputed to the project, the project rate is not a true indication of expectations from the investment. For reasons already given, the project rate would tend in practice to be higher than that for reinvestment, and the rate of return computed for the project thus would tend to be optimistic.

It has already been seen that the pattern of capital recovery affects the average investment for the project over its term. To refresh the reader's memory, the straight line computation yielded an average investment (for Professor Solomon's example, Table 1) of $583.33; the compound-interest model showed an average investment of $629.40. It is also clear that the average investment varies with different amortization patterns. The reason for these differences is that a decline in principal affects all following years; what happens in the earlier years is thus weighted more heavily than the events of later years. The compound-interest model has a higher average investment because less of the principal is recovered in the early years. This leaves more capital to be carried over the rest of the term; to postpone the decline of principal tends to increase the average investment. Straight-line book yields would necessarily be lower than the project rate in the early years of an investment, and they would be higher in the latter years, because of the way in which the "project-rate" of amortization affects investment balances. The choice of method of amortization is, however, not one that should be made because one is concerned only with an average rate of return as opposed to specific annual rates. Rather, capital recovery or amortizations should be based upon the usage of the store or services in the asset. An unrealistic view of the service usage is wrong for that reason, but it is doubly to be guarded against when it affects the carrying amount of the asset and affects the measurement of the rate of return which is desired. The fact that increasing-charge amortizations do not fit the real-world experience pattern is sufficient reason for not using them; but their damping effect upon the measurement of annual rates of return (by raising the average investment to level off the rate) makes them doubly undesirable.

This matter may be put in another way, as when the statement is made that the straight-line pattern of amortization "reduces book value faster than economic value declines"[11]—the real question is, of course, how fast *does* economic value decline in the given case? With reinvestment at the project rate of return assumed as an inherent part of the compound-interest model, it is hard to see how "economic-value-declines" can be established.

One other observation may be made with respect to average investment, (or "carrying" balances) in models of the kind under discussion. On a straight line basis, average investment is one half the capital commitment over the term. With a residual or scrap recovery, the net commitment is scrap value plus half the rest of the principal. In view of this, the figures shown in Table 1 as "beginning of year balances" (after Solomon) are not quite appropriate. The reason why they are shown thus is that investment is assumed to have been made at the beginning of a year, and amortization is figured for a year as a unit. Thus the "average" investment in Table 1 for the straight-line basis is $583.33, which is too high. The difference between $583.33 and the proper average of $500 arises from the use of beginning of the year figures instead of the average investment during the year. For instance, the first year's investment appears in Table 1 for straight line amortization book yield as $1,000. This should be, more correctly, $916.67, computed (1,000+833)/2. The capital recovery in straight-line amortization is assumed to be a continuous constant rate through time: the rate per period is prorated to parts of a period; the depreciation for half a year would be $83.33, one half the annual amount. Centering the book values at the middle of the year (conventionally regarded as a necessary correction) would produce somewhat higher book values and lower yields; but it would result in a correct average investment figure, in keeping with the straight-line assumption.

Strictly speaking, the average investment on a straight-line basis for *any* term ignoring the terminal or disposal values is one half the initial commitment. The length of the term is irrelevant; average investment does not vary with different length of term. Thus Solomon's conclusion that the average investment declines toward a limit of $500 as the term increases is open to question. What is involved in his example is that the error in centering becomes less and less significant as the term is made longer. A half year is a smaller error relative to twenty years than it is to six, and the relative significance of centering thus declines with a longer term. The average investment does not decline toward half the principal as the term is increased; the error in centering approaches zero as it is spread over longer periods.

A word is indicated about the perpetuity case, which appears to be the limit of an increasing-term pattern. Such a view does fit the compound-interest model, in that the compound-interest tables may be set up for any number of "periods"—i.e., "t" may increase without bound. But perpe-

[11] Op. cit., p. 4.

tuity is far removed from this conception; the real world does not contain many cases in which "t" becomes much greater than 20 or 25 (or, with "quarterly compounding") 80 or 100. Perpetuity is really a special class of investment in which there is *no* capital recovery and no problem of amortization of principal; the average investment is simply the initial investment.

The relation of average investment to length of term is, in the compound-interest model, a rather interesting thing which has not received a great deal of attention. Since the average investment seemed so different from the straight-line figure in the six-year case thus far used as an example, the writer tried to follow the calculations of the effect of term length on rate of return given for the straight-line case, with a comparative calculation for the compound-interest model. The average investment for the 15-year project—($1,000 principal, annual receipts $131.47) worked out to $648.10—$18.70 *more* than the $629.40 computed for the six year investment. For 25 years, the average investment computed for a $1,000 principal ($110.17 annual receipts) investment was $701.61, another $43.81 *higher*. While this might have been expected from the "increasing charge" pattern of amortization, it was somewhat greater than had been anticipated. There seemed to be some justification for examining average investment in compound-interest models of this kind.

For a constant annual cash-flow compound-interest investment model, the average investment may be computed from the formula:[12]

$$I_{av}=\frac{I_0}{i}\left(CRF_{i,n}-\frac{1}{n}\right)$$

In this formula, I_{av} is average investment; I_0 is the initial investment; i is the rate of interest per payment interval, n is the number of years in the term, and $CRF_{i,n}$ is the "capital recovery factor" for the given rate and term. Conventionally, this is the reciprocal of the present worth of an annuity of 1 for the given term:

$$CRF_{i,n}=\frac{i}{1-(1+i)^{-n}}$$

For the six year case we have been considering, the capital recovery factor is .2296073, and average investment is $629.41:

$$\frac{\$1{,}000}{.10}(.2296073-\tfrac{1}{6}) = \$10.000(.0629407)$$

$$=\$629.41$$

This figure will be seen to correspond to the average investment in Table 1 above. Using this formula to establish average investment figures for 10% investments covering various terms gives the results presented above in Table 5.

It will be seen from these figures that the average investment starts at $1,000 and falls as the term increases until the eighth year, when it reverses; after year 8 it increases first at an increasing, then at at a decreasing rate. By the 30th year it has

TABLE 5

COMPOUND INTEREST INVESTMENT MODELS
EFFECT OF LENGTHENING TERM ON AMORTIZATION AND AVERAGE INVESTMENT

Term (years)	*Annual (Cash Flow)*	*First Year*		*Average Investment Over the Term*
		Income	*Amortization*	
1	$1,100.00	$100.00	$1,000.00	$1,000.00
2	576.19	100.00	476.19	761.90
4	315.47	100.00	215.57	654.70
6	229.61	100.00	129.61	629.40
7	205.41	100.00	105.41	625.48
8	187.44	100.00	87.44	624.40
9	173.64	100.00	73.64	625.29
10	162.75	100.00	62.75	627.50
15	131.47	100.00	31.47	648.10
20	117.46	100.00	17.46	674.60
30	106.08	100.00	6.08	727.50
40	102.26	100.00	2.26	772.60
50	100.86	100.00	.86	808.60
100	100.08	100.00	.08	900.08

[12] See appendix note on pages 697-8 for derivation.

TABLE 6

COMPOUND INTEREST INVESTMENT MODELS
AVERAGE INVESTMENT, TERM LENGTH WITH
RESPECT TO INTEREST RATES

Rate of Interest	*Number of Periods in the Term with Minimum Average Investment*	*Minimum Average Investment Amount*
1/4	49	$520.39
7/8	35	528.81
1	25	540.67
1 1/2	20	549.71
2	18	557.30
3	14	569.93
4	12	580.48
5	11	589.58
6	10	597.80
8	9	612.10
10	8	624.40

risen to $727.50, after 50 years it is $808.60, and at 100 years the average investment is $900.80. This increasing average investment continues to a limit of $1,000 at an infinite term. The pattern of average investment is not entirely surprising, reflecting as it does the exponential form of the interest factor. But the basic reason for this is the pattern of amortization. As the term is made longer, amortization in the early periods becomes smaller (at a decreasing rate). As the term increases from two to ten years, the first-year amortization falls from 48% to 6%; with a twenty-year term, the first-year amortization has fallen to 1.7% of principal; at 50 and 100 years the percentages are .086 and .008. Although it would be expected that the rate of amortization would fall as the term is lengthened, the compound-interest model exaggerates this, and on long term investments the capital recovery is extremely slow. For the 50 year investment, the unrecovered principal after 25 years (one half the term) is still $915.47—more than nine-tenths of the original amount. In the last six years of the 50 year investment, $439.06 of the original $1,000 must be recovered out of $605.16 expected future receipts.

The average investment in the compound-interest model does not follow the patterns of Table 5 in the same way for all rates of interest. At 10%, an eight-year term produces the lowest average investment figure, but this is shifted to longer terms as the rate of interest is reduced. Table 6 presents this effect for interest rates ranging from ¼ per cent to 10%—in general, the higher the rate of interest, the higher will be the average investment for a given length of term, and the shorter will be the term in which the minimum balance is reached. The carrying amount of the investment under compound-interest procedures will be a function of both the rate of interest and the length of the term; these 49
two variables have opposite, but non-linear effects upon the average investment balance. Thus, the carrying amount of an investment in the compound-interest model is not a simple figure, easily determined. When it is recognized that these patterns are complicated by varying opportunities for reinvestment, and fluctuating market or alternative rates of interest, it is indeed difficult to generalize in this area. Certainly, it is clear that the compound-interest model that stresses the "average internal project rate" is subject to serious limitations for its application to real world conditions.

CONCLUSIONS

Professor Solomon's paper has caused us to consider at some length the characteristics of the compound-interest investment model, to explain the apparent differences between book yield and the project rate of return. The underlying difference is, of course, that the project rate and the book yield are calculated under two different sets of conditions, and with two purposes in mind. The project rate is an average rate of return over the project term, not an annual one; even though it may be expressed as a rate per year, it is established and it refers to the term of the project as a whole, being a nominal rate derived from the way in which calculations are made. The book yield is a figure based only on the data related to a given year, and it has no reference to any other part of the project than that year to which it applies. The project rate is the average of the book yields, as was shown in Table 3.

Second, although it is not always recognized, the compound-interest model which includes capital recovery has built into it a kind of amortization which is known as the annuity, sinking fund, or compound-interest method of amortization. It does produce a constant return for each year of
50 the investment term, but at the cost of an unrealistic pattern of depreciation or amortization—increasing charges for the use of assets as they become older. Although this pattern of amortization maintains the constant (average) project rate of return, it does not fit experience patterns of the real world.

Third, the compound-interest model assumes reinvestment of income and capital recovery funds at the same rate of interest ascribed to the project. This is done via the assumption that the project rate determined what "money is worth," and that therefore reinvestment is so automatic and inherent as to be ignored in the specific calculations. We did examine the effects of reinvestment, and established that it is in fact of some real importance, and that it ought to be considered specifically in any investment decision, because the reinvestment opportunities and returns are likely to be less desirable than for the project which we seriously consider for investment.

Fourth, the question of amounts carried forward from year to year in an investment model brings out the importance of trying to make measurements of capital erosion rather than to allow them to appear by default in the compound interest model. Admittedly this is of less importance in a bond investment that it is in a depreciable asset, but it is of consequence whenever capital recovery is involved. When depreciation is a factor in the measurement of income, one does not really measure that depreciation by treating it as the amount which remains when "income" has been deducted from cash receipts.

Many of the "problems" that arise in the use of book yields stem from the attempt to oversimplify the given situation. A project is "satisfactory" for instance, if it earns a given rate of return—say, 10% on investment. The truth is that every situation is somewhat different; each year of operation of a project is different from the earlier ones; the attempt to force a given rate of return from any and all situations is not likely to succeed. The way to compare a book yield with the project plan is not to use the over-all project rate of return, but to set up for each year of the project that rate of return which applies to it; comparison of the rate expected for that year with the actual experience will not show large discrepancies—certainly not so large as the average-internal-project rate would suggest. Such differences as do appear in the comparisons of expectations with actual results in given years may be traced by reviewing costs incurred, revenues realized, and capital erosion experienced, against the backdrop of the figures that were in the detailed planning model when it was set up. Thus, one may determine what is different as between the operations and the model's expectations; this may be much more useful than merely determining that the hoped for rate of return was not achieved.

It is perhaps unfortunate that neatly averaged project rates cannot be applied without reservation to the actual operations of a single year. And the fact that individual years' rates of return start at a low level and increase over the term is awkward. But these are the rates of return which result when capital erosion is recognized realistically; no problem is raised if the project analysis is carried out in the way it should be—the way actual operations will be measured and reported.

The pattern of annual rates is also upsetting (as Solomon points out) in its apparent effect on an increase in a given portfolio; the over-all effect of an investment does not show until it has been held over its term. But is this a reason for using an average which may have no relevance whatever? Nobody should get overly interested in a cumulative preferred stock with a 6% dividend rate, which is selling for 30% of par; such a quotation usually means that this stock will participate in a reorganization or refinancing, and the 20% yield is a mere accident. Similarly, a 4 per cent bond offered at $120 has a yield of 3 per cent over thirty years, only if there is no default, refunding, or other event to change the situation. The accountant must make his measurements in a given status quo, under constraints that allow only a minimum of dependence upon his own and others' expectations. He does assume a persistence of that status quo in terms of continuity of operations and of the environment in terms of experience standards and observable tendencies. But he cannot assume away the uncertainties of the future by making his figures fit a model. Rates of return are merely derived relationships; they cannot be viewed as absolutes. Too many problems of interpretation lie in the way of those who seek a simple way to make difficult comparisons.

Even though it may be helpful to put such measurements together, the underlying limitations of derived measurements must be understood if they are to be used for interpretation of results. The difficulties in establishing income for a short period, pitfalls in estimating the investment applicable to a project or a division, and the confusions that result from transplanting concepts from one context to another may mislead or misdirect otherwise good judgment.

Above all, the suggestion that progress and success should be measured by such relationships as cash flow in relation to gross assets, ought to be viewed with great care. While we may share Ezra Solomon's concern that we ought to use the best measures we can find, it may be worth noting that it is better to use accountant's estimates of what we really want to know than to use numbers which bear no relationship to the problems we need to solve.

Appendix Note

This formula for average investment does not appear in typical discussions of compound interest. I am indebted to my colleague, Jack D. Rogers, for the following.

At any time, t, the amount invested is the present worth of unrecovered principal; if t payments have been made, the remaining $n-t$ payments are an annuity with present value equal to the unrecovered principal. The annuity payments are each R, which is equal to $CRF_{i,n}\,(I_0)$. The present worth of this annuity of $n-t$ payments is

$$A = \frac{(1+i)^{n-t}-1}{i(1+i)^{n-t}}\,R.$$

The investment at any time, t, is

$$\frac{(1+i)^{n-t}-1}{i(1+i)^{n-t}}\cdot\frac{i(1+i)^n}{(1+i)^n-1}\,I_0.$$

$$I_t = \frac{(1+i)^t[(1+i)^{n-t}-1]}{(1+i)^n-1}$$

$$= \frac{(1+i)^n-(1+i)^t}{(1+i)^n-1}\,.$$

The *average* investment at any time is

$$I_{av} = \sum_{t=1}^{t=n} \left(\frac{I_t}{n}\right)$$

$$= I_0 \sum_{t=1}^{t=n} \left[\frac{(1+i)^n - (1+i)^t}{(1+i)^n - 1}\right] \cdot \frac{1}{n} \cdot$$

Then,

$$I_{av} = I_0 \left[\frac{n(1+i)^n}{(1+i)^n - 1} - \frac{1}{n(1+i)^n - 1} \left\{ \sum_{t=1}^{t=n} (1+i)^t \right\}\right] \cdot$$

But

$$\sum_{t=1}^{t=n} (1+i)^t = \frac{(1+i)^n - 1}{i} \cdot$$

Hence

$$I_{av} = I_0 \left[\frac{CRF_{i,n}}{i} - \frac{1}{n(1+i)^n - 1} \cdot \frac{(1+i)^n - 1}{i}\right]$$

$$= I_0 \left[\frac{CRF_{i,n}}{i} \cdot \frac{1}{ni}\right]$$

$$I_{av} = \frac{I_0}{i}\left[CRF_{i,n} - \frac{1}{n}\right].$$

Alternative rate of return concepts and their implications for utility regulation

Ezra Solomon
Dean Witter Professor of Finance
Graduate School of Business
Stanford University

The rate of return on invested capital is a widely used concept in both regulated and unregulated sectors of the economy. It provides a measure of actual performance as well as required or expected performance (the latter is often termed the "cost of capital"). In the utility field, regulatory agencies often focus on the rate of return as a major instrument for assessing and controlling the performance of firms under 53
their jurisdictions. Unfortunately, two altogether distinct units are employed for measuring rate of return: (1) book rate units and (2) discounted cash flow units. Rarely will the two produce the same result, and the use of one measure as a surrogate for the other may prove highly misleading. This paper indicates the relationship between the two measures and shows the impact of some variations in depreciation and expensing procedures, growth rate, etc. The object is to point out the potential hazards associated with the use of measures of different things in a context that requires the use of measures of the same thing.

The rate of return on invested capital is a central concept in financial analysis. It is widely used as a basis for decisions, both in the unregulated sector and in utility regulation. One essential process for both purposes is an intercomparison between two facets of the rate of return measure:

(1) One facet is a summary measure of actual or prospective performance i.e., a measure of the annual rate at which each unit of capital input generates net financial benefits.

(2) The second facet is a summary measure of a "required" annual rate i.e., the financial standard or target rate against which the performance of prospective or already committed capital inputs can be assayed. In this second form it is also called "the cost of capital" rate.

When factor prices (other than capital) and product prices are taken as given, (as in the competitive pricing model), an intercomparison of these two facets of rate of return determines changes in the level of capital inputs. If, on the other hand, the scale of existing and future investment and factor prices (other than capital) are taken as given (as in the administered pricing model), then an intercomparison of these two facets determines product pricing decisions.

Professor Solomon holds the A.B. degree, with honors (University of Rangoon, 1940), and the Ph.D. degree (University of Chicago, 1950). He was on the faculty of the University of Chicago Graduate School of Business from 1948 to 1960, and was appointed Professor of Finance in 1957. He has been with the Graduate School of Business at Stanford University since 1961, first as Professor of Finance and Director of the International Center for the Advancement of Management Education (1961–'64), and as Dean Witter Professor of Finance since 1965.

Thus, large companies may set prices in order to achieve a target rate of return,[1] and the thrust of utility price regulation is to provide utilities an opportunity to earn some "fair" rate of return on investment.

If the "rate of return on investment" were itself a single, unambiguous concept, the only difficulties we would encounter in using it for either purpose would be difficulties involving correct estimation of the measure. But the concept is not unambiguous: quite apart from trivial variants such as pre-tax vs. post-tax measures or a total capital vs. an equity capital basis for the concept,[2] there is a non-trivial problem which arises from the fact that "rate of return" is measured in terms of two altogether distinct units: book rate units, and discounted cash flow units.

□ **Book rate units.** These are more properly called book-ratio units. The "rate" being measured is defined as the ratio of income during a given period of time (as defined by the usual accounting measure of this term) to the net book-value of invested capital outstanding during the period (as defined by the balance sheet corresponding to the income statement from which the numerator is derived).[3] This version of the rate of return will be symbolized as *b*, and it represents the most commonly used basis for reporting and analyzing "rate of return on invested capital."[4]

□ **DCF units.** Unlike the book-ratio, this measures the return on capital in terms of the annual rate at which the "future" (actual or prospective) net funds flows (or cash flows as these are commonly called) from an investment have a discounted value equal to the value of the investment outlays required to bring about these funds flows. Hence the name DCF units, which refers to the "discounting cash flows" process required to calculate this version of rate of return on investment.

This basis for measuring rate of return is the most commonly used one for theoretical purposes. It will be symbolized by the letter *r*.[5]

Conceptual differences between the DCF rate and the book-ratio

■ There are three major conceptual differences between the two measures, *b* and *r*.

(1) The book-ratio, *b*, defines its flow variable (income) as "cash flow" (meaning funds flow) minus depreciation and minus the expensed portion of current period investment. In contrast, the DCF rate, *r*, defines the flow variable as "cash flow" before these two adjustments.

(2) The book-ratio, *b*, defines its stock variable (investment) as the net book value of capital as this would appear on the balance

[1] See [9].

[2] These are trivial in the sense that they are obvious and therefore lead to no confusion. To simplify the exposition, I shall ignore these two potential differences in definition by assuming, throughout most of this paper, that income taxes and long-term borrowing do not exist.

[3] Another potential, but trivial, ambiguity arises from the fact that we can measure the accounting net book value figure on a beginning-of-period basis, an ending-of-period basis, or somewhere in between.

[4] For reporting, see *Fortune's* 500 Largest Industrials Directory; *Fortune's* 50 Largest Firms in Merchandising, Banking and Transportation; FTC-SEC Quarterly Financial Report on Rates of Return in Manufacturing; First National City Bank of New York's Annual Return on Capital series; FPC and other regulatory agencies' Annual Reports on "Return on Investment."

For analysis, see [3], [8], [11], and [18].

[5] For prospective investments it is equal to the expected marginal productivity of capital (or the marginal efficiency of capital in Keynesian analysis), or the "initial rate of return." For investments in long-term bonds it is called the "effective yield to maturity."

sheet consonant with the definition of the income variable, i.e., the balance sheet number, which is linked by the inexorable rules of double-entry accounting to the income definition. In content, the DCF rate, r, defines the stock variable (investment) as the total initial outlay of funds required for generating the cash flows counted on the flow side of the equation.

(3) Finally, the book ratio, b, defines the rate of return in a given period of time, or over a period of time, as the arithmetic ratio of its flow variable to its stock variable. In contrast, the DCF rate, r, defines the rate of return as that rate of compound discount (or interest) at which the time adjusted (present) value of the flow variable (cash or funds flows) is equal to the time adjusted (present) value of the stock variable (investment outlays).

Given these basic differences in definition between b and r, it is highly unlikely that their numerical values will be equal. Yet both carry the same label "percent per annum rate of return on investment," and the two are frequently used as if they were freely congruent and interchangeable measures of the same thing. Some examples are:

1. For a single company or industry the rate, b, is often treated as if it were an unbiased measure of r;

2. When several companies or industries are analyzed it is generally assumed that differences in b reflect corresponding differences in r;

3. Estimates of fair or reasonable rates are often calculated in DCF units, i.e., in terms of the r measure, and applied to net book value estimates without regard to the essential differences between DCF units and book rate units. Alternatively, a company may set its required rate of return for *ex-ante* capital budgeting purposes in terms of DCF cost of capital units and then measure *ex-post* performance in terms of book rate units.

These, and other forms of confusion between the two conceptually and numerically different yardsticks, can and do lead to considerable confusion in many forms of investment analysis, both in the unregulated sector and, more particularly, in utility regulation.

The rest of this paper is an attempt to explore the nature and magnitude of the differences between the r version and the b version of rate of return measurement and, on the basis of this analysis, to examine potential uses and misuses of the two concepts for interpretive and regulatory purposes.

Measuring performance: the DCF rate of return

■ For a single investment project, the DCF rate, r, is defined as the rate at which net cash flows from the project, over its productive life, have a present value equal to the original investment outlay required by the project. Thus if:

$$C_0 = \text{investment outlay at time } t = 0,$$
$$F_t(t = 1 \cdots n) = \text{net cash flows per period},$$
$$n = \text{project life (zero salvage assumed)},$$

we have

$$C_0 = \sum_{t=1}^{n} F_t(1 + r)^{-t}. \quad (1)$$

The DCF rate, r, is uniquely determined by the configuration of net cash inflows per unit of outlay, where configuration, in this context, refers to the volume, time-pattern, and duration of the net cash inflows F_t.[6]

In the general case, where the configuration of F_t is freely variable, the rate r has to be ascertained by trial and error calculations from compound discount tables. However for a pattern of level cash inflows, equation (1) can be restated more explicitly. Thus if the net cash inflows is a level stream of F a year for n years, we have

$$F = C_0\left[\frac{r(1 + r)^n}{(1 + r)^n - 1}\right]. \tag{2}$$

Regular tables exist for the bracketed items for various values of r and n, and hence the value of r for any ratio F/C_0 can be found readily by inspection. For example, assume

$$C_0 = \$1{,}000,$$
$$F = 229.61,$$
$$n = 6.$$

Then using annual end-of-period discount tables it can be shown that $r = 0.10$ or 10 percent per annum.

Although the DCF rate for a single project is a well known and widely used measure in capital analysis, the corresponding DCF measure for an ongoing company is not generally available. The reason for this is that the pattern and duration of net cash flows for a single project is known or estimated, either retrospectively or prospectively, whereas this is not true for a company, which is an ongoing collection of many projects. However, logic tells us that if a company holds many projects, each of which individually yields a DCF rate r, then the company as a whole will also be generating a DCF rate r on its total portfolio. This is true regardless of the pace at which the projects have been acquired over time and regardless of the practices used in accounting for capital and income.

To compare the results obtained by measuring return on investment in terms of the book ratio b against the underlying DCF rate r, we must therefore use the simulated model in which r itself is known.

Company profitability: *b* vs *r* in the steady state

■ In order to analyze the level of b relative to any given level of r, we take a hypothetical company or companies which acquire or can acquire only a single type of investment whose cash inflow characteristics are known. For illustrative purposes we can take the investment mentioned above: \$1,000 of outlay generates level cash inflows of \$229.61 a year for 6 years, after which the asset is scrapped at zero salvage value. The DCF rate of return on this investment is 10 percent, and hence any company which holds a portfolio con-

[6] More specifically, the configuration of cash inflows per unit of outlay uniquely determines the rate r only if the outlay value is set independently of the rate, r. This is clearly true in the point-input case being discussed. It also holds for investment outlays which themselves have a time duration if the discounted present value of such outlays is calculated through the use of some cost of capital rate, k, which is known or assumed independently of the rate, r, expected from an individual project. However, the rate, r, is frequently (though incorrectly) calculated as that rate, r^*, that equates the present value of inflows with the present value of outlays when both inflows and outlays are discounted at a common rate, r^*. For this method of computation multiple solutions for r^* can exist. For a more complete discussion of multiple solutions, see [15], ch. 10.

sisting exclusively of such projects must be earning a DCF rate of 10 percent per annum.

What book rate b will such a company show? As we shall see, the answer to this depends on several factors. Two factors which have a powerful effect on the size of b relative to r deserve detailed consideration. These are:

1. Accounting practices used in defining book income and net book capital, and
2. The pace at which the company acquires new investments over time.

In order to understand the effect of each of these factors, we will deal with them one at a time. Assume, to begin with, that the company acquires new investments (or projects) by investing an equal amount of money each year. This will be referred to as the "steady-state" condition (it could equally well be called the zero-growth case). Our hypothetical company which invests an equal amount each year in the basic type of project outlined will reach a "steady state" after six years. Beyond this point it will always hold six "investments." When it acquires its seventh investment, the first one it acquired is scrapped, when it acquires the eighth the second is scrapped, and so on.[7]

The book rate of return b. The book rate of return for a company in the steady state, which holds only investments identical to the basic project outlined, will depend on the accounting procedures used—in particular, on the fraction of each original investment outlay which is expensed for book purposes, and the specific depreciation formula which is used in deriving income, period by period, over each project's economic lifetime.

The book rate can be calculated by (1) defining the general value of b in algebraic terms and (2) solving such an equation for any given set of values of the accounting variables. However for any situation other than full capitalization of investment outlays and straight-line depreciation and zero growth, the algebraic expressions for the book rate of return can become exceedingly messy and sometimes complicated. Happily a graphical approach, even though partly intuitive, makes it possible to bypass explicit algebraic solutions and still make the relevant points.

To begin with the simplest situation, assume that the company capitalizes all of its investment outlays and uses a straight-line depreciation formula. The income statement of such a company after it reaches a steady state will show:

Net Cash Flow	= 6 × \$229.61	= \$1,377.66
Depreciation	= 6 × 1/6 × \$1,000	= \$1,000.00
Net Book Income =		= \$ 377.66

Its balance sheet, in the steady state, would show a net book value equal to one-half of the original outlay for the six "investments" it holds in its portfolio. This is shown in Figure 1. The original outlay is \$1,000. This is written-off continuously as time passes, i.e., the net book value of each asset is diminished along the line AB. After $t = 6$ the company holds six vintages of investment ranging from one 0.5

FIGURE 1
STRAIGHT-LINE
DEPRECIATION

\$1000 ORIGINAL
INVESTMENT

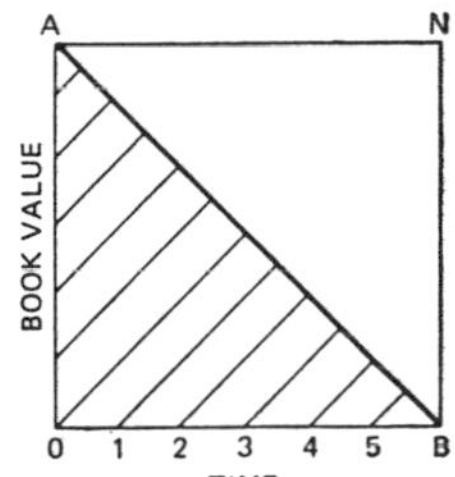

[7] Inflation is assumed to be zero in this portion of the analysis.

year old to one 5.5 years old, and together they have an undepreciated net book value equal to the area under the line *AB*. We can see by inspection and our knowledge of Euclid that this is $1,000 × 6/2 or $3,000.

Thus the book rate of return for this company is $377.66 ÷ $3,000 or 12.6 percent.

We now also have a tool which permits us to vary our accounting procedures and to discover the consequent effect on *b* of doing so *without* engaging in tedious algebraic expressions. (Meanwhile we still retain our basic assumption that all companies are in a "steady state," i.e., that our company acquires its investments through *equal* annual outlays.)

Variation in expensing procedures

58

■ We can begin our analysis by assuming again that all companies acquire only the one basic investment we have outlined ($1000 which generates $229.61 a year for six years) and that all use straight-line depreciation. However, now they are free to alter their expensing procedures, i.e., they may charge off any fraction of the $1000 as current expenses. (Recall that we are ignoring the tax-impact of expensing policies on net cash flows.)

As far as before-tax cash flows are concerned, there is no change if the company's accountant charges part of each year's $1000 outlay to current expenses rather than to book capital. Therefore accounting procedures do not affect the DCF yield *r*. It remains at 10 percent on each investment held, and hence at 10 percent for all of them collectively.

Do these accounting variations in the fraction of each year's $1000 outlay which is expensed affect the flow of company income? In the steady state (equal investment outlays each year) the answer is "No." This can be seen clearly in Table 1. Regardless of the amount expensed each year, the total annual charge of expensing plus depreciation adds up to $1000.

What Table 1 shows is that (in the steady state) the flow of reported income (after depreciation of non-expensed capital and the expensed portion of current investment) does not vary at all with the expensing policy adopted.

Although expensing policy has no effect on book income (ignoring taxes) it does have a profound effect on the net book value of capital. Returning to Figure 1, we see that with a zero expensing policy the straight-line depreciation function (Line *AB*) produces a

TABLE 1
STRAIGHT-LINE DEPRECIATION

EXPENSING POLICY	ANNUAL CASH FLOW	ANNUAL AMOUNT EXPENSED	ANNUAL DEPRECIATION	ANNUAL BOOK INCOME
0	$1377.66	$ 0	$1000	$377.66
20%	1377.66	200	800	377.66
50%	1377.66	500	500	377.66
100%	1377.66	1000	0	377.66

company net book value of $3000, i.e., the net book value figure is equal to the area under the depreciation curve (or line).

With a 100-percent expensing policy, the depreciation function will follow the right-angled line *AOB*. The area under this curve is zero. Such a company would have no net book capital. But, as we have seen in Table 1, its net income is $377.66. Its book rate of return b will therefore be infinity. The corresponding net book value and book rate of return for different expensing policies (straight-line depreciation) are shown in Table 2.

TABLE 2

EXPENSING POLICY	ANNUAL BOOK INCOME	COMPANY NET BOOK VALUE	b (PERCENT)
0	$377.66	$3000	12.6
20%	377.66	2400	15.4
50%	377.66	1500	25.2
90%	377.66	300	125.9
100%	377.66	0	∞

The effects of expensing policies on book rates of return are clearly powerful. What this means is that two companies which are in fact generating the same DCF rate r might in theory show book rates b_a, b_b, b_c, $\cdots$ b_n which range all the way from less than r percent at one extreme to ∞ percent at the other. The empirical question is: Do companies or divisions of companies, in fact, use different expensing ratios as far as investment outlays are concerned. The answer is that they do. Many companies capitalize all or almost all of their investment outlays. Others expense a high fraction. Companies with high research and development expenditures use a high expensing policy. Companies with high long-range advertising expenditures (i.e., expenditures which contribute little to current period cash flow but which contribute to future cash flow) do in effect use a high expensing policy. Producing departments of petroleum companies or primarily producing companies in the oil and gas industry also expense a high fraction of outlays in the form of exploratory, developmental, and intangible drilling costs.

Because our model, thus far, is confined to steady-state situations (equal or approximately equal investment outlays each year) it is premature to extrapolate our findings to the real world, but the results are suggestive. For example, the producing segment of the integrated oil industry, or oil and gas companies which are primarily producers rather than refiners and transporters, tend to have significantly higher book rates of return than the integrated companies. For example, Amerada earned an average book rate on equity capital of 21.6 percent during the period 1964–1968 as opposed to a corresponding rate of about 12.0 percent for the integrated petroleum industry as a whole. Likewise, pharmaceutical companies and cosmetic companies (which also follow a higher-than-typical expensing policy with respect to investment outlays) consistently show significantly higher rates than the rest of the manufacturing sector.

For example, according to the Fortune Directory, the pharmaceutical industry has shown the highest return on invested capital year after year. For 1968 it was again in first place with a median book rate of return of 17.9 percent (compared to the *all*-industry median rate of 11.7 percent). The soaps and cosmetics industry was in second place with a median book rate of return of 16.9 percent.

The conventional explanation for these higher-than-normal rates of return for companies or industries is that they are either:

(1) riskier (this is the standard explanation for the producing sector of the oil and gas industry),

(2) more efficient, or

(3) have monopoly powers (this is frequently applied to the pharmaceutical sector).

While these three conventional explanations may be correct in varying degrees, they all assume that the observable book rates accurately reflect commensurate DCF rates. The fact that many high-book-rate companies or industries also follow high "expensing" policies suggests strongly that a fourth potential explanation is too important to ignore: namely that the observable book rates significantly overstate the underlying DCF rates actually being earned.

Variations in depreciation methods

■ In addition to variations in accounting expensing policies, companies and industries use varying methods of depreciating the capitalized portion of their investment outlays. This is also a potential source of disturbance as far as the book rate of return is concerned. Since "depreciation" is a variant of "expensing" (which is instantaneous "depreciation") or vice-versa (depreciation is a form of "expensing" over time), we can deduce its effects without going through the mechanics of it in detail.

Depreciation, in itself, has no effect at all on before-tax net cash flows. Nor, in the steady state we are examining (equal annual investment outlays), does it affect net income flows. Any depreciation policy, like any expensing policy, or any combination of the two, must lead to a total annual charge equal to the annual outlay. In our arithmetic example this is \$1000. In short, for any combination of depreciation policy or expensing policy, reported income in the steady state will be equal to \$1377.66 less \$1000, or \$377.66.

FIGURE 2

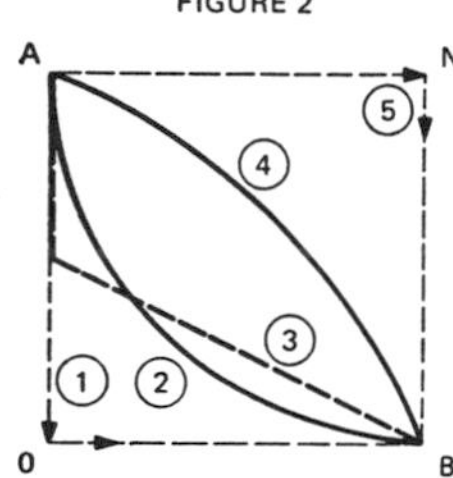

But, like expensing policy, the depreciation policy employed has a profound effect on the amount of net book capital, because this is measured by the area under the expensing-depreciation function. Various functions are shown in Figure 2.

In theory, there are infinitely many ways to go from point A to point B without going out of the rectangle on Figure 2. The five ways shown are not meant to imply that these are the most usual forms—rather they represent potential variants in accounting policy. Each leads to a different estimate of net book value. Given our basic numerical example (that \$1000 of outlay generates \$229.61 of cash flow per year for six years), the level of net income for the company (assuming equal annual investment) is \$377.66, but the level of net book value for the company will range from \$0 for Policy No. 1 to \$6000 for Policy No. 5. Thus the observable book rate of return will

FIGURE 3

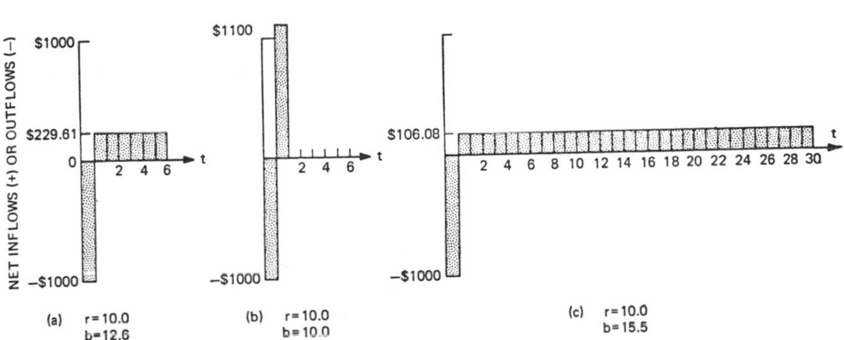

vary from a high of ∞ percent from Policy No. 1 to 6.3 percent for Policy No. 5. Together with expensing policy, depreciation policy produces wide variations in the observable book rate of return for any given DCF rate r (which in this example has been held fixed at 10.0 percent). 61

Other factors affecting the relation of b to r

■ Variations in accounting policies have a powerful effect on the size of rate of return measured in book rate units relative to the size of rate of return measured in DCF units. But they are not the only factors affecting the $(b \sim r)$ relationship. Three other influences are:

1. The economic duration of each investment outlay,
2. The time lag between outlays on the one hand and the commencement of net cash inflows on the other,
3. The time pattern of net cash inflows after they commence.

All three of these items can be summarized under a single caption—"The configuration of net cash outflows and inflows" from each investment.

□ *A.* Figure 3 shows three kinds of assets, all of which yield a DCF rate of 10 percent. Each of these shows outlays (below the horizontal line) and the size and duration of annual inflows (above the line). The first figure, 3a, is a depiction of the standard investment we have used for illustrative purposes thus far: $1000 buys $229.61 a year for 6 years. The DCF rate on this is 10 percent, but the book rate is 12.6 percent.

The second figure, 3b, is a short-duration investment in working capital. $1000 buys an inflow of $1100 in 1 year. The DCF rate (annual compounding basis) is 10 percent. So is the book rate. For this case $b = r$. And possibly this is how someone originated the idea that a rate could be measured accurately by taking the ratio of book income to book value of capital (or possibly it came from another favorite example in elementary commercial arithmetic—the case where $1000 produces a net inflow of $100 a year in perpetuity).

Finally the third figure, 3c, shows a long-duration investment, $1000 outlay producing a net cash inflow of $106.08 a year for 30

FIGURE 4

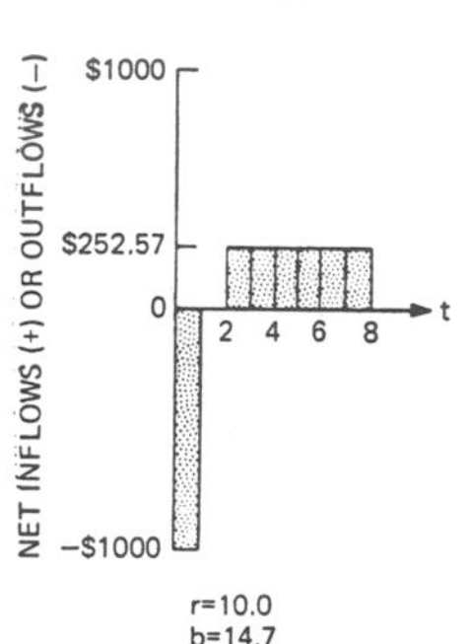

r=10.0
b=14.7

years. The DCF rate is still 10 percent. But the book rate for such a project, or for a "steady-state" company holding different vintages of such projects, would be 15.5 percent.

In short, in the steady state the longer the "duration" of each asset, the greater the discrepancy in the book rate unit measure relative to the DCF rate unit measure. Since, on working capital alone, the book rate is equal to the DCF rate, otherwise similar companies (with identical DCF rates) would show different book rates merely because each uses a different fraction of working capital relative to depreciable fixed capital.

□ *B.* Figure 4 illustrates the effect of time lags. Beginning with the original $1000 outlay which produces $229.61 a year for 6 years starting one year after the outlay is made, (which has a DCF rate of 10 percent and a book rate of 12.6 percent), this is altered in Figure 4 both to introduce a further one-year lag and to retain, in spite of this, a DCF rate of 10 percent per annum. The annual net cash inflow now has to be larger, $252.57 a year, to compensate for the one-year lag in initial receipts. In book rate units the rate of return will rise from 12.6 percent to 14.7 percent.

In the real world, different assets involve different lags. A truck can be productive the minute it is bought. A hydro-electric plant may take years to build, and many manufacturing plants take time to become fully productive even after they are built. The book rate measure will vary because of these differences.

□ *C.* Figure 5 illustrates the effect of the time pattern of cash inflows. Even in the absence of inflation, all net inflows do not follow a level path over the assets' expected life. Some assets, especially those involving new products or processes, require time for full market penetration or de-bugging and are therefore likely to show rising net cash inflows. Others, especially new models of old products—like revised editions of automobiles, or college textbooks, or fashion products, or new detergents, or hula hoops—are likely to show a rapid "decay" pattern.

For any assumed DCF rate, the book rate will vary with the pattern. Thus the level pattern in Figure 3a shows a book rate of

FIGURE 5

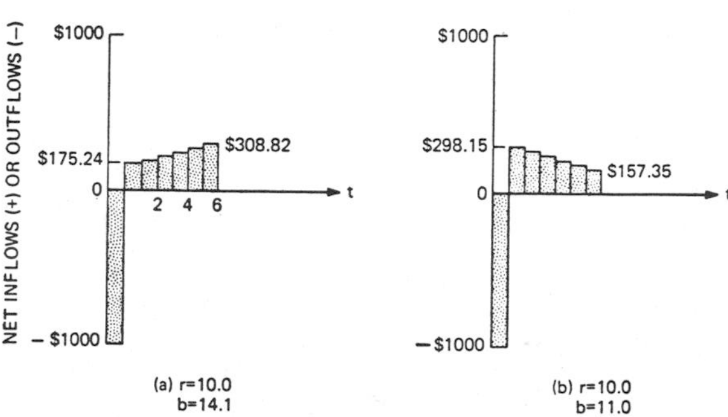

(a) r=10.0
b=14.1

(b) r=10.0
b=11.0

12.6 percent as against the DCF rate of 10.0 percent. The rising pattern in Figure 5a, which starts at $175.24 per annum and rises at 12 percent a year to $308.82 in year 6, also has a DCF rate of 10 percent, but the book rate is 14.1 percent. Finally the "decay" pattern shown in Figure 5b starts at $298.15 in year 1 and "decays" at 12 percent per annum to $157.35 in year 6. The DCF yield is still 10 percent, but the book rate is 11 percent.

The effect of growth

■ We have shown that for a company in a steady-state situation (i.e., no growth) its book ratio or book rate of return is not an unbiased measure of the true DCF rate of return it is making. Instead we have:

$$b = f(r, x, d, n, w, l, \text{and } c)$$

which says that the company's observable book rate is a function of many things,

r the DCF rate it is achieving
x its average expensing policy
d its depreciation policy
n average productive life of assets
w the fraction of working capital to total capital
l the average time lag between the outlay for each asset and the commencement of net cash inflows from its use and
c the time pattern of cash inflows.

In this section we lift the steady-state assumption to deal with another major factor which influences the level of the book rate for any given set of the variables outlined above: This is the pace at which the company invests over time. To keep the analysis straightforward we assume that these outlays increase (or decrease) steadily at a given rate g.[8]

If all of the assets it acquires generate a common DCF rate of return equal to r percent, then clearly a company will be earning a DCF rate of r percent regardless of its growth rate g.

But unless the book rate b for such a company is equal to r in the steady state, variations in the pace of growth will cause changes in the observable book rate. The reason for this is simple and can be illustrated clearly in terms of our original "assumed" asset: namely the $1000 outlay which generates a level net cash flow of $229.61 for six years. Regardless of growth rate, a company holding only this form of asset holds six vintages of capital. In the steady state, the book rate earned on each vintage is a function of (a) the expensing and depreciation policy used and (b) the age of the vintage. With full capitalization and a straight-line depreciation policy, the net cash flow and net income attributable to each vintage is constant—at $229.61 *less* $166.66, or $62.95.

But the midyear net book value of each vintage shrinks with age from [$1000–83.33] for the latest vintage to [$1000–3(83.33)] for the vintage acquired the preceding year, down to $83.33 for the oldest producing asset.

Hence the book rates of return, by vintage, vary: Very low for the mostly undepreciated asset to very high for the almost fully de-

[8] Growth here is defined as real growth; i.e., inflation is still assumed to be zero.

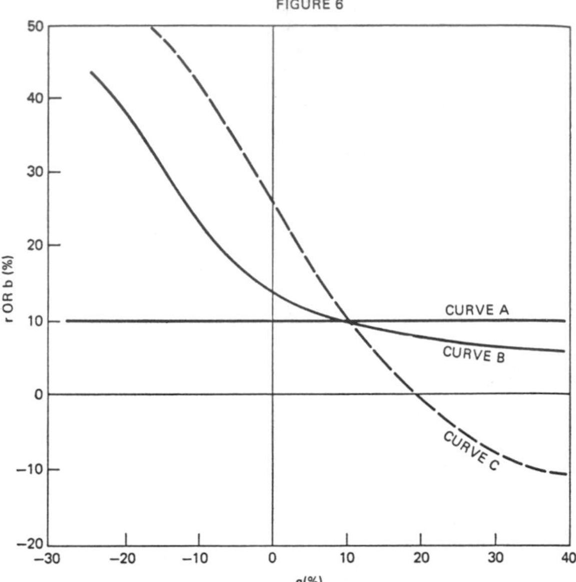

FIGURE 6

preciated asset. The book rate for the company (earlier shown to be 12.6 percent) is simply a weighted average of the individual vintage book rates (with the net book values used as weights).

Introducing positive or negative growth into the analysis leaves the individual vintage book rates unaltered, but it changes the relative weights and, hence, the overall company rate (which is its weighted average). With positive growth, the "low yielding" newer vintages get a higher weight relative to the "high yielding" older vintages. Thus the company's overall book rate falls.

In contrast, when growth is negative (i.e., the company's new investment outlays shrink steadily over time), the opposite phenomenon occurs and the company's overall book rate rises.

The relationship of the book rate to the growth rate is shown in Figure 6. Curve A shows the company's DCF rate, i.e., 10 percent, which is of course invariant to the growth rate (since each asset held is earning 10 percent). Curve B shows what the company's book rate would be at various assumed rates of growth (positive and negative). As growth rates become very large the company's overall rate will be dominated by the newest "low yielding" vintage, i.e., curve *B* approaches the yield for the newest vintage. At very fast rates of decay (negative growth) curve *B* approaches the yield for the oldest vintage.

Curve *C* on the same chart shows the same company, but under the assumption that it expenses 50 percent of each investment outlay when the outlay is made and uses a straight-line depreciation policy for the remaining 50 percent. The individual vintage book rates will now be even further apart. The newest vintage, which has charges of

$500 of its acquistion price as an expense in its first year of life, will show a negative book rate of return, whereas the rate of return for the oldest vintage will now be more than twice as high as it was in the 100 percent capitalized situation. The effect of growth on curve C is therefore even more pronounced.

An interesting point on the growth axis is that at which the book rate b is exactly equal to the DCF rate r. This is the same for both curve B and curve C. And it will also hold for other curves D, $E \cdots Z$, which can be drawn for other combinations of the (x, d, n, w, l, and c) variables which affect the book rate of return. Why should this be so? A rigorous proof is beyond the scope of this paper, but one based on intuition runs as follows.

Taking very small intervals of time, we have by definition:

$$b_t = \frac{F_t - D_t}{B_t} \tag{3}$$

This says the book rate is equal to income (cash flow in period t less depreciation and expenses outlays in period t) divided by net book value. Also 65

$$g_t = \frac{I_t - D_t}{B_t}\,. \tag{4}$$

This says that the growth rate of investment (which is also the growth rate of net book value) is equal to the net additions to net book value (new investment outlay in period t less depreciation and expense outlays in period t) divided by the existing net book value.

Now the condition $g = r$ (the growth rate equal to the DCF rate) exists only when all of net cash flow generated is reinvested. (An easy way to see this is to think in terms of a barrel of wine increasing in value with age. The annual DCF rate of return on holding this barrel of wine is also the rate at which the barrel increases in value each year but only if one does not drink part of the contents!) In short $b = r$ only if all the net cash flow is reinvested, i.e. only if $I_t = F_t$.

But if $I_t = F_t$ we can see from equations (3) and (4) above that the conditions $g = b$ must hold. Hence: If

$$g = r$$

we have

$$g = b$$

and thus

$$b = r.$$

In other words, the book rate is an unbiased and accurate measure of the DCF rate for a company which is growing steadily at a rate equal to r (or b).[9] This remarkable equality holds for all values of the extraneous variables x, d, n, w, l, and c.

Mixed assets, price-level changes and irregular growth

■ The introduction of steady real growth moves our explanatory model one step toward reality. The remaining steps would require the introduction and analysis of three other questions.

[9] The exact condition is that the company has been growing at this rate for at least n years, where n is the length of each underlying asset's productive life.

1. What is the effect on the $b \sim r$ relationship of mixtures of different assets (and associated variables) within a single company?
2. What is the effect of regular and irregular changes in the price-level of inputs and outputs?
3. Finally, what is the effect of cyclical or other irregular growth rates in investment outlays?

The algebra can be stretched to incorporate some of these real-world variables, at least in simplified form, but the exercise gets increasingly tedious at a faster rate than the rewards in understanding grow. It is easier to jump directly to a fully simulated computerized model in order to explore the relationship of b to r under any assumed set of all these variables. But this is a task for a whole new paper. For the present, it is sufficient to suggest that the points we started out to make have been made:

1. The rate of return in conventional book rate units is conceptually and numerically different from the rate of return in DCF units.
2. Two companies with similar DCF rates of return may well show widely differing book rates of return.

Cost of capital counterparts to b and r

■ So far we have dealt with rates of return as measures of performance of real assets and the two basically different units in which these rates can be, and are, counted. The same holds true for the other facet: Rate of return as a measure of the "required," "fair," or "target" standard, also known as the "cost of capital." This facet too can be, and is, measured in terms of the two units of account, namely in DCF units or book rate units.

For example, the concept of the embedded cost of debt capital so widely used in utility regulation is a book rate measure. Likewise the "comparative earnings" approach to setting "fair rate of return" which uses book rate information as its basis, is also a book rate measure.

In contrast, there are other methodologies for "measuring the cost of capital" or setting financial standards for capital usage which are clearly DCF type rates. The most obvious example of such a rate is the yield to maturity of actual outstanding or comparably risky bonds. Another is the current dividend yield plus dividend growth rate formula for calculating the cost of equity funds. A less obvious member of the DCF family is the earnings/stock price ratio (commonly called the E/p ratio). This "looks" like a book rate but only because it is measured as a simple ratio. However, close examination shows that it is a short-cut (and frequently unreliable) procedure for measuring a DCF cost of capital rate. The argument in support of this conclusion is as follows. (a) The cost or price of equity capital in any capital market is the DCF rate at which investors discount (or capitalize) future expected benefits from owning equity securities in order to set a current market price for these securities. (b) For non-level projections of benefit streams, the investors' discount rate can be found only by a trial and error process. For dividend streams that grow continuously at a constant rate the mathematics of the process reduces to a fairly simple form, generally expressed as

$$k = \frac{D_0}{P_0} + g$$

where k is the DCF discount rate being solved for, D_0 is the current rate of dividends per share, P_0 is the current price per share, and g is the rate at which dividends are expected to grow.[10]

With even more restrictive assumptions about future investor expectations, the mathematics of finding the discount rate can be simplified even further. Thus, if future earnings (E) from existing assets can be assumed to be a level, perpetual stream, the present value equation linking current price to future benefits simplifies to[11]

$$k = \frac{E}{p}.$$

In short (quite apart from the validity of the almost impossibly restrictive assumptions underlying this formulation), the E/p basis for estimating k is simply a reduced form of the equation used in solving for a DCF rate.

Thus on the "financial standard" side we are faced with the same kind of confusion as we have on the "performance" side: There are two distinct and numerically different units, one a DCF unit usually 67
symbolized as k, and one a book rate unit, which I will here symbolize as β. Both are called "cost of capital," and both use the label "percent per annum required rate of return."

Uses and misuses of disparate "rates"

■ The rules for the "correct" usage of these concepts and measures are fairly simple. If the actual or prospective performance of any investment is measured in DCF units, and if this rate is being assayed against some target or "reasonable rate standard," it is clear that the relevant standard must itself be calculated in DCF units. In short, r must be matched against k in order to produce rational decisions and judgments. Sometimes adjustments may be required, either to r or to k to allow for perceived differences in riskiness between the kind of investment being assayed and the kind of investments from which the k measure has been derived.

By the same token, if book rate units, b, are used to measure actual or prospective performance, the proper standard of comparison is against β. Here too risk adjustments are legitimate. In addition, adjustments may be necessary if the investment or collection of investments being assayed differ significantly with respect to the set of variables (x,d,n,w,l,c, and g) from the collection of investments from whose performance the estimate of β has been derived.

The potential misuses of these tools of thought involve all the inconsistent comparisons which can be made among the four measures. What is surprising is that almost every conceivable form of misuse is being practiced today. Some examples are:

1. A regulatory authority measures the cost of capital in DCF units (k) and then translates this number into "required revenues" by multiplying it against a net book value estimate (or one based on net book value).
2. The same authority measures the cost of equity capital (k_e) in DCF units and the cost of debt in book rate units (embedded cost), and uses the weighted average of these two rates as the figure to be multiplied against a net book value rate base.

[10] For a proof, see [5].
[11] For a proof, see [15], p. 25, note 7.

But regulation is not the only arena in which the disparate units are used as if they were interchangeable estimates of a common concept. Companies which have moved toward the measurement of investment worth in terms of a promised DCF rate still use book rates as a basis for setting the financial standard rate against which this promised DCF can be compared.

In some cases, DCF rates are used for *ex-ante* capital budgeting purposes, but an unadjusted book rate measure is used for later (*ex-post*) audit purposes, to check whether or not the investment lived up to its promise.

Finally, there is still a great deal of implicit acceptance that widely differing observed book rates are unbiased measures of actual profitability.

Understanding and avoiding these potential misuses of "rates of return" will not in itself provide correct answers. Important differential effects of price level changes on all measures, and the random effects of estimating errors, remain as significant barriers to be overcome, both for regulators and for private managers. Meanwhile, understanding that book rate measures and DCF rate measures are not different estimates of the *same* thing but rather estimates of *different* things should eliminate at least part of the confusion surrounding "rates of return on investment."

References

1. Bierman, H. "Depreciable Assets—Timing of Expense Recognition," *The Accounting Review*, October 1961, pp. 613–18.
2. Carlson, R. *Measuring Period Profitability*. Unpublished doctoral dissertation, Stanford University, 1967.
3. Cottle, S. and Whitman, W. *Corporate Earning Power and Market Valuation*. Durham, N. C.: Duke University Press, 1959.
4. Gordon, M. J. "The Payoff Period and the Rate of Profit," *The Management of Corporate Capital*, edited by Ezra Solomon. New York: MacMillan-Free Press, 1959, pp. 48–55.
5. ——— and Shapiro, E. "Capital Equipment Aanlysis: The Required Rate of Profit," *The Management of Corporate Capital*, edited by Ezra Solomon. New York: MacMillan-Free Press, 1959, pp. 141–47.
6. Harcourt, G. C. "The Accountant in a Golden Age," *Oxford Economic Papers*, New Series, Vol. 17, No. 1 (1965).
7. Johnson, O. "Two General Concepts of Depreciation," *Journal of Accounting Research*, Spring 1968, pp. 29–37 .
8. Kuznets, S., ed. *Income and Wealth, Series II.* Cambridge: International Association for Research into Income and Wealth, Bowes-Bowes, 1952.
9. Lanzilloti, R. F. "Pricing Objectives in Large Companies," *American Economic Review*, Vol. 48 (1968), pp. 921–40.
10. Laya, J. C. *A Cash-Flow Model for Rate of Return.* Unpublished doctoral dissertation, Stanford University, 1965.
11. Minhas, B. S. *An International Comparison of Factor Costs and Factor Use.* Amsterdam: North Holland Publishing Company, 1963.
12. Solomon, E., ed. *The Management of Corporate Capital.* New York: MacMillan, 1959.
13. ———. "Research on Return on Investment: The Relation of Book-Yield to True Yield," in American Accounting Association, *Research in Accounting Measurement*, 1965.
14. ———. "Systematic Errors in Book Rates of Return," Society of Petroleum Engineers, SPE 655 (1963).
15. ———. *The Theory of Financial Management.* New York: Columbia University Press, 1963.

16. ———. "The Variation Between True Yield and Book Rate of Return in the Oil and Gas Producing Industry," Testimony before Federal Power Commission, Area Rate Proceedings AR-61-1 (1961).
17. ——— and LAYA, J. C. "Measurement of Company Profitability: Some Systematic Errors in the Accounting Rate of Return," in *Financial Research and its Implications for Management Decisions*, A. A. Robichek, ed. New York: John Wiley & Sons, 1966, pp. 152–183.
18. STIGLER, G. J. *Capital and Rates of Return in Manufacturing Industry*. Princeton, N. J.: Princeton University Press, 1963.
19. VATTER, W. J. "Income Models, Book Yield and the Rate of Return," *The Accounting Review*, October 1966, pp. 681–98.
20. WRIGHT, F. W. "Toward a General Theory of Depreciation," *Journal of Accounting Research*, Spring 1964, pp. 80–90.

Relationship between the Accounting and the Internal Rate of Return Measures: A Synthesis and an Analysis

JOHN LESLIE LIVINGSTONE and GERALD L. SALAMON*

71

Introduction

Several recent studies have dealt with the relationships between the internal rate of return (*IRR*) and various measures of accounting rate of return (*ARR*), given different sets of conditions. Published studies appear in the literature of accounting, economics, finance, and industrial engineering, with no two of these studies appearing in the same journal. Moreover, none of the studies references any of the others. Hence, there is no coordinated approach to the topic and each adopts a different set of assumptions.

The purpose of the present paper is (1) to summarize and review the prior studies, so that their results can be synthesized into an integrated framework. This process reveals a more general class of cases than those previously considered; (2) to derive some propositions dealing with reinvestment of cash inflows and the rate of growth, and (3) to suggest some directions for future research in this general area.

Previous Research: A Brief Synthesis

Solomon[1] studied the relationship between *ARR* and *IRR* for a firm which consisted solely of projects with the same life and *IRR*. The firm

* Professor of Accounting and Ph.D. student, The Ohio State University. The authors gratefully acknowledge the assistance and helpful comments of several of their colleagues and in particular those of Professors William F. Bentz, Robert S. Carlson, David C. Ewert, René Manès, and Gerald A. Zeisel.

[1] E. Solomon, "Return on Investment: The Relation of Book Yield to True Yield," in *Research in Accounting Measurement*, ed. R. K. Jaedicke, Y. Ijiri, and O. W. Nielsen (American Accounting Association, 1966).

was assumed to operate in a certain and taxless environment. Solomon broke his study into two distinct but not different cases—the case in which annual gross investment was constant and the case in which annual gross investment grew at a constant rate, g. These two cases are alike since the constant annual investment case is the constant growth case with $g = 0$. In the zero growth model Solomon found that the *ARR-IRR* relation was affected by the length of project life, pattern of project cash flow, capitalization policy, and depreciation method. In the growth model, Solomon studied the effect of growth rate and price-level changes on the *ARR-IRR* relation. The growth model was formulated only for the case in which the individual projects generated level cash flows over their lives.

Carlson[2] extended the work of Solomon in several ways. First, he studied the effects in the zero growth and growth models of capitalization policy, depreciation method, length of project life, salvage value of projects, in-
72 vestment time lags, cash-flow pattern, income taxes, and price-level changes on the *ARR-IRR* relationship. This part of his study was conducted under the assumption that the firm was a collection of projects which all had the same life and *IRR*. Second, Carlson formulated expressions for *ARR* in terms of model parameters for the cases in which the firm had (1) invested in projects with different lives and same *IRR*, (2) invested in projects with different internal rates of return and same life, and (3) invested in current assets as well as depreciable assets. Note that both Solomon and Carlson showed the separable effect of each of many variables on the *ARR-IRR* relationship.

Harcourt[3] divided his study into two main cases, with each containing the same two subcases. Like Solomon and Carlson, his main cases were that of either constant annual investment or constant growth in annual investment. Again, we assume that the constant investment case is just the particular instance of constant growth in which the growth rate is zero. The subcases considered by Harcourt were those in which (1) the firm invested solely in projects with the same *IRR*, life, and cash flow pattern and (2) the firm invested in financial assets (i.e., securities) as well as the regular projects. For each of these four models, Harcourt formulated expressions for *ARR* in terms of *IRR*, cash flow pattern, project life, and the growth rate. He reported separate expressions for straight-line depreciation and 150% declining balance depreciation methods. Thus, one of the important differences between the Harcourt study and those previously cited is that the Harcourt study examined the simultaneous effect that asset life, cash flow pattern, growth, and *IRR* had on the *ARR-IRR* relationship.

Sarnat and Levy[4] studied the relationship between *ARR* (calculated by

---

[2] R. S. Carlson, "Measuring Period Profitability: Book Yield Versus True Yield," unpublished Ph.D. dissertation, Stanford University, 1964.

[3] G. C. Harcourt, "The Accountant in a Golden Age," *Oxford Economic Papers* (March 1965), pp. 66–80.

[4] M. Sarnat and H. Levy, "The Relationship of Rules of Thumb to the Internal

using either total or average investment and straight-line depreciation) and *IRR* for investment projects which generated level cash flows. They formulated expressions for *ARR* in terms of project life and *IRR* in order to determine when the *ARR* for the project was a closer approximation to *IRR* than other rules of thumb, such as the payback reciprocal. They found that the relation between *ARR* and *IRR* was not affected by the introduction of income taxes into their model.

Swalm[5] studied the relationship between *IRR*, *ARR*, and the reciprocal of the payback period for projects which generated level cash flows and which were depreciated by the straight-line method. He showed that project *ARR* (based upon the total investment) was a good approximation of *IRR* when asset life and *IRR* were both small and when asset life became very large.

Finally, Ijiri and Robichek[6] studied the relation between *ARR* and *IRR* for single projects and firms with zero growth. They derived the relation 73
for projects with level cash flows given alternative methods of depreciation.

The main conclusions reached in the above studies are similar. As stated by Solomon:

> The main findings are that (1) book yield (ARR) is not an accurate measure of true yield (IRR), (2) that the error in book yield is neither constant nor consistent.[7]

The Comparison of ARR and IRR for a Firm: A Priori Considerations

The *ARR* is a measure of the rate of return that is normally associated with a firm rather than an individual project. The *IRR* is a measure of the rate of return that is normally associated with a project but it can also be used as a measure of a firm's rate of return. Thus, a comparison of *ARR* and *IRR* can be made for an individual project (as was done by Carlson, Harcourt, and Solomon). We have elected to compare these two rates of return measures as they apply to firms.

The notion of a firm implies continued existence or permanence. Therefore, in constructing models for the purpose of comparing firm *ARR* with firm *IRR*, a mechanism for generating the continued existence of the firm must be incorporated into the model. In the studies cited above, firm

---

Rate of Return: A Restatement and Generalization," *Journal of Finance* (June 1969), pp. 479–90.

[5] R. O. Swalm, "On Calculating the Rate of Return on Investment," *The Journal of Industrial Engineering* (March–April, 1958), pp. 99–103.

[6] Y. Ijiri and A. A. Robichek, "Accounting Measurement and Rates of Return," unpublished working paper, Stanford University, Graduate School of Business, 1965 (presented at the Institute of Management Sciences National Meeting, San Francisco, February 3–5, 1965).

[7] E. Solomon, "Return on Investment: The Relation of Book Yield to True Yield," Society of Petroleum Engineers of AIME, paper number SPE 655, p. 4, quoted in R. S. Carlson, *op. cit.*, p. 3.

permanence was assured by explicitly making gross annual investment an amount which was either a constant each year or an amount which grew at a constant rate from one year to the next. In the models used, the disposition of the cash flows generated by firm assets was not treated explicitly. For example, it is not clear what the disposition of these annual flows was in the Harcourt or Solomon models, whereas Carlson assumed that the difference between the annual flows and the annual gross investment was either paid to or received from firm stockholders.[8]

An alternative approach is to formulate the firm's continued existence in terms of the reinvestment of its net cash inflows. Thus, if the reinvestment rate is specified as less than 100% (of total net cash inflows), then the unreinvested funds are paid out to the stockholders. If the reinvestment rate exceeds 100%, we assume that in addition to complete reinvestments additional funds are paid in by the firm's stockholders.

74 Of course, once the reinvestment rate is specified, then the investment growth rate is fully determined. Thus, either the reinvestment rate or the investment growth rate can be made explicit, which then implicitly determines the other. Since these are much different sides of the same coin, we are free to choose which one to specify explicitly.

We prefer to treat reinvestment explicitly for the following reasons. First, we find it intuitively easier to conceive of setting the reinvestment rate and then solving for the investment growth rate, as we will do, rather than vice versa. Also, this approach is consistent with the Hicksian notion of income which is based on how much we can consume (i.e., disinvest vs. reinvest) without expecting to impair future consumption. It is also consistent with valuation models based on dividend rates since they are the complement of reinvestment rates. Later we will examine the relationship between the gross investment, growth rate, and the reinvestment rate, and will show how they are linked to one another.

The Scope of the Present Paper

We propose to add generality to the scope of prior research by considering a wider range of assumptions with respect to the basic features of the problem. For instance, we go beyond the work of Solomon by considering project cash flows that are nonuniform over time, as well as uniform flows. Also, we go beyond Carlson's approach by analyzing simultaneous changes in all parameters, rather than one-at-a-time changes. In addition, we go beyond the assumptions made by Harcourt, who considered only growth rates in gross investment, by dealing also with reinvestment rates.

In some other respects, however, we take a narrower approach than in previous studies. In particular, our study ignores taxes, price changes, and depreciation methods other than straight-line. However we feel that these latter factors are secondary, and that we should first seek generality

[8] R. S. Carlson, *op. cit.*, p. 10.

on the basic features. Future studies can elaborate the analysis to take account of them.

Model Assumptions

To begin we make specific assumptions regarding the firm and its environment. These assumptions are not arbitrarily chosen. They are those used in previous studies, and we adopt them to make our study comparable. Since these assumptions are both strict and limiting, we list the main ones for the convenience of the reader:

(1) The firm is a collection of independent projects and operates in an economy of unchanging prices.
(2) The projects which constitute the firm each have the same life, the same pattern of cash flows, the same *IRR*, and the same salvage value (zero).
(3) All cash outlays relate directly to specific investment projects— 75
the firm has no general or indirect costs.
(4) Accounting income is equal to the cash flow generated by the projects less straight-line depreciation.
(5) There are no income taxes.
(6) All expectations are realized.

In addition, we assume that the annual gross investment results from some constant exogenous amount along with reinvestment of the cash benefits generated by the firm's assets in the prior year. One can assume numerous patterns for the constant amount. Since the primary reason for having exogenous investment in our model is to get the firm started, we have assumed that this investment is made each year for the number of years equal to the length of the project life and is then terminated. Hence, annual gross investment is thereafter determined within the model.

Formulation of the Model

F_t = the cash flows generated by all the assets of the firm in year t
D_t = straight-line depreciation in year t
K_t = accounting net book value of assets at beginning of year t
G_t = accounting gross book value at beginning of year t
I_t = gross investment made at the end of year t
Q_i = the net cash flow generated by a single project at the end of its ith year
b = the factor which describes the pattern of cash flows generated by the project (i.e., $Q_i = b\,Q_{i-1}$, $1 = 2, \cdots, n$. If $b = 1$, the project has level flows)
n = length of project in years
ARR_t = accounting rate of return in year t
r = the IRR for the project
c = the proportion of annual firm flows which are reinvested.

I_0 is the cost of an infinitely divisible asset which generates cash benefits of $Q_1, Q_2, \ldots, Q_n$ and represents the exogenous investment which is made by the firm each year for n years.

For years t such that $t \geq 2n$, the useful life of all projects which have been acquired with exogenous investment has expired. Since an investment of I_0 gives rise to a sequence of cash benefits of $Q_1, Q_2, \cdots, Q_n$ then an investment of an amount A gives rise to a sequence of cash benefits of $A/I_0\, Q_1,\ A/I_0\, Q_2, \cdots, A/I_0\, Q_n$. Therefore, for any year t such that $t \geq 2n$ we have:

$$F_t = \frac{c \cdot F_{t-1}}{I_0} \cdot Q_1 + \frac{c \cdot F_{t-2}}{I_0} \cdot Q_2 + \cdots + \frac{c \cdot F_{t-n}}{I_0} \cdot Q_n$$
$$= \frac{c}{I_0} \sum_{i=1}^{n} F_{t-1} \cdot Q_i . \tag{1}$$

76 We know that $Q_i = b\, Q_{i-1}$ for $i = 2, 3, \cdots, n$. Therefore,

$$Q_2 = b\, Q_1,$$
$$Q_3 = b\, Q_2 = b^2\, Q_1, \quad \text{and in general,}$$
$$Q_i = b\, Q_{i-1} = b^{i-1}\, Q_1 \quad \text{for } i = 2, \cdots, n.$$

Substituting this last result into equation (1), we have:

$$F_t = \frac{cQ_1}{I_0} \sum_{i=1}^{n} F_{t-i} \cdot b^{i-1}.$$

Since the projects acquired with the exogenous investment have all expired by the year $2n$,

$$G_t = \sum_{i=1}^{n} c \cdot F_{t-i}, \quad \text{for } t \geq n.$$

Hence,

$$D_t = \frac{1}{n} G_t = \frac{c}{n} \sum_{i=1}^{n} F_{t-i} .$$

The accumulated depreciation on any investment made i years ago is i/n times the amount of the investment. Therefore, the net book value of any investment made i years ago is $(n/n - i/n)$ times the amount of the investment. Since all projects acquired with exogenous investment have expired by year $t = 2n$ we have:

$$K_t = \frac{n}{n} cF_{t-1} + \frac{n-1}{n} cF_{t-2} + \cdots + \frac{1}{n} cF_{t-n} = \frac{c}{n} \sum_{i=1}^{n} (n + 1 - i) F_{t-i}, \quad \text{for} \quad t \geq 2n.$$

Consequently, for any year $t \geq 2n$, we have:

$$F_t - D_t = \frac{cQ_1}{I_0} \sum_{i=1}^{n} b^{i-1} F_{t-i} - \frac{c}{n} \sum_{i=1}^{n} F_{t-i} = \frac{c}{nI_0} \sum_{i=1}^{n} (nQ_1 b^{i-1} - I_0) F_{t-i} .$$

Also, for $t \geq 2n$

$$
\begin{aligned}
ARR_t &= \frac{F_t - D_t}{K_t} \\
&= \frac{\dfrac{c}{NI_0} \sum_{i=1}^{n} (nQ_1 b^{i-1} - I_0) F_{t-i}}{\dfrac{c}{n} \sum_{i=1}^{n} (n + 1 - i) F_{t-i}} \qquad (2) \\
&= \frac{\sum_{i=1}^{n} (nQ_1 b^{i-1} - I_0) F_{t-1}}{I_0 \sum_{i=1}^{n} (n + 1 - i) F_{t-i}}.
\end{aligned}
$$

Now we know that: 77

$$
\begin{aligned}
I_0 &= \sum_{i=1}^{n} Q_i (1 + r)^{-i} = Q_1 \sum_{i=1}^{n} b^{i-1} (1 + r)^{-i} \\
&= Q_1 \left[\frac{(1 + r)^n - b^n}{(1 + r - b)(1 + r)^n} \right] \qquad (3)
\end{aligned}
$$

assuming that $b \neq 1 + r$.

If we substitute the result of equation (3) back into equation (2) we have:

$$
\begin{aligned}
ARR_t &= \frac{\sum_{i=1}^{n} \left\{ nQ_1 b^{i-1} - Q_1 \left[\dfrac{(1 + r)^n - b^n}{(1 + r - b)(1 + r)^n} \right] \right\} F_{t-i}}{Q_1 \left[\dfrac{(1 + r)^n - b^n}{(1 + r - b)(1 + r)^n} \right] \sum_{i=1}^{n} (n + 1 - i) F_{t-i}} \qquad (4) \\
&= \frac{\sum_{i=1}^{n} [n(1 + r - b)(1 + r)^n b^{i-1} - (1 + r)^n + b^n] F_{t-i}}{[(1 + r)^n - b^n] \sum_{i=1}^{n} (n + 1 - i) F_{t-i}}.
\end{aligned}
$$

From (4) we note that the relation between ARR_t and IRR in our model depends upon n, r, b, and the cash flows generated by the projects for the last n years. Since we could not derive an expression for F_t in terms of the parameters of the model, we were unable to examine the relation between ARR_t and IRR any further analytically. We proceeded instead to the use of a deterministic simulation, varying the model parameters over a set of reasonable ranges.

The Simulation

In our simulation, the values for F_t, D_t, K_t, G_t, and ARR_t were calculated for all possible combinations of the following values for the given model parameters:

n: 5, 10, 20, 30

b: .5, .75, 1.00, 1.25, 1.50

c: .5, .75, 1.00, 1.25, 1.50

r: .05, .10, .20, .30

The calculations were made for all years t such that $t = 1, 2, \cdots, 8n$.

The analysis of the simulation is discussed in terms of the relationship between *ARR* and *IRR* and between the reinvestment rate and the growth rate in gross investment.

Unfortunately, the simulation yielded *nbcr* (or $4 \times 5 \times 5 \times 4 = 400$) combinations for each value of t (and $t = 1, 2, \cdots, 8n$). This large number of outcomes is difficult to present in a compact fashion, and the reader's
78 staying power is about to be put to the test.

The *ARR*-*IRR* Relationship

In all of our examples we found that the *ARR* cycled symmetrically about a constant. The cycle dampens out over time in each case. Figure 1 illustrates this cyclical behavior for one of our examples. The constant about which *ARR* cycles and the amplitude of the *ARR* cycle is affected by the model parameters n, b, r, and c.

The effect of b and c on the behavior of *ARR* for given n and r is shown

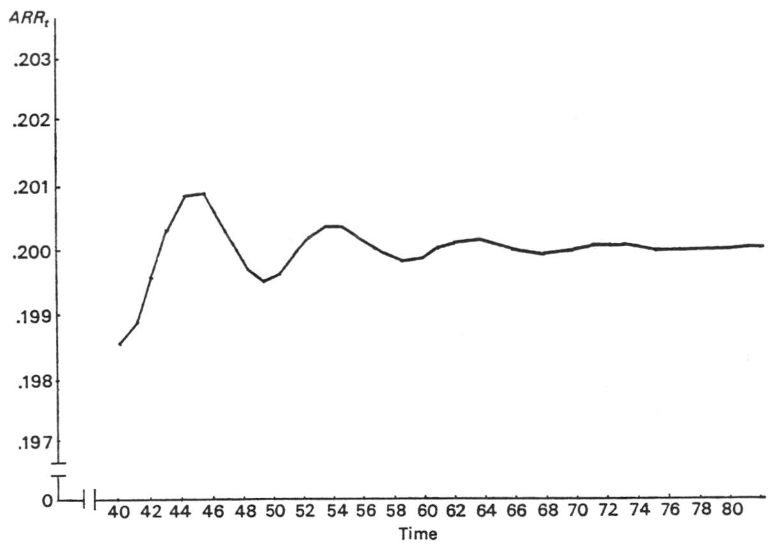

FIG. 1. ARR_t for $n = 10$, $IRR = .20$, $b = 1.5$, $c = 1.0$

TABLE 1

Accounting Rate of Return by Time Periods for $n = 10$, $IRR = .10$ and Given Values of c and b

Time period	c = .50					c = .75					c = 1.00				
b	.50	.75	1.00	1.25	1.50	.50	.75	1.00	1.25	1.50	.50	.75	1.00	1.25	1.50
$3n < t \leq 4n$	−14.05 (−14.05)	1.53 (1.52)	12.09 (12.04)	17.59 (16.97)	20.42 (18.49)	−.17 (−.17)	6.53 (6.53)	10.81 (10.80)	12.89 (12.70)	13.99 (13.03)	10.00 (10.00)	10.00 (10.00)	10.00 (10.00)	10.05 (9.94)	10.24 (9.60)
$5n < t \leq 6n$	−14.05 (−14.05)	1.52 (1.52)	12.07 (12.07)	17.33 (17.25)	19.84 (19.37)	−.17 (−.17)	6.53 (6.53)	10.81 (10.81)	12.79 (12.76)	13.71 (13.53)	10.00 (10.00)	10.00 (10.00)	10.00 (10.00)	10.00 (10.00)	10.05 (9.96)
$7n < t \leq 8n$	−14.05 (−14.05)	1.52 (1.52)	12.07 (12.07)	17.28 (17.27)	19.66 (19.52)	−.17 (−.17)	6.53 (6.53)	10.81 (10.81)	12.78 (12.78)	13.63 (13.59)	10.00 (10.00)	10.00 (10.00)	10.00 (10.00)	10.00 (10.00)	10.01 (9.99)

Time period	c = 1.25					c = 1.50				
b	.50	.75	1.00	1.25	1.50	.50	.75	1.00	1.25	1.50
$3n < t \leq 4n$	17.24 (17.24)	12.53 (12.53)	9.43 (9.43)	8.09 (8.09)	7.72 (7.22)	22.45 (22.45)	14.42 (14.42)	9.01 (9.01)	6.65 (6.61)	5.86 (5.46)
$5n < t \leq 6n$	17.24 (17.24)	12.53 (12.53)	9.43 (9.43)	8.07 (8.07)	7.57 (7.51)	22.45 (22.45)	14.42 (14.42)	9.01 (9.01)	6.64 (6.63)	5.74 (5.70)
$7n < t \leq 8n$	17.24 (17.24)	12.53 (12.53)	9.43 (9.43)	8.07 (8.07)	7.54 (7.53)	22.45 (22.45)	14.42 (14.42)	9.01 (9.01)	6.63 (6.63)	5.72 (5.71)

Cell values are in percentage terms with the maximum ARR in the time period given first and the minimum ARR in the time period in parentheses.

in Table 1. A careful reading of Table 1 reveals several facts which are typical of most of our examples:

(1) If $c < 1$ and $b < 1$ then $ARR_t < IRR$ for all $t > 2n$
(2) If $c < 1$ and $b \geq 1$ then $ARR_t > IRR$ for all $t > 2n$
(3) If $c > 1$ and $b < 1$ then $ARR_t > IRR$ for all $t > 2n$
(4) If $c > 1$ and $b \geq 1$ then $ARR_t < IRR$ for all $t > 2n$
(5) If $c = 1$ then the *ARR* cycles about the *IRR* for all values of b
(6) The amplitude of the *ARR* cycle (the difference between the maximum and minimum values of *ARR* in a given time period) increases as b increases, decreases as c increases, and decreases as t increases.

The results of (1) through (4) are summarized in Table 2.

At this point we note the interdependencies which exist within the model. We see that the effect of the parameter b on the relationship between *ARR* and *IRR* depends upon the value of c and vice versa. There-
80 fore, in attempting to reconcile *ARR* and *IRR* we cannot look at the effect of model parameters one at a time. However, with this caution in mind, we can make some comparisons of wide (although incomplete) generality as follows.

The ordinal relationships between *ARR* and *IRR* outlined above hold for almost all of our examples, no matter what the values of n and r. The exceptions occur when the amplitude of the *ARR* cycle is large.

We also note from an analysis of Table 1 that:

(1) If $c < 1$ then *ARR* increases as b increases
(2) If $c > 1$ then *ARR* decreases as b increases, and
(3) If $c = 1$ then *ARR* is approximately equal to the *IRR* for all values of b.

The effect of n and r on the relationship between *ARR* and *IRR* is depicted in Tables 3 and 4. The values of c and b in Table 3 were chosen so as to reduce the amplitude of the *ARR* cycles. This enables us to illustrate the effect that n and r have on the level of *ARR* but it does not enable us to illustrate the effect than n and r have on the amplitude of the *ARR* cycle. This latter effect is illustrated in Table 4.

In general the effect of n and r on the *ARR-IRR* relation is harder to determine than the effect of b and c. This will become clearer as we analyze Table 3. In Table 3, when *IRR* is held constant the ratio *ARR/IRR* becomes larger as n becomes larger. This result is in direct contrast with one obtained by Harcourt. The case shown is one in which firm projects have

TABLE 2

The Effect of b and c on the ARR-IRR Relationship

	$c < 1$	$c > 1$
$b < 1$	$ARR_t < IRR$	$ARR_t > IRR$
$b > 1$	$ARR_t > IRR$	$ARR_t < IRR$

TABLE 3

Accounting Rate of Return by Time Periods for $c = 1.25$, $b = .75$, and for Given Values of n and IRR

Time period	n															
	5				10				20				30			
	IRR															
	.05	.10	.20	.30	.05	.10	.20	.30	.05	.10	.20	.30	.05	.10	.20	.30
$3n < t \leq 4n$	6.58 (6.58)	11.50 (11.50)	21.37 (21.37)	31.25 (31.25)	7.49 (7.49)	12.53 (12.53)	22.59 (22.59)	32.64 (32.64)	8.61 (8.61)	13.71 (13.71)	23.82 (23.82)	33.87 (33.87)	9.13 (9.13)	14.20 (14.19)	24.25 (24.25)	34.28 (34.28)
$5n < t \leq 6n$	6.58 (6.58)	11.50 (11.50)	21.37 (21.37)	31.25 (31.25)	7.49 (7.49)	12.53 (12.53)	22.59 (22.59)	32.64 (32.64)	8.61 (8.61)	13.71 (13.71)	23.82 (23.82)	33.87 (33.87)	9.13 (9.13)	14.20 (14.19)	24.25 (24.25)	34.28 (34.28)
$7n < t \leq 8n$	6.58 (6.58)	11.50 (11.50)	21.37 (21.37)	31.25 (31.25)	7.49 (7.49)	12.53 (12.53)	22.59 (22.59)	32.64 (32.64)	8.61 (8.61)	13.71 (13.71)	23.82 (23.82)	33.87 (33.87)	9.13 (9.13)	14.20 (14.19)	24.25 (24.25)	34.28 (34.28)

Cell values are in percentage terms with the maximum *ARR* in the time period given first and the minimum *ARR* in the time period in parentheses.

TABLE 4

Accounting Rate of Return by Time Periods for $c = .75$, $b = 1.5$ and Given Values of IRR and n

Time period	n															
	5				10				20				30			
	IRR															
	.05	.10	.20	.30	.05	.10	.20	.30	.05	.10	.20	.30	.05	.10	.20	.30
$3n < t \leq 4n$	7.95 (7.34)	.13.53 (13.01)	24.69 (24.36)	35.87 (35.67)	8.19 (7.02)	13.99 (13.03)	25.84 (24.96)	37.70 (36.05)	8.39 (6.31)	15.57 (11.26)	28.76 (22.17)	40.36 (35.66)	9.68 (5.07)	19.36 (8.41)	33.86 (16.85)	43.46 (31.52)
$5n < t \leq 6n$	7.69 (7.59)	13.29 (13.22)	24.53 (24.49)	35.76 (35.75)	7.85 (7.57)	13.71 (13.53)	25.58 (25.49)	37.49 (37.32)	7.85 (6.67)	14.46 (12.28)	27.05 (25.02)	39.09 (38.46)	8.79 (5.51)	17.06 (9.65)	30.26 (21.25)	40.82 (38.02)
$7n < t \leq 8n$	7.64 (7.62)	13.25 (13.24)	24.50 (24.50)	35.75 (35.75)	7.74 (7.66)	13.63 (13.59)	25.54 (25.52)	37.46 (37.45)	7.60 (7.02)	13.97 (13.07)	26.42 (25.81)	38.79 (38.66)	8.24 (5.85)	15.78 (10.71)	28.41 (24.40)	39.74 (38.81)

Cell values are in percentage terms with the maximum *ARR* in the time period given first and the minimum *ARR* in the time period in parentheses.

declining cash flows ($b = .75 < 1$). For this case and for zero growth, Harcourt derived the result that the ratio ARR/IRR decreases as n increases.[9] He also showed that the introduction of growth causes the ratio ARR/IRR to increase for a given n, but if the growth rate is fixed at a positive level, the ratio ARR/IRR decreases as n increases. Now in our Table 3, c is held constant at a positive 1.25 and we show that the ratio ARR/IRR increases as n increases. The explanation of the conflict is that the effect of n on the ratio ARR/IRR (given a declining cash flow pattern for firm assets) is not independent of the growth rate (or in our model, the reinvestment rate). The effect that n has on the ratio ARR/IRR given a declining cash flow pattern for firm projects can be summarized as follows:

(1) If $c < 1$, then ARR/IRR decreases as n increases
(2) If $c > 1$, then ARR/IRR increases as n increases
(3) If $c = 1$, then $ARR/IRR = 1$ (approximately) for all values of n.

This conflict and its resolution again reveal the danger in examining the 83
effect of an individual model parameter without simultaneously considering the values of the other parameters.

Further analysis of Table 3 reveals that for a given n, the magnitude of the difference between ARR and IRR is not appreciably different for different values of the IRR. This means that the relative deviation of ARR from IRR decreases as IRR increases. In other words, the ratio $(ARR - IRR)/IRR$ decreases as IRR increases (given the values of n, b, and c in Table 3).

From Table 4 we see that the amplitude of the ARR cycle:

(1) decreases as t increases for all values of n and IRR
(2) increases as n increases for any given IRR
(3) decreases as IRR increases for any given n.

The Relationship between the Reinvestment Rate and the Growth Rate

In the models developed in previous studies a constant rate of gross investment was assumed. In our model, we assume a constant reinvestment rate of the firm's cash flows. The relationship between the reinvestment rate and the growth rate will now be explored.

In the Appendix it is shown that if the gross annual investment of a firm grows at a constant rate, g, then for years $t \geq n$ the firm possesses a constant reinvestment rate. Specifically, for $t \geq n$ (see equation (4A) in the Appendix):

$$I_t = k F_t$$

where

$$k = \left[\frac{b^n - (1+r)^n}{(1+r)^n(b-1-r)}\right]\left[\frac{(1+g)^n(b-1-g)}{b^n - (1+g)^n}\right].$$

[9] G. C. Harcourt, *op. cit.*, p. 79. See his graph of the case 1 (2).

This constant reinvestment rate k depends upon n, b, r, and g. Therefore, we conclude that models with a constant growth rate in annual investment do achieve a constant rate of reinvestment after an initial startup period.

Is the converse also true? The question then becomes: Does a constant rate of reinvestment after an initial startup period result in a constant rate of growth in gross investment? Inspection of the results of our simulation shows that the growth rate in gross investment in year t, g_t, tends to cycle about a constant which we designate as g. Illustrative data are shown in Table 5, from which we note that:

(1) If $c < 1$ then $g_t < IRR$ for all values of b and g increases as b increases

(2) If $c > 1$ then $g_t > IRR$ for all values of b and g decreases as b increases

(3) If $c = 1$ then g_t is approximately equal to IRR and g does not change as b increases.

The behavior of the amplitude of the growth rate cycle is similar to the behavior of the amplitude of the ARR cycle. The amplitude of the growth rate cycle decreases:

(1) as t increases for any c and b

(2) as c increases for a given b

(3) as b decreases for a given c.

The conclusion that is reached from this exploration of the growth rate and reinvestment rate seems to be significant. We have shown that a constant rate of growth results after an initial period in a constant rate of reinvestment. We have also seen from our examples that a constant reinvestment rate tends, after time, towards a constant rate of growth. Therefore, it makes no great difference when studying the ARR-IRR relationship whether a model is formulated which includes a constant growth rate or a constant reinvestment rate (since one tends toward the other).

Note also that as long as $c = 1$ (i.e., there is 100% reinvestment) then $IRR \approx ARR$, regardless of the values of the remaining parameters. This result was shown by Solomon for the case of level project cash flows, and now we see that it applies more generally for other project cash flows as well. Therefore there is a class of cases for which ARR is a good proxy measure for IRR.

Concluding Comments

As stated in the introduction to this paper, we have tried to synthesize the scattered literature in this problem area and to analyze with increased generality a basic set of ARR:IRR relationships. The analysis has yielded the following results: First, it is not sufficient to study the effects of the variables in the problem one at a time. Since the variables interact, it is necessary to consider the simultaneous effects of all the variables together. Second, a constant reinvestment rate tends toward a constant gross in-

TABLE 5

Growth Rate by Time Periods for $n = 10$, $IRR = .10$ and Given Values of c and b

Time period	c = .50					c = .75					c = 1.00				
b	.50	.75	1.00	1.25	1.50	.50	.75	1.00	1.25	1.50	.50	.75	1.00	1.25	1.50
$3n < t \leq 4n$	−20.2 (−20.2)	−9.9 (−10.0)	−3.2 (−3.6)	.9 (−1.0)	2.8 (−.7)	−5.0 (−5.0)	.3 (.3)	3.9 (3.7)	6.0 (5.1)	7.0 (5.1)	9.9 (9.9)	10.0 (9.9)	10.0 (9.9)	10.3 (9.8)	10.7 (9.2)
$5n < t \leq 6n$	−20.2 (−20.2)	−10.0 (−10.0)	−3.5 (−3.5)	−.3 (−.6)	1.6 (.3)	−5.0 (−5.0)	.3 (.3)	3.7 (3.7)	5.4 (5.3)	6.3 (5.8)	9.9 (9.9)	9.9 (9.9)	10.0 (9.9)	10.0 (9.9)	10.2 (9.8)
$7n < t \leq 8n$	−20.2 (−20.2)	−10.0 (−10.0)	−3.5 (−3.5)	−.5 (−.5)	.8 (.6)	−5.0 (−5.0)	.3 (.3)	3.7 (3.7)	5.3 (5.3)	6.0 (5.9)	9.9 (9.9)	9.9 (9.9)	9.9 (9.9)	10.0 (9.9)	10.0 (9.9)

Time period	c = 1.25					c = 1.50				
b	.50	.75	1.00	1.25	1.50	.50	.75	1.00	1.25	1.50
$3n < t \leq 4n$	25.0 (25.0)	19.2 (19.2)	15.5 (15.5)	14.0 (13.8)	13.3 (12.3)	40.0 (40.0)	28.4 (28.4)	20.6 (20.6)	17.4 (17.3)	16.7 (15.3)
$5n < t \leq 6n$	25.0 (25.0)	19.2 (19.2)	15.5 (15.5)	13.9 (13.9)	13.4 (13.1)	40.0 (40.0)	28.4 (28.4)	20.6 (20.6)	17.3 (17.3)	16.1 (15.9)
$7n < t \leq 8n$	25.0 (25.0)	19.2 (19.2)	15.5 (15.5)	13.9 (13.9)	13.2 (13.2)	40.0 (40.0)	28.4 (28.4)	20.6 (20.6)	17.3 (17.3)	16.0 (16.0)

Cell values are in percentage terms with the maximum growth rate in the time period given first and the minimum growth rate in the time period in parentheses.

vestment growth rate, and vice versa. Since they are different sides of the same coin, study of the problem area may proceed from either of these alternative characterizations of the firm's continued existence without loss of generality.

It has not been our purpose to examine the relative theoretical merits of *ARR* vs. *IRR* as a measure of economic performance (past or expected). This has already received considerable attention, and has resulted in several published articles reflecting divergent points of view.[10] Our objective was to facilitate a comparison of and conversion between the alternative rate of return measures. This aim does not require that *IRR* must necessarily be the only "true" measure. It is sufficient justification that *IRR* be a desired measure, in which case—as Solomon suggested—it would be useful to have a conversion formula from the (usually available)[11] *ARR* to the (usually not available) *IRR*.

86 With respect to future research, several avenues seem obvious. This study could be extended by relaxing a number of our simplifying assumptions. Thus consideration could be given to factors like the effects of taxes, the presence of current and other nondepreciable assets, the use of alternative depreciation methods and impact of changing prices, to name just a few of the main possibilities. Like the other studies cited, this one also assumes a constant *IRR* for all projects. While convenient, this assumption is certainly limiting and its removal would provide a better approximation to the real world. So, likewise, would the recognition of uncertainty.

Appendix

In this appendix, we show that a constant growth rate in gross investment results in a constant reinvestment rate.

We let g be the constant rate of growth. Then, by definition,

$$I_t = (1 + g)^t I_0 . \tag{1A}$$

[10] See, for instance, Hector Anton, "Depreciation, Cost Allocation, and Investment Decisions," *Accounting Research* (April 1956), pp. 117–34; Harold Bierman, Jr., "Depreciable Assets—Timing of Expense Recognition," *The Accounting Review* (April 1961), pp. 613–18; William J. Vatter, "Income Models, Book Yield, and the Rate of Return," *The Accounting Review* (October 1966), pp. 681–98; Arthur L. Thomas, "Precision and Discounted Services," *The Accounting Review* (January 1962), pp. 67–72 and "Discounted Services Again: The Homogeneity Problem," *The Accounting Review* (January 1964), pp. 1–11; Orace Johnson, "Two General Concepts of Depreciation," *Journal of Accounting Research* (Spring 1968), pp. 29–37; Melvin N. Greenball, "Appraising Alternative Methods of Accounting for Accelerated Tax Depreciation: A Relative-Accuracy Approach," *Journal of Accounting Research* (Autumn 1969), pp. 262–89; Thomas R. Dyckman, "Discussion of Accelerated Depreciation and Deferred Taxes: An Empirical Study of Fluctuating Asset Expenditures," *Empirical Research in Accounting: Selected Studies, 1967*, Supplement to Vol. 5, *Journal of Accounting Research*.

[11] I.e., available to persons outside the organization from published accounting data.

We note that $I_{t+1} = (1 + g)\, I_t$.
Now, for $t \geq n$ cash flows are a function of the last n-years investment; or after $t \geq n$:

$$\begin{aligned} F_t &= Q_1 \frac{I_{t-1}}{I_0} + Q_2 \frac{I_{t-2}}{I_0} + \cdots + Q_n \cdot \frac{I_{t-n}}{I_0} \\ &= Q_1 \cdot (1 + g)^{t-1} + Q_2 \cdot (1 + g)^{t-2} + \cdots + Q_n \cdot (1 + g)^{t-n} \qquad (2A) \\ &= \sum_{t=1}^{n} Q_1 \,(1 + g)^{t-1} \\ &= Q_1 \sum_{i=1}^{n} b^{i-1} \,(1 + g)^{t-i}. \end{aligned}$$

From the last expression in (2A) we see that:

87

$$\begin{aligned} F_{t+1} &= Q_1 \sum_{i=1}^{n} b^{i-1} \,(1 + g)^{t+1-i} \\ &= (1 + g)\, Q_1 \sum_{i=1}^{n} b^{i-1} \,(1 + g)^{t-i} \\ &= (1 + g)\, F_t . \end{aligned}$$

Therefore, we can conclude that for all $t \geq n$:

$$\frac{I_{t+j}}{F_{t+j}} = \frac{I_t(1 + g)^j}{F_t(1 + g)^j} = \frac{I_t}{F_t} = k,$$

where k is some constant. Therefore, $I_t = k\, F_t$ and hence there is a constant rate of reinvestment.

Combining equations (1A) and (2A), for $t \geq n$:

$$\begin{aligned} \frac{I_t}{F_t} &= \frac{(1 + g)^t I_0}{Q_1 \sum_{i=1}^{n} b^{i-1}(1 + g)^{t-i}} \\ &= \frac{I_0}{Q_1 \sum_{i=1}^{n} b^{i-1}(1 + g)^{-i}} . \end{aligned} \qquad (3A)$$

Now it is easily shown that:

$$\sum_{i=1}^{n} b^{i-1}(1 + g)^{-i} = \frac{(1 + g)^n - b^n}{(1 + g)^n(1 + g - b)} \quad \text{if } b \neq 1 + g.$$

We also know from equation (3) that:

$$\frac{I_0}{Q_1} = \frac{(1 + r)^n - b^n}{(1 + r - b)(1 + r)^n} \quad \text{if } b \neq 1 + r.$$

Substituting these two results into (3A) we have:

$$\frac{I_t}{F_t} = \left[\frac{(1+r)^n - b^n}{(1+r-b)(1+r)^n}\right]\frac{(1+g-b)(1+g)^n}{(1+g)^n - b^n} = k. \qquad (4A)$$

We see that I_t is a constant multiple of F_t so that k, the reinvestment rate, is constant.

The measurement of corporate rates of return: a generalized formulation

Thomas R. Stauffer

Research Associate
Center for Middle Eastern Studies,
Harvard University

90

General conditions are derived under which accounting ratios, such as the conventionally defined accounting rate of return, deviate from the economic rate of return for a firm. Cash revenue streams of arbitrary time-shape, non-depreciable capital, and corporate income taxes are considered. The sign and magnitude of the bias in the accounting rate of return depend upon the depreciation schedule, the revenue time-stream, the firm's growth rate, and its capital structure.

There exists a unique depreciation schedule for which the accounting rate of return is unbiased. However, where the firm's capital structure involves working capital, "exact" depreciation yields a biased accounting rate of return. Thus accounting and economic criteria are irreconcilable unless an intuitively unattractive generalization of "depreciation" for financial assets is introduced.

Where pretax and taxable income differ, the error in the accounting rate of return may no longer converge to zero as the growth rate increases. Regulated utilities and mining companies are particularly susceptible to this error component.

1. Introduction

■ In an earlier issue of this journal, Ezra Solomon [16] revealed the inherent discrepancies between the economic rate of return for a firm and the accounting rate of return as conventionally computed. Here we shall both extend and qualify Solomon's results by introducing a more realistic model for the firm. When one allows for non-depreciable assets (working capital) and considers less restrictive shapes for the time stream of the cash flow associated with a given investment outlay, both the magnitude and the sign of the errors in the rate of return are affected. Corporate income taxes further affect the results. Although the net error becomes almost negligible for some cases of empirical interest, a discrepancy does persist. While the thrust of Solomon's argument is in no way blunted, the quantification of the error in the rate of return requires considerable modification, especially where the analysis is to be inverted in order to estimate real rates of return from historical accounting data.

The author received the Sc.B. degree from M.I.T. in mathematics, the M.A. degree from Harvard in Middle Eastern studies, and the Ph.D. degree, also from Harvard, in economics. His present research has been concentrated in the area of oil taxation, and he was a consultant to the Cabinet Task Force on Oil Import Control.

The initial phase of this research was financed by the Foreign Area Fellowship Program of the Ford Foundation, and Resources for the Future supported the final stage. The assistance of both institutions is gratefully acknowledged, and the usual disclaimers obtain.

Our analysis here includes both Solomon's work and the earlier study by Meyer and Peck [10] as special sub-cases. Specifically we have introduced the following generalizations:

(1) *Accounting profitability measures.* Solomon used the ratio of net income to net assets, whereas Meyer and Peck employed the ratio of cash flow to gross (undepreciated) assets. We shall treat the interdependence and properties of each of the accounting profitability ratios.

(2) *Cash flow time-shapes.* All prior work was effectively confined to the very special case where the time-shape of the cash stream which is generated by an investment outlay was assumed to be constant over the lifetime of the asset (a "rectangular[1] profile"). That assumption is empirically implausible and needlessly restrictive. The results prove to be quite sensitive, in some instances, to the specification of the shape of the cash flow profile. We shall consider an unrestricted set of non-negative profiles.

(3) *Capital structure of the firm.* Due allowance will be made for working capital requirements. The introduction of working capital discloses an ostensibly irreconcilable discrepancy between the determination of the depreciation schedule which yields an exact determination of "income" and the schedule which yields an exact value for the accounting rate of return.

(4) *Income taxes.* The effect of corporate income taxes and the implications of using different depreciation schedules for tax and corporate purposes are explored. Tax effects cancel out in the special case treated by Solomon or Meyer and Peck, but otherwise the tax correction itself can be as large as the inherent discrepancy which is determined for the non-tax case. Hence taxes cannot properly be ignored.

This paper will be confined to the case where all non-current outlays by the firm are capitalized; a subsequent paper will extend the same methodology to cases where capital or quasi-capital outlays, such as advertising or research and development, are expensed, rather than carried as capital assets. Once again, the simple consequences of expensing, versus capitalizing, require extensive qualification when a more realistic financial model of the firm is introduced. In particular, it will be shown that capitalization of outlays on non-current account, which are otherwise expensed, does *not* in general eliminate the bias in the rate of return calculation and can actually increase that error.

The next sections will be devoted to a fairly general mathematical formulation of the interrelationship between economic and accounting rates of return, but a non-mathematical summary of the principal results can be found in the final section (8). The reader who wishes to spare himself the methodological demonstrations is urged to pass directly to that final section. In Section 2, we define the financial model of the "firm" and determine its exact economic rate of return. In Section 3, the two alternative accounting profitability ratios are specified mathematically, and their relationship to the economic rate of return is described for the case of an arbitrary growth pattern for

[1] The designation "rectangular" is borrowed from control system theory, and will be used hereafter.

the firm. The intrinsic disparity between the "root" and "ratio" definitions of profitability is demonstrated.

Sections 4 and 5 are then devoted to deriving the properties of the conventional accounting rate of return and the "gross profitability ratio" (the ratio of cash flow to gross assets) for the special case of steady-state growth. The impact of working capital is studied in Section 6, and the effects of corporate income taxes are introduced in Section 7, including several alternative accounting treatments. A non-mathematical recapitulation of results is given in Section 8, which is followed by a glossary of symbols and notation.

2. Financial model of the firm

■ We must perforce introduce an idealized representation of the firm, while retaining those financial or structural features which might have material effect upon the conclusions. It is obvious that many of the important real-world complications will necessarily be assumed away, but we note in passing that most of the complexities which we shall hereafter ignore would have been further extra parameters in the system equations, all tending to reduce the likelihood that the accounting measures of the economic rate of return would be unbiased.

Specifically, we restrict our attention to a firm which invests each year in a bundle of capital projects with the same composition, i.e., the mix between different types of fixed assets remains constant even though the total outlays may increase. For most industries—excluding conglomerates—this assumption is not unreasonable, since the relative proportions of expenditure for buildings, warehouses, machinery, office equipment, etc., would not be expected to shift rapidly over time.

Each such bundle of assets is assumed to generate a future stream of quasi-rents, the time pattern of which is constant, being proportional only to the size of the initial investment and quite independent of either prior or subsequent investments. This assumption that investments are not mutually interdependent ("separability") assures us, qualitatively speaking, that the contributions of incremental investments can be identified and hence analyzed.

More precisely, we assume that the firm can be represented by a convolution-type investment process, whereby the cash flow in any year t is the sum of the investment outlays made in all prior years, each investment outlay being weighted by the cash flow associated with a unit investment of age τ.[2] This is a "point-input, flow-output" process, described by a Volterra integral equation of the second kind:

$$Y(t) = K(t) + \int_0^t \pi(t-\tau)Y(t-\tau)K(t,\tau)d\tau\,, \qquad (1)$$

where

$Y(t)$ = cash flow for firm,
$K(t, \tau)$ = cash flow generated in year $t + \tau$, from a unit investment in year t, and
$\pi(t)$ = fraction of firm's cash flow which is reinvested in any year.

[2] The convolution, or *Faltung*, of two functions is defined as:

$$F \otimes G = \int_0^t F(t)G(t-\tau)d\tau\,.$$

The above representation embodies the assumption that sequential investments are separable, but the relationship is still not particularly productive in its generalized form, because the cash flow $K(t, \tau)$ depends both upon asset age and the time of investment. So we must introduce further assumptions:

(1) The process is stationary, i.e., $K(t, \tau)$ equals $K(t - \tau)$. In other words, the cash flow pattern produced by a unit investment is independent of the time at which the investment is made and is also independent of all prior or subsequent investments made by the firm.[3]

(2) $K(t)$ is a bounded, non-negative function of t for $1 \leq t \leq N$ and vanishes for all $t > N$.

This ensures that there exists one and only one real internal rate of return for $K(t)$, i.e., a unique, positive discount rate, r, for which the present value of the cash flow stream $K(t)$ equals unity.[4]

(3) Expectations are always realized; if the firm invests one dollar now, the resulting cash flow will be precisely that given by $K(t)$.[5] 93

(4) $\pi(t) = \pi_0$; the reinvestment fraction is taken to be constant.

Under these assumptions, irrespective of the functional form of $K(t)$, we have the following theorem:

ONE: The internal rate of return of a firm described by a stationary, separable convolution investment process is equal to the internal rate of return of the projects in which the firm invests.[6]

Thus, for this case, we know precisely that the real, economic rate of return for the firm equals r, where $k(r) = 1$, and $k(s)$ is the Laplace transform of $K(t)$. The thrust of the subsequent analysis can thus be directed towards determining the accounting rate of return exhibited by such a firm, since we know its real rate of return.[7]

---

[3] See [9], pp. 69–72.

[4] See articles cited in [6] and [7]. This condition can be relaxed to allow a single crossing of the axis by $K(t)$; the contingencies where multiple roots are mathematically possible have thus far been of trifling practical interest. The sufficiency of this condition is shown collaterally in [18], Appendix 1.

[5] This assumption plays two roles; first, if we choose to value the firm by terminating reinvestment in any year, it stipulates that the firm will continue to collect the residual revenues from prior investments, even while winding down its operations. Second, the fact that the firm realizes *ex post* the *ex ante* rate of return upon its annual investment outlays injects behavioral content into the model. The *ex post* rate r is thus the rate which is employed in resource allocation decisions.

[6] Stock-valuation models such as those pioneered by Myron Gordon use a special case of this theorem, where $K(t)$ is either rectangular or a step function of infinite duration.

[7] This theorem may be proved as follows: If we specialize equation (1) by introducing assumptions (2) and (4) above:

$$Y(t) = K(t) + \pi\int_0^t Y(t - \tau)K(\tau)d\tau\,. \tag{2}$$

Take the Laplace transform of equation (2). This results in

$$y(s) = k(s) + \pi y(s)k(s)\,, \tag{3}$$

where

$$y(s) = \mathcal{L}[Y(t)] = \int_0^N e^{-st}K(t)dt\,,\ \text{etc.},$$

A second aspect of this investment process is the fact that the firm ultimately grows asymptotically at a constant rate which is a function only of the cash flow profile, $K(t)$, and the re-investment coefficient, π; we state the theorem here without proof:

TWO: Under the assumptions enumerated above, the cash flow in a convolution investment process, $Y(t)$, *assumes the asymptotic form* $Y(t) \sim Y_0(1 + g)^t$, *where* g *is the unique root of the transcendental equation* $k(g) = \pi^{-1}$.[8]

Consequently, insofar as we consider the special case of steady-state growth, the formal apparatus developed in the preceding paragraphs assures us that the economic rate of return for the firm in question is unique and equal to r, the internal rate of return of the unit project mix.[9]

3. General properties of accounting profitability metrics

■ Under the assumptions developed in the preceding section, the economic rate of return for the firm is uniquely defined. In contrast, there are two important alternative *accounting* metrics for the rate of return. These different accounting ratios of "income" to "assets" are (1) the ratio of cash flow to gross assets, or gross profitability ratio (GPR), and (2) the ratio of net income to net assets, or net profitability ratio (NPR). In this context, "cash flow" designates the net revenues after all non-capital charges but before deducting any depreciation; it therefore includes interest. Cash flow less depreciation is then equal to "net income." "Gross assets" means the total historical cost of all plant and equipment which has not been scrapped (retired), while "net assets" denotes the remainder when cumulative depreciation reserves have been deducted from the "gross assets" figure. In this section it will be assumed that the firm consists only of depreciable assets.

Of these two accounting profitability ratios, only the second—NPR—has achieved wide currency, as it defines the conventional accounting rate of return. The GPR has only occasionally been recommended, based on the assertion that using that ratio obviates

---

using the fact that the Laplace transform of the convolution of two functions is the product of the Laplace transforms of the functions themselves. (Cf. [3], *in passim*, and [11].) In equation (3), let $s = r$, where r is the root of $k(r) = 1$; then $k(s) = k(r) = 1$, and we have, upon rearranging:

$$y(r) = (1 - \pi)^{-1}.$$

However, the fraction π of that gross revenue stream had been reinvested, so that the disposable cash stream equals $(1 - \pi)Y(t)$, and the present value of that disposable cash stream, discounted at r, equals unity. The internal rate of return of the firm is therefore identical to that for the unit project.

[8] See [18], Appendix 1.

[9] More generally, even where π is a function of time, the internal rate of return of a firm characterized by a convolution investment process equals r. The investment flow becomes: $I(t) = \pi(t)Y(t) + \delta(t)$, and the present value of the gross cash flow *minus* the investment stream equals:

$$y(r) - i(r) = k(r) + \mathcal{L}[K \otimes (\pi Y)] - \mathcal{L}[\pi k] - \mathcal{L}[\pi\{(\pi Y) \otimes K\}] - \mathcal{L}[\delta(t)].$$

Noting that $k(r)$ and the Laplace transform of the Dirac function both equal unity, we have, upon substituting the equation for $Y(t)$ into $\mathcal{L}[\pi Y]$:

$$y(r) - i(r) = 1 - 1 = 0.$$

Thus, the internal rate of return equals r, since the present values of revenue and investment streams are equated when discounted at that rate.

the need to specify depreciation schedules—no depreciation is deducted from the cash flow, and, symmetrically, no accumulated depreciation is deducted from the cumulative historical cost of the assets still in service. Since an exact depreciation schedule is quite elusive, so the argument runs, one can eliminate that source of error by using none whatsoever.

In order to arrive at a comparative assessment of the merits of both metrics, in terms of their relationship to the underlying economic rate of return, we examine the general properties of each metric first for the case of a quite general growth pattern in the firm and then subsequently for the more special case of steady-state growth. In particular, we shall derive the conditions under which each of the metrics approximates the real rate of return—if at all.

Turning first to the GPR, let $I(t)$ represent an arbitrary stream of investment flows in the firm, except that $I(t) \leq Y(t)$, i.e., investment never exceeds cash flow. Then the general expression for the GPR becomes

$$\mathrm{GPR}(t) = \frac{\text{Cash Flow}}{\text{Gross Fixed Assets}} = \frac{\int_0^N I(t-\tau)K(\tau)d\tau}{\int_0^N I(t-\tau)d\tau}. \tag{4}$$

If the GPR is to be a useful measure of the economic rate of return, it must be time-invariant, independent of the prior investment pattern, since we showed above that the economic rate of return of the firm under these conditions is exactly equal to r. Let us assume that $\mathrm{GPR}(t)$ equals a constant, ϕ, and solve for the conditions which this imposes upon $K(t)$. Substituting ϕ into equation (4) and clearing, we find

$$\int_0^N I(t-\tau)\{K(\tau) - \phi\}d\tau \equiv 0\,. \tag{5}$$

If the definite integral must be identically zero for all investment time patterns—i.e., if ϕ is to be independent of the firm's investment history, $I(t)$—then the bracketed term itself must vanish, from which we conclude that the GPR can be invariant if and only if $K(t) = \phi$ for $1 \leq t \leq N$. In other words, a necessary and sufficient condition that the GPR be constant for all $I(t)$ is that the cash flow profile be rectangular.

However, even in this very special case where $K(t)$ is rectangular, the GPR is still inherently biased. Let r be the internal rate of return for a rectangular cash flow profile with duration N; then

$K(t) = \left\{\dfrac{r}{1-(1+r)^{-N}}\right\}$ and the GPR equals $r[1-(1+r)^{-N}]^{-1}$.

Since the term in brackets is less than unity, the GPR is seen to be always biased upwards: GPR $> r$, and it overstates the economic rate of return even in the one special case for which the ratio is independent of the time path of the firm's investments. This result suggests that the GPR should prove to be of limited utility as a measure of the economic rate of return, since a constant cash flow stream, the rectangular profile, is applicable only to rather special kinds of equipment—such as light bulbs, telephone poles, etc.—and even then the ratio is biased.

An analogous result obtains for the conventional accounting profitability ratio, NPR; it too, yields a correct value for the economic rate of return only for the special case of a given profile shape. We shall demonstrate the following theorem:

THREE: Under the assumptions outlined in Section 2, the accounting rate of return will exactly equal the economic rate of return, for an arbitrary growth path, if and only if the cash flow profile, K(t), *and the book depreciation schedule,* D(t), *jointly satisfy the integral equation*

$$D(t) = K(t) - re^{rt}\left[1 - \int_0^t K(\tau)e^{-r\tau}d\tau\right]. \qquad (6)$$

Thus, if $K(t)$ is given, $D(t)$ is uniquely specified. Although this condition appears even more restrictive than that imposed upon the GPR, we will show later that the implicit shape for $K(t)$ is empirically rather more plausible than the rectangular profile associated with the GPR. Moreover, the NPR will be seen to have additional properties which ensure that it is normally a more precise and more readily interpretable measure of the economic rate of return.

In order to demonstrate this central result, let us first define the general equations for net income and net assets:

$$\text{Net Income }(t) = \int_0^N I(t-\tau)K(\tau)d\tau - \int_0^N I(t-\tau)D(\tau)d\tau\,, \qquad (7)$$

$$\text{Net Assets }(t) = \int_0^N I(t-\tau)d\tau - \int_0^N I(t-\tau)\,\text{Res}(\tau)d\tau\,, \qquad (8)$$

where

$$\text{Res}(\tau) = \int_0^\tau D(x)dx = \text{depreciation reserve}\,.$$

The conventional accounting profitability, NPR, equals, by definition, the ratio of net income to net assets (which is the same as the conventional accounting rate of return):

$$R^{acc} = \frac{\displaystyle\int_0^N I(t-\tau)K(\tau)d\tau - \int_0^N I(t-\tau)D(\tau)d\tau}{\displaystyle\int_0^N I(t-\tau)d\tau - \int_0^N I(t-\tau)\,\text{Res}(\tau)d\tau}\,. \qquad (9)$$

Let us postulate that R^{acc} equals r, the economic rate of return, and then solve for the conditions under which that identity is possible; substituting r into equation (9), clearing fractions, and regrouping, we obtain an integral condition which defines the necessary relationship between $K(t)$ and $D(t)$:

$$\int_0^N I(t-\tau)\{K(\tau) - D(\tau) - r - r\,\text{Res}(\tau)\}d\tau \equiv 0\,. \qquad (10)$$

If the NPR exactly equals r for a piece-wise continuous but otherwise arbitrary time pattern for the investment flows $I(t)$, then the bracketed term in equation (10) must vanish identically, i.e.,

$$K(t) = r + D(t) - r\,\mathrm{Res}(t)\,. \tag{11}$$

Upon substituting $D(t) = \dfrac{dR(t)}{dt}$, multiplying through by $\exp(-rt)$, and integrating by parts, we find:

$$\mathrm{Res}(t) = e^{rt}\int_0^t K(\tau)e^{-r\tau}d\tau - e^{-rt} + 1 \tag{12}$$

since $R(0) = 0$. If equation (12) is differentiated with respect to time, we regain an expression in terms of $D(t)$:

$$D^e(t) = \frac{d}{dt}\,\mathrm{Res}(t) = K(t) - re^{rt}\left[1 - \int_0^t K(\tau)e^{-r\tau}d\tau\right], \tag{13}$$

where $D^e(t)$ denotes the "exact" depreciation function in the sense of the theorem. Thus, for any given profile $K(t)$, a unique depreciation schedule is defined by equation (13) for which the accounting rate of return will be exact.[10] Otherwise, if $K(t)$ and $D(t)$ are not related to each other as stipulated by that equation, the accounting rate of return will in general diverge from the economic rate of return.

We have previously stipulated conditions upon $K(t)$ which ensure that the economic rate of return, r, is unique. Equation (13) accordingly defines a unique relationship between $K(t)$ and $D(t)$; thus, for any given $K(t)$ there is one and only one depreciation schedule, $D(t)$, for which the accounting rate of return exactly equals the economic rate of return, which proves the theorem.

The "exact" depreciation function which is embodied in equation (13) admits of a direct economic interpretation.[11] Consider a function, $V(t)$, which equals the present value, referenced at time t, of those revenues generated by the unit investment made at $t = 0$ between year t and its scrapping in year N; $V(t)$ is the present value of the area shown shaded in Figure 1. In a perfectly competitive capital market, $V(t)$ represents the value of the remaining services of that asset to an entrepreneur whose opportunity cost of capital equals r:

FIGURE 1

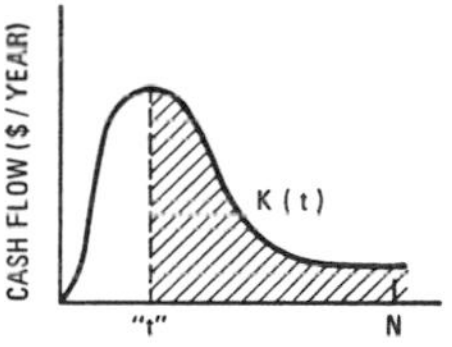

$$V(t) = e^{rt}\int_t^N K(\tau)e^{-r\tau}d\tau \qquad 0 \le t \le N\,. \tag{14}$$

The time derivative of $V(t)$ is equal to the rate of change of the financial value of the asset:

$$\frac{dV}{dt} = re^{rt}\int_t^N K(\tau)e^{-r\tau}d\tau - K(t)\,, \tag{15}$$

---

[10] One may verify that $D^e(t)$ is non-negative and that its integral over the range 0 to N equals unity; it thus satisfies the mathematical restrictions upon a depreciation function.

[11] One must distinguish carefully between (1) our designation of "exact" to denote a depreciation schedule for which the accounting rate of return is unbiased and (2) a special criterion for "neutrality" of depreciation used by tax accountants. The latter refers to schedules such that the same fraction of the initial value is depreciated independent of the lifetime, i.e., the depreciation reserve must be a function solely of the fractional life (t/N); see [4].

or

$$\frac{dV}{dt} = re^{rt}\left\{1 - \int_0^t K(\tau)e^{-r\tau}d\tau\right\} - K(t)\,, \tag{16}$$

since

$$\int_t^N K(\tau)e^{-r\tau}d\tau = 1 - \int_0^t K(\tau)e^{-r\tau}d\tau\,,$$

where we have exploited the condition that $k(r)$ equals unity. However, upon comparing equation (16) with the expression for $D^e(t)$, equation (13), we find:

$$D^e(t) \equiv -\frac{dV(t)}{dt}. \tag{17}$$

The "financial depreciation" defined in equation (14) is equal to the "exact depreciation" as derived in equation (13). Accordingly, the only form of depreciation for which the accounting rate of return is invariant and identically equal to the "true" economic rate of return is the time pattern of depreciation charges defined by equation (16) —i.e., a depreciation charge which will in general vary during the lifetime of the project, and which equals the time rate of change of the present value of the future stream of quasi-rents which remain to be collected at each point in time.[12]

If the depreciation schedule actually used in the firm's accounts deviates from the "exact" depreciation function, $D^e(t)$, as defined above, the accounting profitability will not in general equal the economic rate of return. Since depreciation schedules and lifetimes are in large measure arbitrary, being established by convention or through conformity with standards specified by fiscal authorities, it would be purely fortuitous if the two rates of return were identical in actual cases. In particular, straight-line depreciation, the form most commonly employed in the United States for corporate reporting, is consistent with only one cash flow profile, as defined by equation (13); it would be a heroic assumption to presume that all capital investments made by U. S. industry just happen to generate cash flows with precisely that time shape.

In recapitulation, we have shown thus far that both of the principal accounting profitability ratios, GPR and NPR, are theoretically inadequate.[13] Both can yield exact or usable measures of the economic rate of return only in very special instances, and we have no basis for claiming that those special cases are usefully representative of real-world circumstances. The general result—that neither measure is ordinarily exact—is clear enough, but whether the size and direction of the error may be more precisely defined and the extent to which the discrepancies are significant remain to be determined. Consequently, one must examine the numerical implications of different shapes for the cash flow profile and different degrees of mismatch between cash flow profile and depreciation schedule.

[12] Samuelson [13], [14] has shown that this depreciation function is the only form for which the present value of a stream of quasi-rents will be independent of the tax rate.

[13] A third accounting profitability ratio—net income divided by gross assets—has been used occasionally, most notably by Dupont [1]. An analysis exactly parallel to that used above suffices to show that this ratio, too, is faulty.

4. Properties of the accounting rate of return (steady-state growth)

■ Let us now restrict our attention to the case of steady-state growth and determine the properties of the conventional accounting profitability ratio: let $I(t)$ in equation (9) be replaced by $I_0 \exp g(t_0 - \tau)$. The NPR for the steady-growth case becomes

$$R^{acc}(g) = \frac{I_0 e^{gt_0} \int_0^N K(\tau) e^{-g\tau} d\tau - I_0 e^{gt_0} \int_0^N D(\tau) e^{-g\tau} d\tau}{I_0 e^{gt_0} \int_0^N e^{-g\tau} d\tau - I_0 e^{gt_0} \int_0^N \text{Res}(\tau) e^{-g\tau} d\tau}, \quad (18)$$

or, simplifying,

$$R^{acc} = \frac{k(g) - d(g)}{\frac{1}{g}[1 - e^{-gN}] - \int_0^N \text{Res}(\tau) e^{-g\tau} d\tau}, \quad (19)$$

where $k(g)$ and $d(g)$ are defined as the Laplace transforms (present values) of $K(t)$ and $D(t)$, respectively, evaluated at the growth rate of the firm g.[14]

The equation may be further simplified if we express the second integral in the denominator in terms of $d(g)$: when we integrate the expression by parts, the result is

$$\int_0^N \text{Res}(\tau) e^{-g\tau} d\tau = \int_0^N \frac{dD(\tau)}{d\tau} e^{-g\tau} d\tau - \frac{1}{g}[d(g) - e^{-gN}], \quad (20)$$

using $\text{Res}(0) = 0$ and $\text{Res}(N) = 1$ as the end conditions on $\text{Res}(t)$ and the assumption that all depreciable assets are retired automatically N years after their acquisition. If equation (20) is substituted into equation (19), we obtain the following general expression for the accounting rate of return of a steadily growing firm:

$$R^{acc}(g) = \frac{k(g) \quad d(g)}{\frac{1}{g}[1 - d(g)]}. \quad (21)$$

This formulation is both compact and computationally convenient, since the Laplace transforms for the various profiles or depreciation schedules are tabulated functions.[15]

An important asymptotic property of the accounting rate of return may be deduced immediately; let $g \to r$ in equation (21), i.e., consider a firm whose rate of growth approaches its real rate of return:

$$\lim_{g \to r} R^{acc}(g) = \frac{1 - d(r)}{1 - d(r)} \lim_{g \to r} \frac{1}{1/g} = r. \quad (22)$$

---

[14] Although the functions assume the form of a present value there is no economic significance to that fact, and it is misleading to interpret g here as a discount rate.

[15] If the cash flows and depreciation charges are discrete, rather than continuous, the Laplace transforms are to be interpreted as z-transforms. The derivation would proceed in a parallel fashion. However, where depreciation is computed and charged at discrete intervals, the "net assets" are to be interpreted as the *beginning-of-period* figures.

Thus, as $g \rightarrow r$, $R^{acc} \rightarrow r$, which means that the accounting rate of return converges to the real rate in such measure as the growth rate approaches the accounting rate of return.[16] This result holds for *all* cash profiles, $K(t)$; its empirical significance lies in the suggestion that the errors may in fact be quite small for that class of firms or industries whose growth rates and indicated rates of return do not differ greatly.

More generally, if $g \neq r$, it is possible to derive an equation for the error in the accounting rate of return. Let R^i denote the accounting rate of return corresponding to a given depreciation schedule $D^i(t)$ used in conjunction with a specific cash flow profile $K(t)$, while $D^e(t)$ denotes the exact depreciation schedule associated with that same cash profile. Then, from equations (13) and (21), we can express $d^e(g)$ in terms of $k(g)$, as

$$d^e(g) = \frac{r - gk(g)}{r - g}. \tag{23}$$

Using the result in equation (23), one then obtains the following expression for the difference between the accounting and the economic rates of return:

$$\delta R = R^i - r = \frac{g[k(g) - 1]}{[1 - d^i(g)][1 - d^e(g)]}\{d^i(g) - d^e(g)\}. \tag{24}$$

The Laplace transforms of both depreciation functions lie between zero and one, i.e., $d^e(g), d^i(g) < 1$. Then, if $g < r$, $k(g) > 1$, and we therefore know that the sign of δR, the error in the book rate of return, is governed only by the sign of the term $[d^i(g) - d^e(g)]$. Hence we can conclude:

$$\begin{aligned} &\text{If } d^i(g) > d^e(g), \text{ then } \delta R > 0. \\ &\text{If } d^i(g) < d^e(g), \text{ then } \delta R < 0. \end{aligned} \tag{25}$$

[17]

We may draw two conclusions from this relationship:

(1) The error in the accounting rate of return is proportional to the difference between the Laplace transforms of the actual depreciation schedules used in the accounts and the exact function associated with the cash flow profile.

(2) If the accounting depreciation schedule is not "exact," there will *always* be an error in the accounting rate of return, except when $g = r$. This follows from the fact that Laplace transforms are unique, i.e., no two functions can have identical Laplace transforms unless they are themselves identical.[18]

Having demonstrated the existence in general of an error in the rate of return, it is useful at this juncture to examine a set of illustrative cases in order to indicate representative magnitudes for the

---

[16] This phenomenon was observed by Solomon and Laya for the special case of the rectangular cash profile and described as the "magic switching point" ([17], p. 174).

[17] If $g > r$, the two sets of inequalities must be reversed, but that situation is rarely encountered in practice.

[18] More generally, they can differ at most over a set of points whose measure is zero.

errors. Figure 2 illustrates a family of truncated exponentials, where the decay rate is treated as a parameter. Then $K(t) = a(r)(1 + d)^{-t}$, $1 \leq t \leq N$, where $a(r)$ is chosen so that the internal rate of return equals r. This family of cash flow profiles ranges from a rectangular function ($d = 0$) to a steeply declining, exponential-shaped profile ($d = 0.08$). Let us further assume that $r = 10$ percent; the corresponding accounting rates of return are plotted in Figure 3 as a function of g and for three values of d.

FIGURE 2

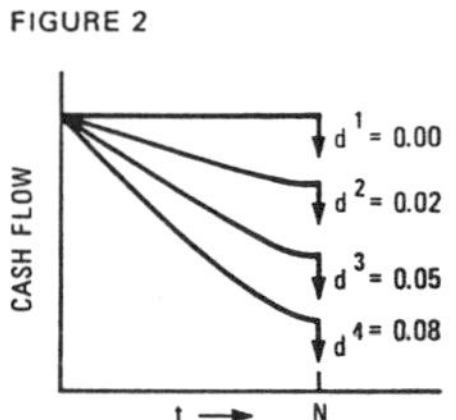

The topmost curve in Figure 3 shows how the book rate of return varies with the growth rate of the firm for the case of a rectangular cash flow profile ($d = 0$), where the exact rate of return equals 10 percent. The book rate overstates the real rate by 2.8 percentage points for the no-growth case, but the disparity falls steadily as g increases. For example, the error amounts to some 0.6 points if the growth rate equals 7 percent per annum; the error vanishes when g equals 10 percent.

FIGURE 3

ACCOUNTING RATE OF RETURN:
STEADY-STATE GROWTH AND DIFFERENT PROFILES

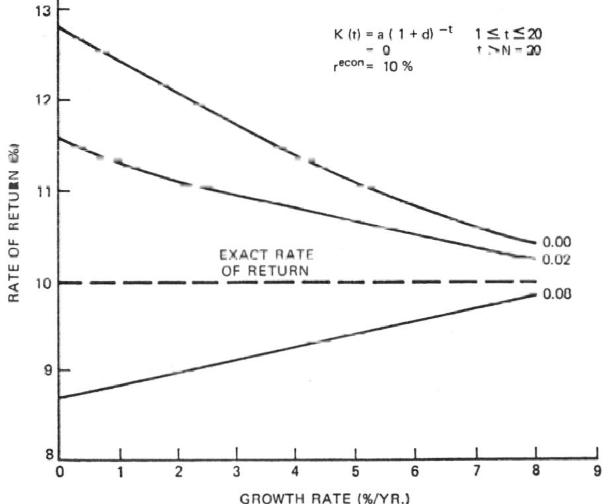

If the cash profile declines slightly with increasing asset age ($d = 0.02$), the dependence of the indicated accounting rate of return upon the firm's rate of growth is similar. However, the magnitude of the error is reduced to almost half of what was observed for the case of a rectangular profile; this is shown by the middle curve in Figure 3. Finally, when an exponential cash flow profile with a relatively high decay rate ($d = 0.08$) is considered, we see exemplified the case where the accounting profitability actually *understates* the real rate of return.[19] For the latter alternative, if $g = 0$, the *negative*

[19] If $d = 0.05$, for this pair of values of r and N, the accounting error is quite small, but such a happy conjunction of parameters is accidental.

bias in the rate of return is some 1.3 percentage points. This error, too, declines in magnitude as g increases, and in all three cases the accounting profitability converges to the exact rate of return, $r = 10$ percent, as g approaches 10 percent.[20]

This small set of examples illustrates two further conclusions: first, the errors can be of significant magnitude, i.e., the inquiry into the disparity is not trivial; second, the error in the rate of return is seen to be strongly dependent upon the time-shape of the cash flow which is generated by the firm's individual projects. Since quite a wide variety of such time-shapes is admissible *a priori*, we must attempt to quantify this dependence more carefully. In particular, two related questions are relevant here:

(1) For each of the standard depreciation schedules, what is the time-shape of the cash flow profile for which the accounting rate of return would be exact?

(2) How does the "exact" profile which is associated with each standard depreciation schedule compare with the profiles which are likely to be encountered in practice?

Let us first determine the "exact" forms of $K(t)$ corresponding to the cases of straight-line depreciation (SLD) and sum-of-the-year's-digits depreciation (SYD). We demonstrated earlier that the "exact" depreciation function in each case was related to the cash flow profile via an integro-differential equation—equation (14)—which is repeated below

$$D^e(t) = \frac{dV(t)}{dt},$$

where

$$V(t) = e^{rt} \int_t^N K(\tau) e^{-r\tau} d\tau \,. \tag{26}$$

In this instance, $D^e(t)$ is given, and we must solve for the shape of the cash flow for which the given depreciation schedule will result in calculation of the correct rate of return, rather than vice versa. For the case of straight-line depreciation, the result is

$$-\frac{dV^e(t)}{dt} = \frac{1}{N} \qquad 0 \leq t \leq N \,. \tag{27}$$

Integrating equation (27) with respect to time, we obtain an expression for $V^e(t)$ which satisfies the initial conditions and implicitly defines $K^e(t)$:

$$V^e(t) = 1 - \frac{t}{N} \qquad 0 \leq t \leq N \,. \tag{28}$$

V^e defines the curve of the "net assets" of the project as a function of time.

Upon combining equations (26) and (28), we obtain an integral equation for the unknown profile, $K^e(t)$, which is consistent with

[20] If $g > 10$ percent, the signs of the errors are reversed. Since this case is infrequent, we do not plot values of g greater than r^{econ}.

straight-line depreciation:

$$\int_t^N K^e(\tau)e^{-r\tau}d\tau = \left(1 - \frac{t}{N}\right)e^{-rt}. \tag{29}$$

Differentiating both sides with respect to t, we obtain:

$$re^{-rt} + \frac{e^{-rt}}{N} - \frac{rte^{-rt}}{N} = K^e(t)e^{-rt},$$

and then

$$K^e(t) = \left(r + \frac{1}{N}\right) - \frac{rt}{N}. \tag{30}$$

FIGURE 4

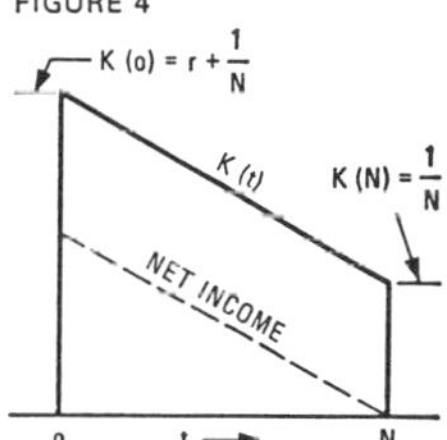

One may readily verify by direct integration that the present value of the kernel $K^e(t)$, discounted at r, equals unity.

The cash flow profile and the net accounting income are shown in Figure 4. Since the annual depreciation equals $1/N$, "net income" vanishes for $t = N$. We note that the form of this normative profile is more plausible than the rectangular profile, since the stream of quasi-rents here declines as the asset becomes older, a feature which one intuitively expects.

In practice, one usually deals with discrete, rather than continuous, functions, corresponding to the accounting periods in which income is recognized. In this case, it is desirable to choose the *beginning-of-year* net asset figure as the denominator of the accounting profitability ratio, in order to prevent indeterminacy. Then it may be shown that the "exact" profile is:

$$K^e(t) = \frac{1}{N}\{1 + r(N - t + 1)\} \quad t = 1, 2, 3 \cdots N.$$

This differs from the result for the continuous case, equation (30), in that the "net income" in year N is r/N dollars, as distinguished from the instantaneous value of zero when $t = N$ for the case of continuous cash flow streams.

Similarly, if

$$D(t) = \frac{(N - t + 1)}{N(N + 1)},$$

the sum-of-the-year's-digits schedule, the corresponding exact form for $K(t)$ becomes

$$K^e(t) = \frac{2}{N}\left(1 - \frac{t}{N + 1}\right) + r\left\{1 - \frac{(t - 1)[2(N + 1) - t]}{N(N + 1)}\right\}. \tag{31}$$

Both forms for $K^e(t)$, corresponding to SLD and SYD, are plotted in Figure 5. One notes that SYD implies a very much more rapid falloff in the cash flow with increasing asset age than does SLD. For the case shown—r = 10 percent and N = 15—SLD presumes that the cash flow is down 50 percent at the end of 15 years, whereas SYD assumes that the end-of-life cash stream has declined to less than one-twentieth of its initial value.

Three other possible functional forms for $K(t)$ are shown in Figure 5 and tabulated in Table 1; all of these illustrative profiles

FIGURE 5
SELECTED CASH FLOW TIME PROFILES

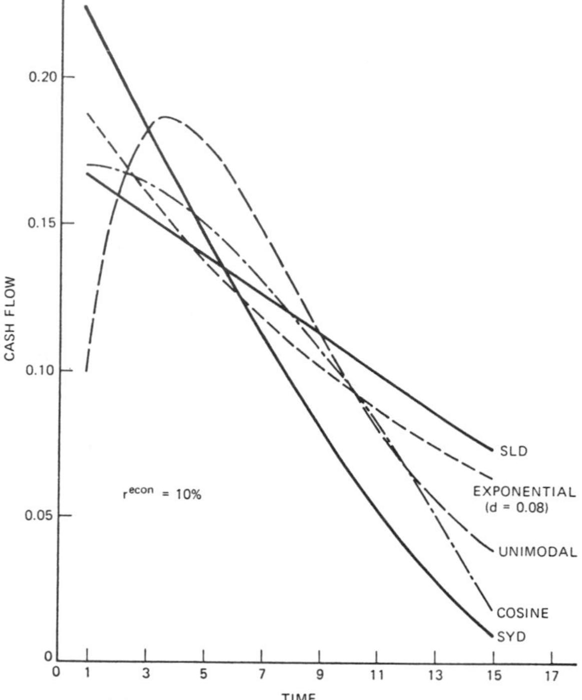

are monotonic except for the unimodal, which peaks strongly for $t = 4$ and declines quite steeply thereafter. The forms are quite diverse, but the disparities in the associated accounting rates of return are less than one might have expected from the large differences in the time shapes. This effect becomes apparent if we plot the values of the Laplace transforms of the depreciation functions associated with each profile, recalling that it is the difference between the Laplace transforms of the depreciation functions, rather than the difference between the time profiles themselves, which influences the errors in the accounting rate of return.

The Laplace transforms of the two conventional depreciation functions, SLD and SYD, are plotted as heavy, unbroken lines in Figure 6 in order to highlight their role as benchmarks in determining the direction and magnitude of error in the accounting rate of return. We note first that the plots of the "exact" depreciation function for both the rectangular and the slowly declining exponential ($d = 0.02$) lie *below* that for SLD; thus if one employs SLD for firms characterized by either of the two aforementioned cash flow profiles, the bias in the rate of return will be positive. If the firms used SYD, the error in the accounting profitability ratio would be still greater.

TABLE 1

CASH FLOW PROFILE FUNCTIONS*

LAPLACE TRANSFORM	TIME DOMAIN**	Z –TRANSFORM*** (DISCRETE)
$\frac{C_1}{r+d}\left[1-e^{-N(r+d)}\right]$	1. EXPONENTIAL $K(t)=C, e^{-d(t-1)}$	$\frac{C_1(1+d)}{d+r+dr}\left[1-(d+r+dr)^{-N}\right]$
$\frac{C_2}{r}\left[1-e^{-Nr}\right]$	2. RECTANGULAR $K(t)=C_2$	$\frac{C_2}{r}\left[1-(1+r)^{-N}\right] \triangleq cS(N_1 r)$
$C_3\left[\frac{N+1}{r(1+r)}-\frac{(Nr^2+1)S(N,r)}{Nr^2(1+r)}\right]$	3. TRIANGULAR (TERBORGH) $K(t)-C_3\left[N-\frac{(t-1)}{N}\right]$	$\frac{C_3}{r}\left[1-\frac{1}{r}\left\{1-(1+r)^{-N}\right\}\right]$
$C_4\left\{\frac{Ne^{-(r+b)N}}{r+b}+\frac{S(N, r+b)}{r+b}\right\}$	4. UNIMODAL $K(t)=C_4\, t\, a^{-t}$	$\frac{C\beta}{(\beta-1)^2}\left\{1-\frac{N\beta-N+\beta}{\beta^{N+1}}\right\}, \beta=a(1+r)$
$C_5\left\{\frac{1-e^{-rN}}{(1+r)\left[r^2+\frac{\pi^2}{4N^2}\right]}\right\}$	5. TRUNCATED COSINE $K(t)=C_5 \cos\frac{\pi(t-1)}{2N}$	$\frac{C_3}{1+r}\;\frac{1-\frac{\cos \pi/2N}{1+r}+\frac{\sin \pi/2N}{(1+r)^{N+1}}}{1-\frac{2\cos \pi/2N}{1+r}+\left(\frac{1}{1+r}\right)^2}$

PRIMARY SOURCE: J. RAGAZZINI & G. FRANKLIN [11]

* ALL FUNCTIONS VANISH FOR $t > N$.

** IF K (t) IS A CONTINUOUS FUNCTION FOR FUNCTIONS 1, 3, OR 5, THE TERM (t–1) IS TO BE REPLACED BY "t".

*** $Z = 1 + r$; THE FUNCTIONS ARE EXPRESSED DIRECTLY IN TERMS OF r, SINCE IT IS THE VARIABLE WITH DIRECT ECONOMIC SIGNIFICANCE; IN THE DISCRETE CASE, THE FUNCTION VANISHES FOR $t < 1$.

More interesting, however, is the fact that the curves for the Terborgh profile,[21] the unimodal, and the steeply declining exponential ($d = 0.08$) are all clustered closely together. In spite of their quite disparate time-shapes, each of these profiles would result in essentially the same *understatement* of the economic rate of return in the case where SLD is used for the corporate accounts, or all would produce essentially the same *overstatement* if the firm uses SYD.

Qualitatively, one observes that the likelihood of positive bias appears to decrease in such measure as one relaxes the condition that the cash flow be constant over the physical lifetime of the asset. Even though the three profiles mentioned above are quite differently shaped for the early years, all are characterized by rapid decay in later years—in marked contrast to the unvarying level embodied in the rectangular profile or the quite modest decline for the exponential where $d = 0.02$ (only some 25 percent after 15 years).

[21] This special form of a triangular profile has been so designated since George Terborgh of MAPI has argued over the years that it best represents the likely shape of the stream of quasi-rents from an investment in industrial machinery. See [19] and [20].

FIGURE 6

PRESENT VALUES OF DEPRECIATION FUNCTIONS

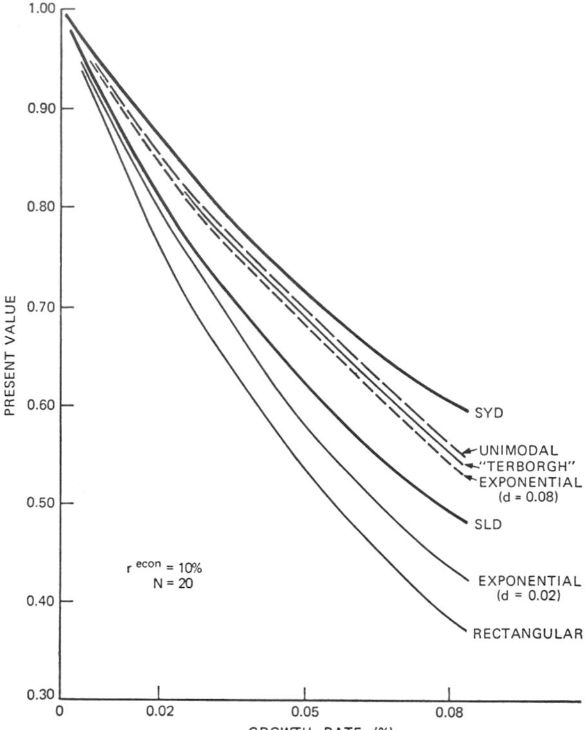

Estimates of the error in the rate of return depend strongly upon knowledge of the shape of $K(t)$, yet it does not appear practicable to estimate that shape econometrically.[22] Nonetheless, insofar as we can reject on purely intuitive grounds the possibility that industrial assets resemble the deacon's "one-horse shay," cash profiles akin to the cosine, unimodal, or Terborgh appear to be more likely than the rectangular. Hence, we conclude tentatively that any bias in the accounting rate of return is more likely to be *negative* than positive—in stark contrast to Solomon's earlier results; in any case, the error will be less than that shown by Solomon. Parametric studies where r and N are varied over the empirically relevant ranges do not contradict this assessment.[23]

---

[22] Griliches [5] discusses the econometric obstacles in general, while Mendelowitz [8] and Sampson [12] illustrate two cases where such difficulties arose; see also Stauffer [18], Section I, pp. 13–16, and Section IV, pp. 6–12.

[23] Later, when we allow for working capital, we shall see that the errors are very much reduced. We mention again that the sign of the error *reverses* if $g > r$; since this case is exceedingly rare in practice, we do not treat it explicitly.

5. Properties of the gross profitability ratio

■ Having demonstrated that the conventional accounting rate of return is inherently biased—significantly so, under certain adverse circumstances—we shall now examine the alternative "accounting" measure equally carefully. For the case of a steadily growing firm, the gross profitability ratio, defined as the ratio of cash flow to the undepreciated historical cost of all fixed assets, is obtained directly from equation (4) if we substitute $I_0(1 + g)^{t_0+t}$ for $I(t)$:

$$\text{GPR} = \frac{k(g)}{\frac{1}{g}[1 - (1 + g)^{-N}]} = \frac{k(g)}{S(N, g)}. \tag{32}$$

The GPR is mathematically equal to the ratio of the Laplace transform of the cash flow profile and a term equal to the present value of one dollar per period for N periods, discounted at the rate g.

Here we wish to concentrate upon three different attributes of the GPR which have been proposed in the earlier literature, in order to establish whether this measure is in any way more useful than the conventionally defined accounting rate of return (NPR): 107

(1) One line of thought claimed that the GPR is a "better" metric for economic profitability because depreciation charges have been excluded symmetrically from both the numerator and the denominator:

> A further problem, which has been avoided in my investigation by defining both profits and capital gross, is how to treat depreciation. Any attempt to include it must face the problem that historic costs introduce inequities between the foreign subsidiaries recently established, whose fixed assets are but 10 percent depreciated, and the older established, mainly British firms, whose plant and other assets are, on average 50 percent depreciated. [2]

(2) Meyer and Peck [10], following a different tack, argued that the GPR has two useful properties: (*a*) it converges to the true rate of return as the asset lifetime increases; and (*b*) the bias is constant as a function of N and r. They then concluded that one can construct tables from which the real rate of return corresponding to a given value of the GPR can be read off directly or computed by interpolation.

(3) Solomon [17] commented, without further discussion:

> . . . and in extreme cases the measure [the NPR] may have to be abandoned altogether in favor of an alternative measure, such as the ratio of cash flow before depreciation to gross book value.

We have already demonstrated, in Section 3 above, that the GPR is in general biased; here, paralleling the preceding analysis of the NPR, we shall assess the magnitude of that bias and its dependence upon the true shape of $K(t)$ in order to be able to compare the relative merits of the GPR versus the NPR.

Let us first examine the asymptotic properties of this profitability metric. An important property of the accounting rate of return is the fact that any disparity between it and the economic rate of return is reduced in such measure as the firm's rate of growth approaches the economic rate of return. The GPR does not exhibit such convenient behavior; if we let $g \to r$ in equation (32), we have:

$$\lim_{g \to r} \text{GPR} = \frac{\lim_{g \to r} k(g)}{S(N, r)} = \frac{r}{1 - (1 + r)^{-N}}, \tag{33}$$

TABLE 2

ASYMPTOTIC VALUES FOR GROSS PROFITABILITY RATIO (GPR)

	N = 10			N = 20		
r = g	0.05	0.10	0.15	0.05	0.10	0.15
GPR	0.129	0.163	0.199	0.080	0.117	0.159
% ERROR	+158	+63	+33	+61	+17	+6

FIGURE 7

"GROSS" ACCOUNTING RATE OF RETURN: STEADY-STATE GROWTH AND DIFFERENT PROFILES

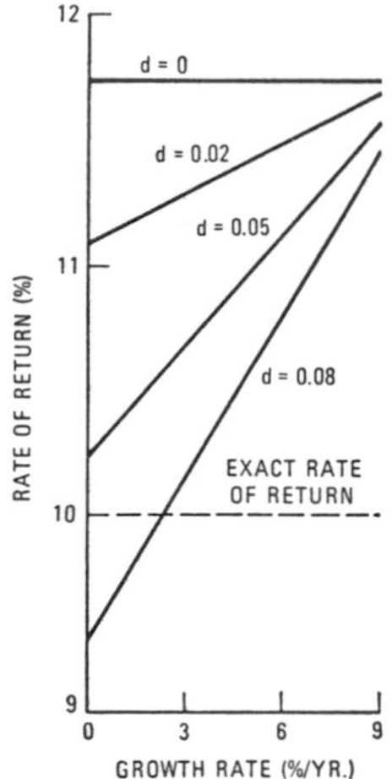

since $k(r) = 1$ by definition. The limiting value of the GPR depends upon both N and r. The results are clear: the asymptotic value of the GPR always is greater than r, and the relative error in the asymptotic value decreases as N, the asset lifetime, or r increases. Table 2 illustrates the effects of r and N.

The GPR is seen to possess no particularly useful asymptotic property. More generally, where $g \neq r$, the GPR remains biased. The dependence of the GPR upon g and $K(t)$ is illustrated in Figure 7, using the same family of exponential profiles which was used in Figure 3 to display the sensitivity of the NPR to g and to the functional form of $K(t)$. For the case $d = 0$, i.e., where $K(t)$ is rectangular, the bias is constant at *plus* 1.75 percentage points, completely independent of the growth rate. However, for non-zero values of the decay rate, d, the bias is seen to depend upon the growth rate. Indeed, if $d = 0.08$ and $g < 2$ percent per year the bias is in fact negative. More generally, as either N or r is larger, the range of values of g for which the bias is negative also increases, but no useful general properties of the GPR have been derived.

Even though it has not proved possible to derive any *explicit* relationship between r and the GPR, one can exhibit the interdependence between the conventional accounting rate of return and the GPR for the one case where SLD is used, from which certain general relations may be deduced indirectly. The equation for the conventional rate of return may be reshuffled to give

$$\text{NPR} = \left\{ \frac{g}{\dfrac{1}{S(N, g)} - \dfrac{1}{N}} \right\} \left[\text{GPR} - \frac{1}{N} \right], \tag{34}$$

from which one obtains

$$\begin{aligned} \text{GPR} &= \frac{1}{N} + \frac{\text{NPR}}{gS(N, g)} \left\{ 1 - \frac{S(N, g)}{N} \right\} \\ &= \frac{1}{N} + \text{NPR} \left\{ 1 - \frac{\text{Reserve}}{\text{Ratio}} \right\}, \end{aligned} \tag{35}$$

where the reserve ratio is defined as the ratio of the depreciation reserve to the total acquisition cost. The bracketed term, while dependent upon both N and g, ordinarily lies in the range 0.5 — 0.6 for most firms. However, it can rise to as high as 0.7 — 0.8 for rapidly growing utilities (where assets are long-lived) or drop to 0.4 or less for firms which are not reinvesting.

Even though equation (35) does not explicitly contain r, the economic rate of return, we nonetheless can deduce that the gross profitability ratio is almost as sensitive to the specification of the time-shape of the cash flow profile, $K(t)$, as is the conventional accounting profitability. If N and g are known, as would be the case empirically, the GPR is equal to a constant, $1/N$, plus the NPR multiplied by a coefficient which is less than one. Thus, for any given value of r, the dispersion in values of the GPR is proportional to the dispersion in the values for the accounting rate of return for the same set of functional shapes of $K(t)$.

More precisely, let K^a and K^b be two cash flow profiles which are non-zero for $1 \leq t \leq N$; unless one of the two happens to be "exact,"[24] the accounting rates of return for the firm will not equal r but some other values, R^a and R^b. Then the associated values of the GPR can be obtained by substituting R^a and R^b into equation (35), where g and N remain fixed; if we subtract GPR^a from GPR^b, the result is

$$\delta GPR = GPR^b - GPR^a = \delta NPR\{1 - \text{Reserve } R^a\} . \quad (36)$$

Thus, any dispersion in the accounting profitability is reflected into the gross profitability ratio, but reduced in magnitude by the bracketed term above.

The error in the GPR can be large and depends strongly upon N and g. Let us consider an extreme case where $N = 10$ and both the economic and the accounting rate of return is zero; according to equation (35) the GPR would then be 10 percent, a quite extraordinary bias. If $N = 30$ and the accounting rate of return is 15 percent, then the GPR would be approximately 12.5 percent, low by some 2.5 points as compared with the NPR. In the latter example, the actual error vis-à-vis the real rate of return would be somewhat less or greater, depending upon the precise form one chooses for $K(t)$ and the value of g.

One question remains to be settled whether the Meyer and Peck[25] method of computing real rates of return from values of the GPR has any general validity. It was shown earlier that the GPR is independent of the past history of the firm only in the very special case where the cash flow profile is rectangular. Similarly, for the case of a steadily growing firm, the GPR is independent of the growth rate if, and only if, $K(t)$ is rectangular. Theoretically, therefore, we have already demonstrated that the method is of restricted utility. It is nonetheless useful to illustrate the magnitude of the errors which can result from mis-specification of the form of $K(t)$, in order to show that the theoretical inadequacy is empirically significant.

Let us consider a numerical example, following Meyer and Peck's procedure; let there be three different firms whose rates of return we wish to determine, with asset lives of 10, 20, and 30 years respectively, and for which the corresponding GPR's are given in Table 3. If we interpret the GPR's within Meyer and Peck's framework, assuming that the underlying profile is rectangular, we determine that the "real" rate of return in each instance is precisely 10 percent.

However, if the underlying profile were not rectangular—contrary to the implied situation—but were instead, say, a declining-triangular profile (Terborgh), the equivalent real rates of return would be ap-

[24] See equation (13), above.
[25] Described in [10].

TABLE 3

GPR'S FOR THREE FIRMS

ASSET AGE (YEARS)	10	20	30
GROSS PROFITABILITY RATIO	0.163	0.132	0.117
RATE OF RETURN (%)			
–MEYER AND PECK	10.0	10.0	10.0
–ECONOMIC	12.0	12.2	12.4
% ERROR (MEYER AND PECK)	20.0	22.0	24.0

preciably different, and the Meyer and Peck procedure would involve a significant error. Illustrative results are shown for the economic rate of return in Table 3, for a Terborgh-shaped cash flow profile and a steady-state growth rate of 5 percent per annum. The Meyer and Peck
110 technique leads to an understatement of the real rate of return by between 2.0 and 2.4 percentage points, or from 20 to 24 percent of the estimated value. This error is approximately equal in magnitude, but of *opposite* sign, to the error which would have arisen if one had simply used the uncorrected accounting rate of return.

The magnitude and the sign of the discrepancy inherent in Meyer and Peck's procedure depends intimately upon the growth rate, the asset lifetime, and the shape of the cash flow stream. Consequently, the Meyer and Peck method offers no general assistance to the person computing rates of return, unless he is somehow in the happy position of knowing—or being able to determine—the shape of the cash flow profile. But if $K(t)$ is known, the accounting rate of return too can be correctly inverted to yield the economic rate of return, and the whole problem is reduced to a bagatelle.

We conclude, therefore, that the GPR offers no advantage compared with the standard definition of the accounting rate of return because:

(1) Its inherent bias is of comparable magnitude and unpredictable sign.

(2) The bias does not decrease with increasing values of g, a consideration of some practical relevance.

(3) The bias does not vanish for an empirically plausible shape of $K(t)$.

Both rate of return measures are in general biased, but the conventional accounting rate of return at least has useful asymptotic properties.[26]

6. The effect of non-depreciable capital

■ Let us now assume that for every incremental dollar invested in physical assets there will be associated an additional incremental component of working capital α. This component represents the additional amount of money which would be tied up in inventories,

[26] As $g \rightarrow r$, the dispersion of values of GPR is reduced commensurately, irrespective of the form of $K(t)$, and all values converge to the asymptote. In the case of the GPR, the asymptotic value does *not* equal r. Nonetheless, both measures contain the same information, so that both are potentially manipulable in the same fashion.

accounts receivable, trade investments, etc. These funds will be treated as circulating capital in the literal sense—i.e., the incremental infusion of working capital is assumed to be associated with the given project for its lifetime, and the magnitude of that infusion of working capital will be recovered when the associated asset is retired. This flow-of-funds relationship is shown schematically in Figure 8.[27]

FIGURE 8

FLOW OF WORKING CAPITAL OVER ASSET LIFETIME

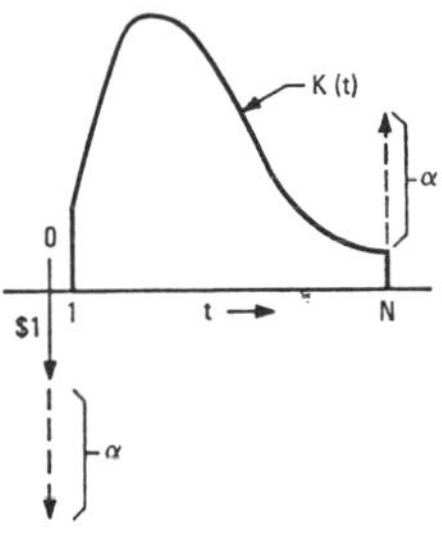

If we further assume that the annual level of investment outlays for fixed assets grows exponentially at an annual rate g, we obtain directly an expression for the stock of working capital, $\mathrm{WC}(t)$, as a function of the gross plant, property, and equipment (GPP&E) account in any given year:

$$\Delta \mathrm{WC}(t) = \alpha[I(t) - I(t-N)] ,$$

$$\mathrm{WC}(t) = \alpha \mathrm{GPP\&E}(t) = \alpha \frac{(1+g)}{g}[1-(1+g)^{-N}]I(t) . \qquad (37)$$

Equation (37) provides a unique relationship between the stock of working capital and the three parameters α, N, and g. The firm's net assets (NA) are the sum of net GPP&E plus working capital:

$$\mathrm{NA}(t) = \frac{1+g}{g} I(t)[1-d(g)] + \frac{\alpha(1+g)}{g} I(t) S(N, g) . \qquad (38)$$

Let us use the same cash flow profiles as we used in Section 5, in order to preserve comparability. Then, if working capital is added, $K(t)$ must here be multiplied by a scale factor h, in order that the internal rate of return still equals r, providing additional cash to cover the return on the working capital. The condition that the present values of inflows and outflows are equal when both are discounted at r is

$$1 + \alpha = hk(r) + \alpha(1+r)^{-N} .$$

Solving for h, we obtain

$$h = 1 + \alpha\{1-(1+r)^{-N}\} , \quad \text{since } k(r) = 1.0. \qquad (39)$$

The cash flow for the steadily growing firm equals

$$I(t)(1+g)hk(g) ,$$

and the accounting rate of return for a firm in which the ratio of non-depreciable capital outflows to those for fixed assets equals α, and where the financial, discounted cash flow (DCF) rate of return is exactly equal to r, becomes

$$R^{acc} = \frac{\{1+\alpha[1-(1+r)^{-N}]\}k(g) - d(g)}{\frac{1}{g}\{1-d(g)\} + \alpha S(N, g)} . \qquad (40)$$

The properties of this equation are not obvious. Let us first examine the effect of working capital upon R^{acc} in the special case where $K(t)$ is a rectangular profile. The accounting rate of return is dis-

[27] We defer for the present time the precise quantification of "working capital" as used in this context. Once a consistent definition has been selected, the analyti-

FIGURE 9

ACCOUNTING RATE OF RETURN: EFFECT OF WORKING CAPITAL*

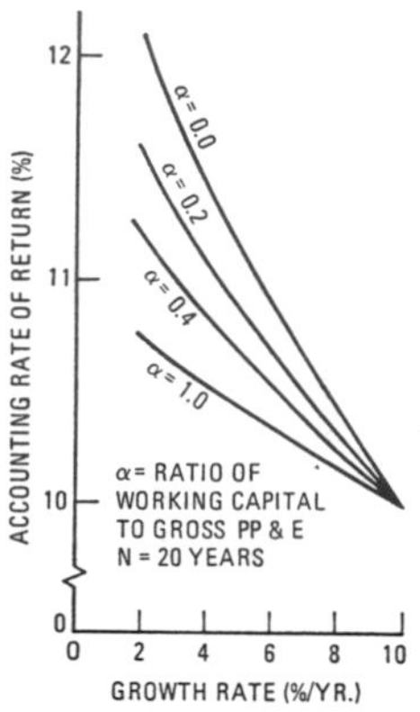

*RECTANGULAR CASH PROFILE

FIGURE 10

ACCOUNTING RATE OF RETURN VS. WORKING CAPITAL*

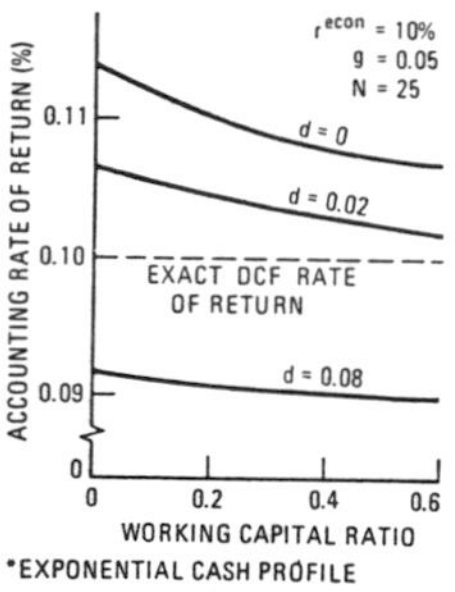

*EXPONENTIAL CASH PROFILE

placed in Figure 9 for the case where $r = 10$ percent, $N = 20$ years, and for a range of values of α and g.

Non-depreciable capital in the firm's capital structure significantly reduces the disparity between the accounting and economic rates of return. Thus, if $g = 4$ percent/year and $\alpha = 0.40$, the discrepancy in the book rate of return is diminished by almost 0.6 percentage points—i.e., the indicated rate of return falls from 11.5 percent to 10.9 percent, as compared with the case where no working capital is involved ($\alpha = 0$). If $\alpha = 1.0$, corresponding to a case where non-depreciable capital made up two-thirds of the total capital employed in the firm, the error is reduced to some 40 percent of its magnitude in the absence of any working capital.

A similar effect is observed if one considers more general cash profiles, such as the set of truncated exponential profiles examined earlier. Three of these are plotted in Figure 10 for the case $N = 25$, $g = 0.05$, and $r^{DCF} = 10$ percent.[28] The effect of working capital is largest for the case where the decay rate d is zero, which is the rectangular cash profile discussed above. A "representative" level of working capital, $\alpha = 0.5$, reduces the error by 50 percent or more. However, working capital in this case lowers the apparent rate of return over the full range of both parameters, α and d, so that an increased share of working capital in the capitalization of the firm can actually *increase* the error in the accounting rate of return. The latter effect occurs only for those profiles where the bias in the rate of return would have been negative in the absence of any working capital. Where $d = 0.08$, the discrepancy *increases*, but only slightly, as α, the share of working capital, is raised from zero to 0.6.

Certain general properties of the accounting rate of return, analogous to those derived in the absence of working capital, can be identified in this more general case. Taking the limit of equation (40) as $g \to r$, we find

$$\lim_{g \to r} R^{acc} = \frac{[1 + \alpha\{1 - (1 + r)^{-N}\}]k(r) - d(r)}{\frac{1}{r}\{1 - d(r)\} + \alpha S(N, r)},$$

$$= r\frac{[1 + \alpha r S(N, r) - d(r)]}{[1 - d(r) + \alpha r S(N, r)]},$$

$$= r\,. \tag{41}$$

Thus, $R^{acc} \to r$ as $g \to r$. This asymptotic result, analogous to that in the fixed-asset case, obtains irrespective of the forms of $K(t)$.

More generally, where g can lie anywhere between zero and r, the direction of the impact of working capital upon R^{acc} will depend

cal relationships to follow will obtain independently of the exact form of that quantification.

It may also be shown that the formulation outlined above, i.e., where working capital is treated as a circulating fund which is recovered at the end of each "project" with which the infusion was associated, is entirely equivalent to the alternative formulation in which one postulates a pool of working capital related in some functional way either to the total sales volume or to the total capital employed by the enterprise.

[28] The magnitude of the indicated error will be reduced (increased) as g is larger (smaller) or N is lowered (raised).

upon the profile and the values of g and r. This may be shown by factoring the term $\bar{R}$ out of equation (40):

$$R^{acc} = \frac{k(g) - d(g) + \alpha\{1 - (1+r)^{-N}\}k(g)}{\frac{1}{g}\{1 - d(g)\}\left[1 + \frac{\alpha S(N,g)}{\frac{1}{g}\{1 - d(g)\}}\right]},$$

$$= \bar{R}\frac{\left\{1 + \frac{g\alpha k(g)[1 - (1+r)^{-N}]}{R[1 - d(g)]}\right\}}{\left\{1 + \frac{\alpha S(N,g)}{\frac{1}{g}[1 - d(g)]}\right\}}, \tag{42}$$

where

$$\bar{R} = \frac{k(g) - d(g)}{\frac{1}{g}\{1 - d(g)\}},$$

the rate of return for the given profile in the case of depreciable capital only. Thus:

$$R^{acc} > \bar{R} \quad \text{if} \quad k(g) > \frac{\bar{R}}{r}\frac{S(N,g)}{S(N,r)},$$

$$R^{acc} < \bar{R} \quad \text{if} \quad k(g) < \frac{\bar{R}}{r}\frac{S(N,g)}{S(N,r)}.$$

There does not appear to be any ready interpretation for the preceding pair of inequalities, but the first could hold only in the case of an extremely rapidly declining profile for which the bias in the basic case would be markedly negative. Consequently, working capital ordinarily reduces the accounting rate of return, but no usable criterion has yet been derived which defines the conditions under which it will reduce the error in the measurement of the economic rate of return.

It is possible, however, to determine the depreciation schedule for which the accounting rate of return would be exact. If we stipulate that $R^{acc} = r$ in equation (40), we obtain, after some manipulation, an expression for the Laplace transform of the "exact" depreciation function in the presence of working capital, $d^e(g,\alpha)$, in terms of $d^e(g)$ and other system parameters:

$$d^e(g,\alpha) = d^e(g) + \frac{\alpha r g}{r - g}S(N,r)\{k^{rect}(g) - k(g)\}. \tag{43}$$

This expression reduces to the previously determined value of the exact depreciation function, $d^e(g)$, only if one of two conditions is satisfied:

(1) α itself vanishes, i.e., the trivial case of no working capital; or,

(2) The cash flow time profile is rectangular, i.e., $k(g) \equiv k^{rect}(g)$, in which case the bracketed term on the right vanishes identically, independently of the value of α.

Thus the depreciation schedule which would yield an exact value for the economic rate of return in this more general case is *not* identical with the "exact" depreciation schedule associated with the investment in fixed assets.[29] This poses a fundamental dilemma for accounting theory, in the sense that the specification of an "exact" depreciation schedule for fixed assets cannot be made independently of the level of working capital employed in the firm, since $d^e(g,\alpha)$, as defined in equation (43), contains α explicitly.

For the special case examined by Solomon or Meyer and Peck, where $K(t)$ is rectangular, working capital will not affect the form of the "exact" depreciation function, since the correction term vanishes when $K(t)$ is rectangular. More generally, however, we have the following theorem:

FOUR: If the cash flow profile is not rectangular, the exact depreciation schedule associated with any given cash flow profile, K(t), *as defined in Theorem Three,*[30] *yields a biased measure of the economic rate of return if the financial structure of the firm contains non-depreciable working capital.*[31]

Although the definition of "depreciation" can be so modified that this result can be reconciled with the earlier analysis,[32] the theorem signifies in practice that the depreciation schedule which is appropriate for the definition of income may not necessarily be consistent with an exact representation of the rate of return, and conversely. The accounting and economic specifications thus remain incompatible in this special sense.

Incorporation of working capital into our model of the firm leads us then to three broad conclusions:

(1) The magnitude of the error in the accounting rate of return, if positive, is substantially reduced.

(2) If the error is negative in the absence of working capital, the error can increase slightly as the level of working capital is raised.

(3) If one uses the exact depreciation schedule associated with a given investment in fixed assets, the accounting rate of return will in general still be biased downwards by an amount which is not insignificant.

---

[29] We recall from the prior discussion that two functions are not identical if their Laplace transforms are not identical. It may be verified that $\int_0^N D^e(t)dt = 1$: let $g \to 0$ in equation (43). Then $\lim d^e(g,\alpha) = \lim d^e(g) \to 1$, so that $D^e(t,\alpha)$, defined as the inverse Laplace transform of $d^e(g,\alpha)$, is a proper depreciation function.

[30] See equation (6), Section 3, above.

[31] If we set $\alpha = 0.5$, for example, and examine the case of a Terborgh profile, the error is 1.2 points ($g = 0$) or one-half point if $g = 5$ percent per year.

[32] If one attributes a component of the cash flow equal to $\alpha r S(N, r) k(g)$ to the working capital, it can be interpreted as the "earnings" of the non-depreciable capital, where the recovery of the increment α after N years is to be interpreted as a generalized form of "salvage value." One can then interpret the second term in equation (43) as the "depreciation" implicit in the carrying of working capital. Such a reformulation of depreciation does still greater violence to existing accounting conceptions, so that the practical thrust of the theorem is unimpaired.

The effect of working capital is sufficiently large compared with the "basic" error in the rate of return calculation that it cannot be ignored.

7. The effect of taxes

■ Three distinct cases must be identified when we introduce income taxes into the model of the firm, these cases being differentiated in terms of how depreciation is treated in the determination of pre-tax corporate income versus the firm's taxable income:

(1) Tax accounting congruent with corporate accounting.
(2) Tax accounting distinct from corporate accounting:
 —Flow-through accounting
 —Normalization reserve.

In the first case, it will be assumed that the same depreciation schedule is used for both corporate and tax accounting. This is not common practice, and more typically the firm avails itself of some form of accelerated depreciation schedule for tax purposes while retaining a more "conservative" schedule for corporate income determination. In the second case, two further options arise. The firm may opt to let the resultant tax saving flow through into its computed income, making no allowance for the fact that an accelerated depreciation schedule only defers an otherwise unchanged incremental tax liability until a later period. Alternatively, the firm may follow the presently recommended practice of reserving against reported income a provision which is equal to the difference between the current-year tax liability as determined under each depreciation schedule. The effect of the three different procedures upon the accounting rate of return varies considerably, and each case must be examined separately.

□ **Corporate and tax accounting congruent.** Turning first to the case where tax and corporate depreciation accounting practices are congruent, we can derive the accounting profitability ratio as a generalization of equation (21), where we assume no non-depreciable assets in the firm's capital structure. Let $K(t)$ be an arbitrary, non-negative cash flow time profile (*pre*-tax) such that its unique internal rate of return equals r. Let h be a scale factor which remains unspecified for the present; then the *after*-tax cash flow, $Y'(t)$, is defined below:

$$\begin{aligned} Y'(t) &= hK(t) - \mathrm{Tax}(t), \\ \mathrm{Tax}(t) &= T[hK(t) - D(t)], \\ Y'(t) &= (1 - T)hK(t) + TD(t), \end{aligned} \tag{44}$$

where

$$T = \text{tax rate.}$$

If we now stipulate that the present value of the after-tax cash flow also equals unity when discounted at r, we obtain a value for the scale factor expressed in terms of the tax rate T and the present value of the depreciation schedule:

$$h = \frac{1 - Td(r)}{1 - T}. \tag{45}$$

Thus the post-tax cash flow from a unit investment made at time t_0 is

$$Y'(t - t_0) = \{1 - Td(r)\}K(t - t_0) + TD(t - t_0) .$$

By analogy with the prior results, for a firm which is growing steadily at rate g, the accounting rate of return becomes

$$R^{acc} = \bar{R} + \frac{T}{\frac{1}{g}[1 - d(g)]}\{d(g) - d(r)k(g)\} . \tag{46}$$

The accounting rate of return in the presence of a corporate income tax thus equals the value computed in the absence of any corporate income tax, $\bar{R}$, plus a correction term which is proportional to the tax rate, T:

$$\delta R = g\frac{T}{1 - d(g)}\{d(g) - d(r)k(g)\} . \tag{47}$$

The sign of the correction term depends upon the ratio of the present values of the depreciation schedule evaluated at g and r and the present value of the cash flow profile evaluated at g:

$$\begin{aligned} \delta R > 0 \quad \text{if} \quad k(g) < \frac{d(g)}{d(r)} , \\ \delta R < 0 \quad \text{if} \quad k(g) > \frac{d(g)}{d(r)} . \end{aligned} \tag{48}$$

For the special case where straight-line depreciation is used, the preceding equation reduces to:

$$R^{acc} = \bar{R} + T\frac{S(N, g)}{N - S(N, g)}\left\{1 - \frac{k(g)}{k^{rect}(g)}\right\} , \tag{49}$$

where $k^{rect}(g)$ denotes the Laplace or z-transform of the rectangular cash flow profile. This special case exhibits two properties:

(1) If SLD is used for both tax and corporate accounting, the correction term due to income taxes *vanishes* if the cash flow profile, $K(t)$, is rectangular.

(2) Otherwise, if $K(t)$ is not rectangular, the correction term is positive as long as $k(g) < k^{rect}(g)$.

In equation (49), above, if $K(t) = K^{rect}(t)$, then $k(g) = k^{rect}(g)$ and the bracketed term vanishes, which proves the first property. Solomon's initial studies were confined to the special case of the rectangular cash flow profiles, so that his results, as such, would have been unaffected if he had embodied an allowance for income taxes in his calculations. More generally, if the shape of $K(t)$ is unrestricted, the second term will not vanish, and one must accordingly recognize the effect of corporate income taxes upon the interpretation of the accounting rate of return.

The corrections resulting from tax effects are illustrated in Figure 11 for a family of truncated exponential profiles;[33] straight-line

[33] This is the same set which was used earlier in Figure 7 to illustrate the impact of different profile shapes upon the bias in the accounting rate of return.

FIGURE 11

IMPACT OF CORPORATE INCOME TAX UPON BOOK RATE OF RETURN

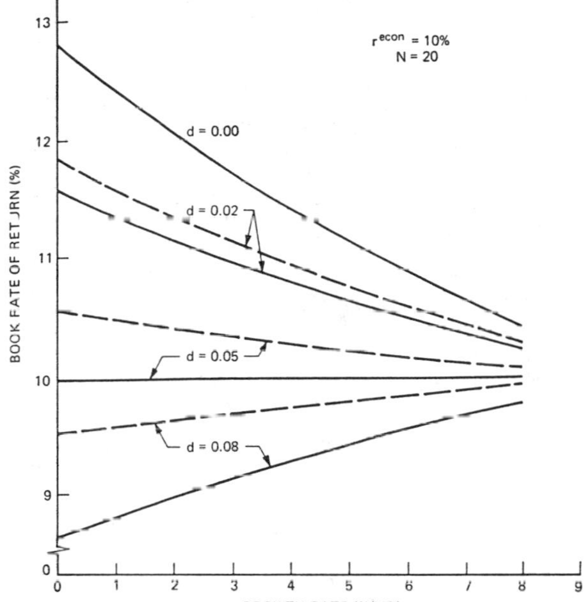

depreciation has been used for both tax purposes and corporate income accounting. The dotted curves show the accounting rate of return in the presence of income taxes, while the associated solid curves duplicate the earlier results in the absence of any income tax effect.

As the decay rate d of the exponential profile increases, the magnitude of the correction resulting from income taxes increases as well. Although the correction to the accounting rate of return is positive in all four cases illustrated in Figure 11, the impact upon the sign of the error in the exact economic rate of return (10 percent) is more complicated. For the case of the most rapidly declining profile, $d = 0.08$, recognition of tax effects means that the error in the accounting rate of return is reduced by about two-thirds. On the other hand, for $d = 0.05$ and $d = 0.02$ tax effects increase the error in the accounting rate of return. Only for the special case where d equals zero—equivalent to a rectangular cash flow profile—do taxes leave the accounting rate of return unaffected.

The inequalities relating the Laplace transforms of the cash flow profile and the depreciation schedule describe the general conditions which determine the sign of the correction term; since the sign and magnitude depend intimately upon the specific shape of $K(t)$ and the other parameters, little more can be said in general. However, it must be noted that the tax-induced corrections are comparable in magnitude to the error resulting from mis-specification of the depreciation profile, so that these effects cannot be ignored except in the very special case which Solomon had examined originally.

We must pose two further questions: (1) Does the error disappear in the limit as $g \rightarrow r$? and (2) Does there still exist a depreciation schedule associated with each form of $K(t)$ for which the accounting rate of return will still be exactly correct? The asymptotic property of the accounting rate of return still holds when taxes are included; referring to equation (49), we note that the correction term vanishes when $g \rightarrow r$, because $k(r)$ equals unity. Since $\bar{R}(g)$ itself approaches r in the limit, as $g \rightarrow r$, so does the post-tax accounting rate of return.

With regard to the second question, there does exist a unique depreciation schedule for each $K(t)$ for which the accounting rate of return is unbiased, but it is not identical to the schedule which results from the no-tax case. We shall demonstrate the following theorem:

FIVE: In the presence of corporate income taxes, there exists one and only one depreciation schedule, D*(t), *associated with any given functional form for the cash flow profile,* K(t), *for which the accounting profitability ratio is exactly equal to the economic rate of return:*

$$D^*(t) = \tilde{K}(t) - \frac{re^{rt/(1-T)}}{1-T}\int_t^N \tilde{K}(t)e^{-rt/(1-T)}dt\,, \tag{50}$$

where

$$\tilde{K}(t) = cK(t)$$

and

$$c = \left[k\left(\frac{r}{1-T}\right)\right]^{-1}.$$

The above integral expression for $D^*(t)$ is identical in form to that for the no-tax case, equation (13), except that r is everywhere replaced by the term $\left(\frac{r}{1-T}\right)$, and $K(t)$ is multiplied by a scale factor so defined that the Laplace transform of $K(t)$ equals unity for $s = \frac{r}{1-T}$ (rather than when $s = r$).

This theorem may be proved rather compactly; let us consider a growing firm characterized by a pre-tax cash flow profile for each unit investment equal to $\tilde{K}(t)$. Then the accounting rate of return is

$$R^{acc} = (1-T)\frac{\tilde{k}(g) - d(g)}{\frac{1}{g}[1-d(g)]}\,. \tag{51}$$

Rearranging terms, we have:

$$\frac{R^{acc}}{1-T} = \frac{\tilde{k}(g) - d(g)}{\frac{1}{g}[1-d(g)]}\,. \tag{52}$$

If R^{acc} is to equal r, then the second ratio can equal $\frac{r}{1-T}$ if and only if $d(g)$ is defined to be the exact depreciation schedule associated with

$\tilde{K}(t)$, where the internal rate of return for $\tilde{K}(t)$ equals not r but $\left(\frac{r}{1-T}\right)$, in accordance with Theorem Three of Section 3, above. If $D^*(t)$ is defined in this fashion, the accounting rate of return will equal r exactly, and it remains to be shown only that the present value of the *after-tax* cash flow stream, where the depreciation schedule is defined by equation (50), equals unity when discounted at r. Taking the Laplace transform of the after-tax flow, we find

$$y'(s) = (1 - T)\tilde{k}(s) + Td^*(s)\,. \tag{53}$$

The Laplace transform of $D^*(t)$ may be derived directly from equation (50) after rather lengthy manipulations, so that

$$d^*(s) = \frac{\rho - s\tilde{k}(s)}{\rho - s}\,,$$

where

$$\rho = \frac{r}{1 - T}\,. \tag{54}$$

Substituting $d^*(s)$ from equation (54) into equation (53) and setting $s = r$, we have

$$\begin{aligned} y'(r) &= (1 - T)\tilde{k}(r) + 1 - (1 - T)\tilde{k}(r)\,, \\ &= 1\,. \end{aligned} \tag{55}$$

This proves that the internal rate of return of the after-tax cash flow stream equals r, when $D(t) \equiv D^*(t)$; since $D^*(t)$ has been constructed so that the accounting profitability ratio equals r, this proves the theorem. Q.E.D.

One may further verify by direct substitution that $D^*(t)$ equals the time-derivative of the present value of the remaining after-tax cash receipts, so that the definition is consistent with the earlier definition of the criterion for economic depreciation. However, in this instance, where taxes are included, one cannot readily derive the specification for $D^*(t)$ directly from the definition, since the latter involves the value of $d^*(r)$ as well as $d^*(g)$, thereby considerably complicating the inversion of the Laplace transforms. It may also be shown that the exact depreciation schedules with and without corporate income taxes are not in general identical.

□ **Corporate and tax accounting not congruent.** When tax and corporate accounting for depreciation differ, one must distinguish between the depreciation schedule, $D^T(t)$, which enters the after-tax cash flow calculations, and the other schedule, $D(t)$, which is debited against the after-tax cash flow in order to determine corporate net income. The components of the calculation are summarized in the left-hand column of Table 4 for the sub-case where the tax-saving from use of accelerated depreciation flows through into the corporate accounts. Where a normalization reserve is used, an additional element must be debited against net income, equal to the difference in the tax liability under the two different depreciation schedules, as shown in the right-hand column of Line 4 of the table.[34]

[34] Since we restrict our attention here to the uses of funds, examining the return upon total resources employed in the firm, there is no associated reserve

TABLE 4

DIFFERING CORPORATE AND ACCOUNTING METHODS

	FLOW–THROUGH	NORMALIZATION RESERVE
CASH FLOW	$(1+g)\frac{1-Td^T(r)}{1-T}k(g)$	$(+g)\frac{1-.Td^T(r)}{1-T}k(g)$
TAX	$(1+g)T\left[\left\{\frac{1-Td^T(r)}{1-T}\right\}k(g)-d^T(g)\right]$	
DEPRECIATION	$(1+g)d(g)$	
DEFERRED TAX RESERVE PROVISION	ϕ	$(1+g)T\left[d^T(g)-d(g)\right]$
ACCOUNTING PROFITABILITY RATIO	$\bar{R}+\frac{gTd^T(g)}{1-d(g)}\left[1-k(g)\frac{d^T(r)}{d^T(g)}\right]$	$\bar{R}+\frac{gTd(g)}{1-d(g)}\left[1-k(g)\frac{d^T(r)}{d(g)}\right]$

120

The resulting forms for the accounting profitability under the two alternative modes of treating incongruities between tax and corporate depreciation schedules are tabulated in the last line of Table 4.

In most instances of practical relevance, the depreciation schedule which is adopted for tax purposes will permit more rapid write-offs than the schedule which is employed for the corporate accounts, although some firms do use "accelerated" depreciation for both. Thus, ordinarily, $d^T(s) > d(s)$, and the following chain of inequalities obtains as long as $g < r$:

$$\frac{d^T(r)}{d(g)} > \frac{d^T(r)}{d^T(g)} > \frac{d(r)}{d(g)}. \tag{56}$$

Again, the sign and magnitude of the corrections depend upon the form of $K(t)$, the two depreciation schedules involved, and the values of g and r. Two cases may be delineated:

(1) $k(g) < \dfrac{d(g)}{d^T(r)}$ Then $\delta R > 0$, and the correction for the "flow-through" case is greater than that for the normalization reserve, while both are less than that for the "congruence" case treated earlier.

(2) $k(g) > \dfrac{d(g)}{d(r)}$ Then $\delta R < 0$, and the magnitude of the correction in the case of the normalization reserve exceeds that for the "flow-through" case, which in turn is greater than the correction where tax and corporate depreciation practices coincide.

---

debited against the net asset figure in the denominator of the rate of return equation, so that the correction for the normalization reserve enters only into the specification of net income in the numerator.

FIGURE 12

ALTERNATIVE TAX ACCOUNTING PROCEDURES: IMPACT UPON RATE OF RETURN CALCULATIONS

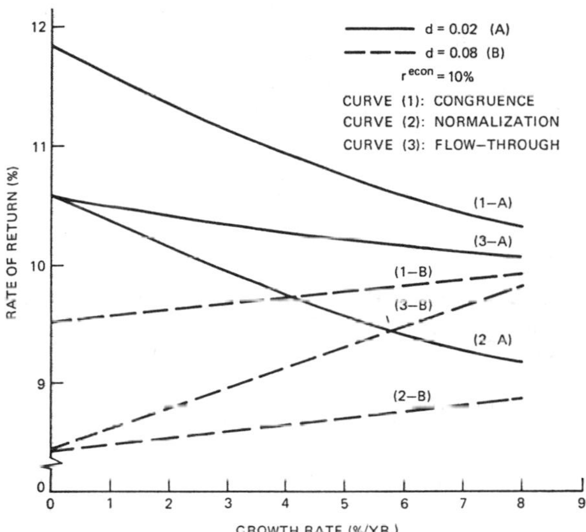

If $\frac{d(g)}{d^T(r)} < k(g) < \frac{d(g)}{d(r)}$, nothing at all can be said about even the signs of the corrections to the accounting profitability, while the relation to the economic rate of return can be determined only on a case-by-case basis.

The different effects are illustrated numerically in Figure 12 for the same set of truncated exponential profiles which were used earlier. The family of solid curves (A) represents the three tax-accounting alternatives applied to the case where the exponential decay rate is 0.02. The disparity between the "congruent" case, curve (1-A), and the "flow-through" case, curve (3-A) is almost one full percentage point when the growth rate of the firm is 5 percent, although both converge toward the true rate of 10 percent as the growth rate g increases. If the firm creates a normalization reserve in order to compensate for the use of accelerated depreciation in computing the firm's tax liability, curve (2-A), the effect is quite different. The normalization and flow-through cases coincide when $g = 0$, but the book rate of return in the normalization case falls with increasing g and does *not* converge to r as $g \to r$. Rather, for $g = 10$ percent (not shown in the figure), the error in the rate of return is *minus* 1.1 points and increases still further with rising values of g.

The same phenomenon is observed when one considers a much more rapidly declining exponential—$d = 0.08$—as illustrated by the family of dashed curves (B). For the congruent and flow-through cases—curves (1-B) and (3-B), respectively—the bias is initially negative, but decreases to zero as $g \to 0.10$. For the normalization case, curve (2-B), the error decreases very slowly with increasing values of g, and still equals 1.2 percentage points when $g = 0.08$. For this case, too, the error in the accounting rate of return does *not* vanish as $g \longrightarrow r$.

In general, as long as one measures the return upon total resources employed in the firm, this additional error component introduced by the normalization reserve will not vanish as the growth rate approaches the economic rate of return. This result follows immediately if we let $g \longrightarrow r$ in the expression for the accounting rate of return:

$$\lim_{g \to r} \bar{R}^{acc} = \lim_{g \to r} \left[\bar{R} + \frac{gT}{1 - d(g)} \{ d(g) - k(g) d^T(r) \} \right]$$
$$= r \left[1 - \frac{T}{1 - d(r)} \{ d^T(r) - d(r) \} \right]. \qquad (57)$$

If the tax depreciation schedule is accelerated, then $d^T(r) > d(r)$, and the correction term to the asymptotic value of the rate of return is negative. The negative shift in the accounting rate of return, in the case of a normalization reserve, vanishes only if T equals zero or if the two depreciation schedules are in fact identical.[35]

Since the corrections to the accounting rate of return which result from the several different ways of embodying income taxes are significant, compared with the basic error, taxes cannot be excluded from consideration.

8. Recapitulation

■ The model of the firm which has been used in this rate-of-return analysis presumes that the firm invests each year in a homogeneous mix of projects which yield the same rate of return. The stream of cash generated by each such incremental annual investment is nonnegative and independent of either prior or subsequent investment outlays by the firm.

Consequently, the economic rate of return of the firm is defined uniquely as the internal rate of return of the basic project mix; it is therefore the root of an algebraic or transcendental equation obtained by discounting the cash flow to unity.

The accounting rate of return is specified as one of two ratios, and the problem is to establish the conditions, if any, under which the ratio approximates the "root," or the economic rate of return. The two ratios—net income divided by net assets (NPR) and cash flow divided by undepreciated assets (GPR)—were investigated in detail, and neither ratio provided in general an accurate representation of the root except under quite restrictive conditions.

The gross profitability ratio (GPR) is in general biased and does not equal the economic rate of return. Only in the very special case where the cash flow stream generated by a fixed asset is constant will the bias in the GPR even be time-invariant.

The conventionally defined accounting profitability ratio (NPR) can exactly equal the economic rate of return. However, this condition holds only if the depreciation schedule used in the firm's ac-

[35] If net assets are redefined and the normalization reserve is deducted from gross investment along with the depreciation reserve, the accounting rate of return is raised, and the revised rate of return does converge to r as $g \longrightarrow r$. A bias still does persist, however, and is comparable in magnitude to that in the no-tax case.

counts is defined as the time-rate-of-change of the present value of the cash flow stream. Otherwise, the NPR too is biased, and the error is proportional to the difference between the Laplace transform of the depreciation schedule actually employed and the exact schedule defined above. The error in the NPR is thus proportional to the magnitude of the mis-specification of the depreciation schedule in the basic case.

If the firm is growing steadily, the GPR still remains biased, and in no way provides a better measure of the real rate of return. However, in this case the NPR converges to the exact economic rate of return in such measure as the growth rate of the firm approaches the accounting rate of return. Thus, the accounting rate of return, in spite of the intrinsic error, is preferable to the GPR because any error diminishes insofar as (R^{acc}-g) is small or the depreciation mismatch is reduced. The GPR exhibits no such useful properties.

The magnitude and sign of the error in the NPR depend intimately upon the time-shape of the cash flow stream. Solomon's work had been confined to constant level streams; if the revenue stream declines with increasing asset age, as is more probable *a priori*, there is increasing likelihood that the sign of the error reverses, and its absolute magnitude will generally be less.

When working capital is included, the error in the NPR is either reduced significantly (for the case of slowly declining cash flow patterns) or increased slightly (if the cash profile declines rapidly with increasing asset age). If the firm's financial structure involves working capital, using the exact depreciation schedule will *not* yield an exact measure of the economic rate of return. In general, the depreciation schedule for fixed assets cannot be specified independently of the level of non-depreciable capital, and the fundamental disparity between economic and accounting measures of the return on capital persists even if an exact depreciation schedule, as defined conventionally, were employed.

Three alternative treatments of the corporate income tax were considered. An error in the accounting rate of return exists in all cases, the additional component due to taxes being comparable in magnitude to the basic error. If the firm reserves against its deferred tax liability, when different depreciation schedules are used for corporate and tax purposes, the error does not vanish as the growth rate and the book rate of return converge. This effect can be important for certain utilities.

We have shown that the accounting rate of return is generally a very poor proxy for the economic or DCF rate of return, which is relevant either for capital budgeting decisions within the firm or for the external assessment of the firm/industry's market performance. The simulation analysis can be inverted, using observed values for the accounting rate of return and financial parameters, in order to estimate empirically the underlying economic rate of return.[36]

Most firms or industries are little affected by the corrections, which partially vindicates the accounting rate of return as a practical tool. There are certain egregious counter-examples, however: the rate of return for the pharmaceutical industry is reduced dramatically, while that for chemical and non-ferrous metals firms drops some-

[36] As discussed in [18].

what, but the accounting rate of return for Polaroid or IBM apparently *understates* their real profitability.

It is clear that further theoretical and empirical research is needed before rates of return can be computed reliably and interpreted with certainty.

Glossary of symbols and notations

■ Definitions

Profile	The time pattern of cash receipts; $K(t)$.
Terborgh profile	A stream of cash revenues which declines linearly from a non-negative value at $t = 1$ to zero at $t = N + 1$.
Rectangular profile	A stream of cash revenues which is constant over the period $1 \leq t \leq N$ and is zero elsewhere.
Laplace transform	An integral operator; see $\mathcal{L}[F(t)]$.
z-transform	A special case of the Laplace transformation; see $\mathcal{L}[F(t)]$. Applicable to functions defined for discrete values of the argument.
Convolution	An integral of two functions, $F(t)$ and $G(t)$, defined as: $\int_0^t F(\tau)G(t - \tau)d\tau \equiv F(t) \otimes G(t)$.

□ Notation

$D(t)$	Depreciation schedule.
$D^e(t)$	The depreciation schedule for which the accounting rate of return is exact.
$D^T(t)$	A depreciation schedule used for tax purposes.
$d(g)$	Laplace/z-transform of a depreciation schedule.
GPR	Gross profitability ratio, equaling cash flow divided by gross assets.
h	Scale factor which corrects cash flow profiles for effects of working capital or tax effects.
$K(t)$	The time stream of net cash revenues from a unit investment.
$k(g)$	The Laplace/z-transform of $K(t)$.
$\mathcal{L}[F(t)]$	Laplace transform: $\mathcal{L}[F(t)] = f(s) = \int_0^\infty F(t)e^{-st}dt$.
$NA(t)$	Net assets.
NPR	Net profitability ratio: the conventionally defined accounting rate of return, i.e., "net income" divided by "net assets."
R^{acc}	The accounting rate of return; see "NPR" above.
$\bar{R}$	The value of the accounting rate of return in the "basic" case, i.e., in the absence of taxes or working capital.
r	The economic rate of return; defined analytically as the values of r for which $\int_0^N K(t)e^{-rt}dt = 1$ or $\sum_{i=1}^{N} K(i)(1 + r)^{-i} = 1$.

$S(N,g)$	Present value of one dollar per period for N periods, discounted at g percent. Discrete case: $\frac{1}{g}[1 - (1 + g)^{-N}]$, Continuous case: $\frac{1}{g}[1 - e^{-gN}]$.
SLD	Straight-line depreciation.
SYD	Sum-of-the-years'-digits depreciation.
$WC(t)$	Working capital.
$\delta(t)$	Dirac delta function.
$\pi(t)$	Fraction of a firm's cash flow which is reinvested in year t.
$F \otimes G$	Denotes the convolution of $F(t)$ and $G(t)$; see above.

References

1. AMERICAN MANAGEMENT ASSOCIATION. "How the DuPont Organization Appraises Its Performance," Financial Management Series, No. 94, 1950. 125
2. COOPER, M. H. *Prices and Profits in the Pharmaceutical Industry*, London: Pergamon, 1966.
3. DOETSCH, G. *Handbuch der Laplace Transformation*, Basel, 1956, Vols. I-III.
4. FERNSCHREIBER, R. "Accelerated Depreciation: A Proposed New Method," *Journal of Accounting Research*, Vol. VII (Spring 1969), pp. 17–21.
5. GRILICHES, Z. "Distributed Lags: A Survey," *Econometrica*, Vol. 35, No. 1 (January 1967), pp. 16–49.
6. JEAN, W. H. "On Multiple Rates of Return," *Journal of Finance*, Vol. XXIII (March 1968), pp. 187–91.
7. LEFKOVITS, H. C., et al. "On Multiple Rates of Return," 5th World Petroleum Congress, New York, 1959, Vol. IX, pp. 67–74.
8. MENDELOWITZ, A. I. "The Measurement of Economic Depreciation," paper presented to AEA, December 1970.
9. PARZEN, E. *Stochastic Processes*, San Francisco: Holden Day, 1964.
10. PECK, M. J. and MEYER, J. R. "The Determination of a Fair Return on Investment for Regulated Industries," *Transportation Economics*, New York: National Bureau of Economic Research, 1965, pp. 199–244.
11. RAGAZINNI, J. R. and FRANKLIN, G. F. *Sampled-Data Control Systems*, New York: McGraw-Hill, 1958.
12. SAMPSON, A. A. "Measuring the Rate of Return on Capital," *Journal of Finance*, Vol. XXIV, No. 1 (March 1969), pp. 61–74.
13. SAMUELSON, P. A. "Some Aspects of the Pure Theory of Capital," *Quarterly Journal of Economics*, Vol. LI, No. 3 (May 1937), pp. 469–96.
14. ———. "Tax Deductibility of Economic Depreciation to Insure Invariant Valuations," *Journal of Political Economy*, Vol. LXXII (December 1964), pp. 604–6.
15. SOLOMON, E. "Return on Investment: The Relation of Book Yield to True Yield," *Research in Accounting Measurement*, American Accounting Association, 1966.
16. ———. "Alternative Rate of Return Concepts and Their Implications for Utility Regulation," *The Bell Journal of Economics and Management Science*, Vol. 1, No. 1 (Spring 1970), pp. 65–81.
17. ——— and LAYA, J. C. "Measurement of Company Profitability: Some Systematic Errors in the Accounting Rate of Return," *Financial Research and Management Decisions*, A. A. Robicheck, editor, New York: John Wiley and Sons, Inc., 1967, pp. 152–83.
18. STAUFFER, T. R. *Measurement of Corporate Rates of Return*, unpublished Ph.D. dissertation, Harvard University, 1971.
19. TERBORGH, G. *Accelerated Depreciation as an Offset to Inflation*, Washington, D. C.: Machinery Allied Products Institute, 1970.
20. ———. *Business Investment Policy: A MAPI Study and Manual*, Washington, D. C.: Machinery Allied Products Institute, 1958.

ACCOUNTANTS, TOO, COULD BE HAPPY IN A GOLDEN AGE: THE ACCOUNTANTS RATE OF PROFIT AND THE INTERNAL RATE OF RETURN[1]

By J. A. KAY

IT is now generally accepted that the correct way to estimate the prospective yield from a project is to find that rate of discount at which the present value of the flow of receipts and expenditures attributable to the project is zero. When accountants assess the actual performance of an activity or a firm, however, the methods they use are very different. They subtract some rather arbitrary depreciation figure from the receipts to give a net profit figure, and they assess the value of the capital employed by cumulating expenditures and subtracting these depreciation allowances from them. The rate of return is then measured as the ratio of these two figures.

It is recognized from time to time that these two rates of return concepts are rather different, and some analyses of the relationship between them exist.[2] Their conclusions make rather depressing reading: Harcourt considers that 'as an indication of the realized rate of return, the accountant's rate of profit is greatly influenced by irrelevant factors, even under ideal conditions':[3] Solomon that 'book yield is not an accurate measure of true yield; the error in book yield is neither constant nor consistent'.[4] Though there are some dissenting views,[5] their arguments carry little conviction, and R. Turvey's dogmatic claim that 'the accounting rate of return on total assets of a public enterprise means little. In particular it does not approximate the average of the d.c.f. rates of return on past investments and so does not indicate whether these past investments were, on average, reasonably successful' is probably representative of the currently prevailing opinion.

[1] I am grateful to G. C. Harcourt, M. A. King, M. F. Scott, A. Silberston, and F. K. Wright for comments on earlier versions of this paper.

[2] Major contributions include those of G. C. Harcourt, 'The accountant in a golden age', *OEP* xvii (1965), pp. 66–80; E. Solomon, 'Return on investment: the relation of book yield to true yield', in *Research in Accounting Measurement*, ed. R. K. Jaedicke, Y. Ijiri, and O. W. Nielsen, American Accounting Association, 1966; J. L. Livingstone and G. L. Salamon, 'Relationship between the accounting and the internal rate of return measure: a synthesis and an analysis', *Journal of Accounting Research*, 8 (1970), pp. 199–216; T. R. Stauffer, 'The measurement of corporate rates of return—a generalised formalisation', *Bell Journal of Economics and Management Science*, 2 (1971), pp. 434–69.

[3] Op. cit., p. 80.

[4] Op. cit., 1966.

[5] Notably W. J. Vatter, 'Income models, book yield and rate of return', *Accounting Review*, 41 (1966), pp. 681–98.

If these views were justified, the problem raised for economists is a serious one. There are rather many studies in which accounting profits have been used as indicators of rates of return. But the implications go much wider. If the accountant's rate of profit is influenced by irrelevant factors, what will be the effect on it of adopting policies which are profitable in the economist's sense, policies which increase the present value of the firm? Is it possible that these policies could reduce profitability as conventionally measured? For example, in recent years the rate of inflation has increased with the result that, while nominal interest rates have risen, real interest rates have fallen. It is a rational response to this situation to increase borrowings and accelerate purchases of fixed assets, but that response is one which reduces accountant's profits in the short term.[1] In the long term it may be expected to increase accountant's profits,[2] but it is not clear, if an arbitrary depreciation scheme is used, that this increase will offset, or
128 indeed bear any fixed relationship to, the initiating reduction. These arguments are disturbing for managers who may accept the arguments for d.c.f. criteria, because it suggests that adopting rational policies of this kind will not necessarily imply an improvement in the conventional indicators of a firm's performance. And they are disturbing for those economists who believe that firms are led to maximize profits as much by external pressures as internal motivation, because it is clearly to these conventional indicators that such external pressures respond.

The purpose of this paper is to explore the relationship between the economist's and the accountant's rate of profit. It is shown that, in balanced growth (as considered by Harcourt and others), there is, in fact, a simple relationship between the d.c.f. rate of return and the accountant's rate of return: that it is possible to deduce a d.c.f. rate of return from a sequence of accounting data without knowledge of either the amount or the scheme of depreciation allowances: and that under quite plausible circumstances a simple average accountant's rate of return will be a good estimator of the true rate of return. It follows from these that there is in fact a close connection between the two measures, and that the problems raised above can be satisfactorily resolved: the shrewd accountant will indeed advise his client to maximize the net present value of his firm.

We should begin by noting that the accountant's rate of profit (ARP) is defined at a point in time, whereas the d.c.f. internal rate of return (IRR) is defined over an interval. We do, however, have the following relationship:

[1] Because the rise in interest charges is debited to profits while the unrealized capital gains on fixed assets are not credited.

[2] Because depreciation allowances will be based on the lower historic cost of the assets whose purchase was brought forward.

(i) *If the ARP on a project is constant, it is equal to the IRR.*

The following notation is maintained throughout this paper. A t-year-old machine generates cash flows at a rate $f(t)$ and requires expenditures at a rate $g(t)$. Accountants depreciate it at a rate $d(t)$, so that its book value at t will be $v(t) = \int_0^t (g(x)-d(x))\,dx$. The accountant's rate of profit $a(t)$ is the ratio of the net profit, $\{f(t)-d(t)\}$ to the book value at t. I adopt the convention that $v(0) = 0$: thus $t = 0$ is the instant before the first expenditure on the machine is incurred. All expenditures are written off sooner or later, so that $\int_0^\infty g(t)\,dt = \int_0^\infty d(t)\,dt$ and $v(t) \to 0$ as $t \to \infty$. The internal rate of return r is defined[1] by the equation

$$\int_0^\infty f(t)e^{-rt}\,dt = \int_0^\infty g(t)e^{-rt}\,dt \tag{1}$$

and the economic value of a t-year-old machine, $w(t)$, is the present value at t of subsequent net cash flows, discounted at the project's own internal rate of return.

If $a(t)$ is constant and equal to a, we have $f(t) = av(t)+d(t)$ and so

$$\int_0^\infty f(t)e^{-at}\,dt = \int_0^\infty av(t)e^{-at}\,dt + \int_0^\infty d(t)e^{-at}\,dt \tag{2}$$

and since $\dot{v}(t) = g(t)-d(t)$ integration by parts gives

$$\int_0^\infty f(t)e^{-at}\,dt = \int_0^\infty g(t)e^{-at}\,dt \quad \text{and hence} \quad a = r. \tag{3}$$

This result makes no assumptions about the shape of the f, g, and d schedules. For any particular set of cash flows and expenditures, there will be only one depreciation scheme[2] which results in a constant accountant's rate of return, and that will be economic depreciation in the sense of Hotelling,[3] under which the book value of assets is at all times equal to their economic value, as defined above. It is well known that in this case the ARP is not a misleading indicator,[4] but our version of the result is much more powerful. We can now deal quite easily with the problem posed by Solomon,[5] who was concerned by the consequences of the use of the ARP

[1] Not necessarily uniquely defined. See J. S. Flemming and J. F. Wright, 'Uniqueness of the internal rate of return: a generalisation', *E.J.* 81 (1971), pp. 256–63, for a discussion of the issues here. Non-uniqueness poses no special problems for the analysis of this paper, though care is required to ensure that each r is associated with the appropriate w.

[2] If r is unique. In general, there will be as many such schemes as there are real roots of the equation defining r.

[3] H. Hotelling, 'A general mathematical theory of depreciation', *J. American Stat. Assn.* xx (1925), pp. 340–53.

[4] T. R. Stauffer, op. cit.

[5] E. Solomon, 'Alternative rate of return concepts and their implications for utility regulation', *Bell Journal of Economics and Management Science*, 1, 1970, pp. 65–81.

by regulatory agencies in assessing the fair rate of return for regulated utilities. If a firm earns accounting profits in line with the fair rate of return, the result above shows that the internal rate of return will be equal to the fair rate, and that this follows whatever depreciation scheme the utility employs. The utility can depreciate over-quickly, relative to economic depreciation, if it chooses—but the consequence is that its capital base is reduced for the purpose of subsequent calculations. In effect, the utility can in this way make its customers invest in the firm, but since it must pay the fair rate of return on any such investment it cannot increase its rate of profit by doing so.

A similar case is that of non-competitive government contracts, where it is the common practice to pay to the firm a constant ARP on the book value of the capital employed on government work. It follows that the internal rate of return earned on such projects will be independent of
130 depreciation conventions and equal to the target rate of profit. In a competitive industry, we can envisage firms employing the same (arbitrary) depreciation conventions, and in equilibrium earning an ARP equal to the rate of return prevailing in the economy generally. If their earnings are determined on this basis, the correctly calculated rate of profit on their activities will be equal to the general rate of return.

In fact, we can strengthen these arguments by showing that they hold even if the fair rate of return, the target rate of profit, or the yield implied by 'normal profits' vary over time.[1] We can generalize the internal rate of return concept[2] by noting that there are infinitely many valuation functions $q(t)$ such that $\int_0^\infty f(t)q(t)\,dt = \int_0^\infty g(t)q(t)\,dt$. Any such function is defined by a sequence of rates of return $r(t)$ and the conditions

$$q(0) = 1, \qquad \dot{q}(t) = -r(t)q(t).$$

The internal rate of return describes that particular valuation function for which $r(t)$ is constant. In general, we can show that

(ii) *Every sequence of accounting rates of return defines a valuation function under which the present value of the cash flows of the project is zero.*

Since $f(t) = a(t)v(t)+d(t)$ and $\dot{v}(t) = g(t)-d(t)$,

$$\int_0^\infty f(t)\exp\left(-\int_0^t a(x)\,dx\right)dt = \int_0^\infty a(t)v(t)\exp\left(-\int_0^t a(x)\,dx\right)dt - \int_0^\infty \dot{v}(t)\exp\left(-\int_0^t a(x)\,dx\right)dt + \int_0^\infty g(t)\exp\left(-\int_0^t a(x)\,dx\right)dt. \quad (4)$$

[1] This result is suggested by Vatter, op. cit.

[2] Along lines indicated by Flemming and Wright, op. cit.

Integrating by parts gives

$$\int_0^\infty f(t)\exp\left(-\int_0^t a(x)\,dx\right)dt = \int_0^\infty g(t)\exp\left(-\int_0^t a(x)\,dx\right)dt \tag{5}$$

and $q(t) = \exp\left(-\int_0^t a(x)\,dx\right)$ has the properties $q(0) = 1$ and

$$\dot{q}(t) = -a(t)q(t);$$

hence $a(t)$ defines an appropriate valuation function.

Suppose now the government varies the target rate of profit on government contracts from time to time, to keep it in line with prevailing yields being earned in other activities. The above result indicates that in this situation the firms involved will receive payments such that the present value of all receipts and expenditures, discounted at the rates of return applicable to industry as a whole at the time, will be zero: and that this 131
will be true whatever depreciation scheme the firm uses. Similarly, if the fair rate of return is equal to the cost of short-term capital at all points in time, the present value of an investment whose returns are regulated will be just equal to the present value of the expenditures involved, where both streams are discounted at the rates appropriate to the cost of capital at the time: no distortion results from inaccuracies in the measurement of the appropriate regulatory base due to divergences of actual and economic depreciation.

This result also suggests a rather natural sense in which one might consider the IRR to be the average ARP of the project. Sequences of accounting rates of return all generate functions which discount the present value of the net cash flow of the project to zero. The IRR is merely the rate of return corresponding to that particular sequence in which the rate is constant. While the IRR is the average ARP in this sense, it is not particularly helpful as a means of computing the IRR from accounting data, and this is a question to which we now turn. Is the average rate equal to the IRR in a more obvious sense of average? The general answer is no: it will not normally be true that

$$\bar{a} = \frac{\int_0^\infty a(t)v(t)\,dt}{\int_0^\infty v(t)\,dt} = r \tag{6}$$

where $\bar{a}$ is the natural definition of an average ARP. But we might suggest that it would be appropriate to discount future capital employed. Two possible rates suggest themselves for this purpose: a, the average ARP itself, or r, the IRR. It makes no difference which we choose, since

(iii) *If the value of capital employed is discounted at a or r, the weighted average ARP is equal to the IRR.*

More formally, if

$$a = \frac{\int_0^z a(t)v(t)e^{-at}\,dt}{\int_0^z v(t)e^{-at}\,dt},$$

then

$$\int_0^z f(t)e^{-at}\,dt = \int_0^z g(t)e^{-at}\,dt. \tag{7}$$

Integration and substitution of $(g-d)$ for $\dot{v}$ gives this result on the same lines as previous proofs.

TABLE I

The accountant's data

132

Year	*Av. book value of assets*	*Net profit*	*Profit rate*
	(£m)	(£m)	(%)
1960	8119	1618	19·93
1961	8601	1434	16·67
1962	9167	1355	14·78
1963	9641	1542	15·99
1964	10039	1804	17·97
1965	10900	1860	17·06
1966	11492	1680	14·62
1967	11159	1940	17·39
1968	11870	2243	18·90
1969	12329	2206	17·89
mean	10332	1768	17·11

SOURCE: DTI, Business Monitor M3.

Av. book value of assets: shareholders' interest + minority interest less preference shares and goodwill, average of beginning and end year figures for compatible data.

Net profit: dividends + retentions + tax – (until 1967) ⅔ of net preference dividends. (Preference shares are considered equivalent to fixed interest loans and goodwill considered meaningless.)

This is not, perhaps, a very appealing definition of average. But it does suggest that it is possible to set up a procedure by which the economist can derive the information he requires from data supplied to him by an accountant. We may consider the position of the economist exploring the profitability of U.K. manufacturing industry in the 1960s. The accountant provides him with data as in Table I: in terms of the notation above, Table I gives $a(t)$ and $v(t)$. What he would really like is information on $f(t)$, gross profits, and $g(t)$, net capital expenditures, as in Table II: but relation

(7) indicates that he does not need to know this to estimate r. He need only compute a, b such that

$$a\sum_{t=0}^{n}\frac{v_t}{(1+b)^t}=\sum_{t=0}^{n}\frac{\pi_t}{(1+b)^t}, \tag{8}$$

$$e^a=(1+b), \tag{9}$$

where π is net accounting profit. This yields an answer of 17·12 per cent, which differs negligibly from the undiscounted average, and indeed from the figure one gets by summing the annual profit rates and dividing by ten.

TABLE II

The economist's data

Year	*Gross profit*	*Gross expenditure on assets*	*Net cash flow*
1960	2073	957	1116
1961	1920	1163	757
1962	1887	944	943
1963	2126	993	1133
1964	2435	1308	1127
1965	2570	1618	952
1966	2442	167*	2275
1967	2701	1604	1097
1968	3104	1414	1090
1969	3113	1282	1831

Initial value of assets = 7755. Terminal value of assets = 12516.

Gross profit: Net profit from Table 1+depreciation.

Gross expenditure on assets: difference between successive beginning of year figures as in Table 1+depreciation during year.

* The smallness of this figure is the result of steel nationalization.

The pointer is significant, and we discuss it further below. The correction implied in (9) is important, and failure to make it is in part the source of Harcourt's difficulties. The profit rate is a continuous concept, and continuous compounding at 17·12 per cent is equivalent to annual compounding at 18·64 per cent: this latter figure is the appropriate discount rate for (8).

The algorithm above is rather more complicated than we need. While it is not possible to deduce the first two columns of Table II from Table I, it is (almost) possible to deduce the third, and that is all that is required. Since $\dot{v}(t)=g(t)-d(t)$, and $a(t)v(t)=f(t)-d(t)$, it follows that

$$f(t)-g(t)=a(t)v(t)-\dot{v}(t).$$

The discussion above assumes that the economist accepts the accountant's estimate of the initial and terminal capital stock. Unless he has estimates of his own, he has little choice: if he does, they can readily be incorporated.

In the example above, the average ARP is a very good approximation to the IRR: and this suggests we might consider when this is likely to be so. From (7) we have

$$r = \frac{\int_0^z \pi(t)e^{-rt}\,dt}{\int_0^z v(t)e^{-rt}\,dt}. \tag{10}$$

If we define $\phi(t) = \pi(t) - \alpha v(t)$ where $\alpha = \left\{\int_0^z \pi(t)\,dt \Big/ \int_0^z v(t)\,dt\right\}$ we have

$$r - \alpha = \frac{\int_0^z \phi(t)e^{-rt}\,dt}{\int_0^z v(t)e^{-rt}\,dt}. \tag{11}$$

$\phi(t)$ now represents the difference between the observed profit level and that predicted by the average level of profitability over the whole period. If there is no time trend in these residuals, then the expected value of the RHS of (11) is zero and the expected value of a is equal to r. This condition is more or less fulfilled for our data from the 1960s. If there is a time trend, then a decline in profitability (as measured by the accountant) will mean that his naïve average rate of profit will underestimate the true rate of return, while a rising trend implies overestimation. Relation (1) allows a rapid check of whether trends are in this context significant: if $\left\{\int_0^z \phi(t)e^{-at}\,dt \Big/ \int_0^z v(t)e^{-at}\,dt\right\}$ is small, one need not consider the matter further.

This is a special case, however, and in practice approximate constancy of the accountant's rate of profit is much more likely for a sequence of projects, or for the activities of a firm taken as a whole, than it is for an individual project. The obvious case to consider is that of steady state growth. Here we have:

(iv) *For a firm in steady state growth at rate n, the ARP is constant and the book value of capital grows at n.*

Suppose the number of machines installed at time T is y_T and the economic life of a machine is z years. Then the accountant's rate of profit at T is

$$a(T) = \frac{\int_0^z y_T\, e^{-nt}(f(t) - d(t))\,dt}{\int_0^z y_T\, e^{-nt}v(t)\,dt} = \frac{\int_0^z (f(t) - d(t))e^{-nt}\,dt}{\int_0^z v(t)e^{-nt}\,dt} \tag{12}$$

since f, d, and v are assumed independent of T, $a(t)$ is thus independent of T and constant, and his valuation of the capital stock is

$$V(T) = \int_0^z y_T\, e^{-nt} v(t)\, dt, \quad \text{which yields } \dot{V}(T) = nV(T). \tag{13}$$

It would be erroneous to conclude from this result and (i) that the ARP is equal to the IRR. Consider a segment (T_1, T_2) of the steady state growth path. Then the ARP is constant along it. However, in deriving relation (3) from (2) we used the assumption that initial and terminal values of v were zero, which will not be true on such a segment. Integrating (2) with limits (T_1, T_2) we now obtain

$$\int_{T_1}^{T_2} f(t)e^{-at}\, dt + V(T_2')e^{-a(T_2-T_1)} = \int_{T_1}^{T_2} g(t)e^{-at}\, dt + V(T_1'). \tag{14}$$

Thus if the economist were willing to accept the accountant's valuation 135
of the capital stock at T_1 and T_2, we would again have $a = r$. In general, however, there will be some discrepancy. Since the discrepancy will grow at n, we immediately have another special case: that where $r = n$, and initial and terminal divergences cancel since the effect of discounting exactly offsets the effect of growth. On a golden rule path, then, we have equality of the accountant's rate of profit, the economist's rate of return, and the natural rate of growth.[1] More generally, the relationship is given by

(v) *For a firm in steady-state growth the relationship* $(n-a)/(n-r) = W/V$ *holds, where* W *is the economist's valuation of the firm and* V *that of the accountant.*

W and V will both grow over time at a rate n in steady state, so that their ratio will be constant. $w(t)$ is the economic value of a t-year-old machine—then

$$w(t) = \int_t^z (f(x)-g(x))e^{-r(x-t)}\, dx \tag{15}$$

and so

$$\dot{w}(t) = rw(t)-f(t)+g(t). \tag{16}$$

Since

$$av(t) = f(t)-d(t) \quad \text{and} \quad \dot{v}(t) = g(t)-d(t)$$

we also have

$$\dot{v}(t) = av(t)-f(t)+g(t). \tag{17}$$

Integrating over all machines and subtracting (17) from (16) yields

$$\dot{W}-rW = \dot{V}-aV. \tag{18}$$

Since

$$\frac{\dot{W}}{W} = \frac{\dot{V}}{V} = n \tag{19}$$

$$(n-r)W = (n-a)V \tag{20}$$

[1] As noted by Solomon, op. cit., 1966.

and so
$$\frac{n-a}{n-r} = \frac{W}{V}. \tag{21}$$

Obvious special cases are those in which $n = r$ or $W = V$, in which case $a = r$. If $n = 0$, then $aV = rW$, so that the profits as computed by the accountant are equal to the permanent income of the firm as computed by the economist. In general, if we suppose that considerations of dynamic efficiency imply $r \geqslant n$ and the accountant's principle of conservatism implies $W \geqslant V$ we will have $a \geqslant r$: the accountant will overestimate profitability. If we define rW, the rate of distribution sustainable from the assets of the firm as the permanent income of the firm, the accountant will succeed if the objective of his conservatism is to induce expenditure below permanent income. The difference between this figure and perceived accounting income is $rW - aV = n(W-V)$: so that if he ensures $V < W$ he
136 will succeed, for expanding firms.

Extension of this analysis to the case of balanced growth is straightforward. We now define $f(t)$ and $g(t)$ as the aggregate cash flows and expenditures which arise from a unit inventory of machines of all kinds, t years after their installation, and it is then natural to define the average profitability (in the economist's sense) of the stock of machines by $\bar{r}$ such that
$$\int_0^\infty f(t)e^{-\bar{r}t}\,dt = \int_0^\infty g(t)e^{-\bar{r}t}\,dt. \tag{22}$$

Then our earlier results can be reinterpreted in terms of the relationship between the ARP which will result from this process and $\bar{r}$.

The simplicity of our result contrasts with those of Harcourt, and it may be worth stressing that it holds for any arbitrary depreciation scheme, provided only that it is consistently applied. The differences may be attributable to our use of continuous time, which is a good deal easier to handle analytically—and the shift from continuous to discrete time involves approximations which must be handled with care, if the introduction of errors, which may in certain circumstances be substantial, is to be avoided. An example of this was illustrated above. Harcourt also considers the case where depreciation provisions are reinvested in financial assets which yield r. This adds little of substance to the analysis: there will now exist in addition to the V and W considered above an additional set of assets whose value and yield are measured in the same way by both accountant and economist. The accountant's estimate will now be an appropriately weighted average of a and r, so that this consideration will always reduce the magnitude of the error in the accountant's estimates, while leaving its sign unchanged.

We can now return to the issues raised in the introduction to this paper. How will a firm concerned with its image as portrayed by accountants behave? Imagine an accountant-dominated economy in which firms can borrow or lend at rate r. In such an economy, a firm will seek to maximize its accounting profits: but both investment analysts and the firm will wish to take some account of capital employed. They will naturally measure this at book value, so that the relevant magnitude will be $\pi(t)-rv(t)$, the difference between actual profits and the perceived opportunity cost of capital. We shall call this the 'residual income' of the firm, following the terminology of those U.S. management accountants who advocate it as an appropriate performance measure for decentralized organizations.[1]

(vi) *Consider a policy which will increase the present value of the firm. Then*

(*a*) *A depreciation scheme exists which would increase residual income at all times.*

(*b*) *The policy will increase the present value of residual income under every depreciation scheme.* 137

For (*a*) we may propose a depreciation scheme

$$d^*(t) = f(t)-rv^*(t)-rm \tag{23}$$

where m is the net present value of the proposed policy. Multiplying through by e^{-rt} and integrating gives

$$v^*(T) = e^{rT}\left[m-\int\limits_0^T \{f(t)-g(t)\}e^{-rt}\,dt\right] \tag{24}$$

so that v^* is zero at the beginning and end of the economic life of the machine and d^* is therefore a feasible depreciation scheme. Under it, net accounting profit at t will be

$$f(t)-d^*(t)-rv^*(t) = rm \tag{25}$$

so that proposition (*a*) follows.

The present value of residual income of the project is:

$$\bar{V} = \int\limits_0^\infty \{f(t)-d(t)-rv(t)\}^{-rt}\,dt. \tag{26}$$

Integration of the final term shows that

$$\bar{V} = \int\limits_0^\infty \{f(t)-g(t)\}e^{-rt}\,dt \quad \text{and } (b) \text{ follows.}$$

The criterion implicit in (vi) (*b*) is a natural one for judging between different time streams of accounting profit, but it is not self-evidently the appropriate one. The economist's case for maximizing net present value is that it is possible to enjoy more consumption in every year by combining

[1] See J. J. Mauriel and R. N. Anthony, 'Misevaluation of investment center performance', *Harvard Business Review*, 44, 1966, pp. 98–105. It is also proposed as a basis for corporate taxation in J. W. Bennett and G. C. Harcourt, 'Taxation and business surplus', *Econ. Record*, 36 (1960), pp. 425–8.

a higher n.p.v. with an appropriate pattern of borrowing and lending. The accountant, however, would wish to restrain consumption in any year to profit in that year. If he would allow one to borrow in anticipation of future profits, then maximization of the present value of residual income would be appropriate—it would allow higher consumption at all times—but he would probably regard that as an unsound policy, at least if applied on any scale.

But there are financial policies which will enable the economist to circumvent the accountant's restrictions. In criticizing the practices of accountants as applied to depreciation, economists have normally had fixed assets in mind, and we have followed this tradition here. It is less commonly noted that their treatment of financial assets is equally eccentric: and in particular, that they adopt the practice of valuing fixed interest liabilities at their nominal value regardless of the redemption date. Thus at present, when
138 the market value of most companies' debt lies well below its nominal value, accounting practices overstate the capital burden of the debt and understate the real cost of financing it. They ignore the fact that the debt could be discharged at a figure well below its balance sheet value, and equally ignore the fact that the cost of so discharging it increases with each year it is held. The results we have derived apply equally to these financial assets: accounting practice represents one particular arbitrary depreciation scheme (that of not allowing the assets to appreciate or depreciate at all). Conventional borrowing and lending transactions do not allow the firm to manipulate the time profile of net accounting profit (since they add proportionately to profits and to capital employed), but these accounting practices make it possible. The recently common practice of repurchasing immature debt raises current profits at the expense of the future.

Bearing this in mind, we can now strengthen the case for present value maximization in an accountant dominated world.

(vii) *Suppose a firm can issue debt at a coupon other than r. Then by combining a policy which increases the present value of the firm with an appropriate financial strategy it can earn a higher residual income in every year.*

Without loss of generality, we consider a zero coupon bond (since any other bond can be regarded as a combination of a zero coupon bond and borrowing and lending at r).

If the firm is obliged to adopt a depreciation scheme $d(t)$ and the present value of the policy is m, it should immediately borrow ϵ and continue to borrow to maintain debt y according to the rule

$$\dot{y} = g(t) - d(t) - \frac{1}{r}(\dot{f}(t) - \dot{d}(t)). \tag{27}$$

Since $\int_0^\infty \dot{y}e^{-rt}\,dt = -m$, this is a feasible policy: the firm will be able to redeem debt on terms which return r to bondholders. Since

$$y(t) = \int_0^t \{g(x)-d(x)\}\,dx - \frac{1}{r}\{f(t)-d(t)\}+\epsilon \tag{28}$$

the book value of capital employed will be $(1/r)\{f(t)-d(t)\}-\epsilon$. Hence the net accounting profit will be higher for all t.

What conclusions can be drawn from this analysis? It provides a justification for the use of accountants' rates of return, in appropriate circumstances, as an *ex post* indicator of the economic return on investment. Harcourt's warning[1] that 'any "man of words" who compares rates of profit of different industries, or of the same industry in different countries, and draws inferences from their magnitudes as to the relative profitability of investments in different uses or countries, does so at his own peril' is much over-dramatized.

We should realize that the way in which accountants' calculations are misleading is a subtle one. The compilation of accounts is an attempt to represent the cash flows of a business in a more economically relevant way, so that they attribute to a year's activities not only the receipts and outgoings of that particular year but also the future receipts and outgoings which will result from these activities. There can be no doubt that accountants make a very bad job of doing this. But it follows from the nature of double-entry book-keeping that this will not imply, over a period of years, any systematic over- or understatement of profitability. Distortions in one year will be offset in due course by opposite distortions, so that it is essentially the timing of changes which is in error. The accountant's rate of profit, measured over a period of years, will be an acceptable indicator of the true rate of return: it is over a single year that it may prove seriously misleading.

Our analysis of the balanced growth case suggests that Solomon is right and Stauffer wrong in assessing the general bias in accountants' estimates: it is likely to be in the direction of overstating the rate of return. If $r > n$, this will certainly occur if accountants understate the value of capital employed, and there seems little doubt that this is typically the case. There are three factors at work here: the relationship of the true pattern of decline in value to that implicit in the accountant's depreciation scheme: the accountant's tendency to write off machinery over a period shorter than its economic life: and the impact of inflation. We illustrate this in Fig. 1, which shows values and depreciation rates for a 'one-hoss shay', which maintains a constant quasi-rent until it suddenly disintegrates.

Even if the accountant chooses the length of life correctly, the w schedule

[1] Op. cit., p. 80.

lies everywhere above the v schedule for straight-line depreciation. For most equipment, however, there will be some deterioration in performance (either absolute or relative) during its lifetime, and this will push the w curve downwards. Against this, however, are the effects of conservatism in steepening the slope of the v schedule, and the impact of inflation, which operates so as to raise w and to increase the gradient of the true depreciation schedule.

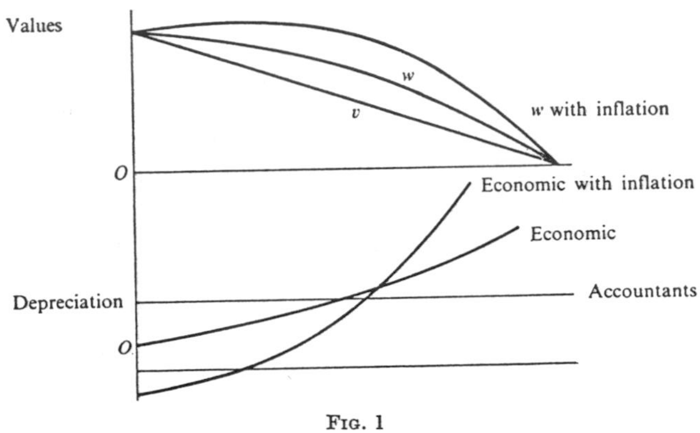

FIG. 1

In the light of this, we can assess the significance of these results for 'inflation accounting'. Inflation affects reported rates of return in two ways: by inserting a wedge between real and nominal rates of return, and by altering the relationship between conventional and economic depreciation. The first of these is easily dealt with by simply subtracting the rate of price increase[1] from the money rate. Fig. 1 shows that inflation implies an increase in the extent to which the depreciation of new equipment is overstated and that of older equipment underestimated: an acceleration in the rate of inflation will have the same effect of initial overstatement, subsequent understatement. If the inflation rate rises, then, the first effect is to reduce reported profits below the true rate: over time, this reported rate will rise until a new steady state is reached in which the profit rate is systematically overestimated.

St. John's College, Oxford.

[1] Presumably of consumer prices, though there are some who would argue for some index related to the particular assets held by the firm.

ACCOUNTING RATE OF PROFIT AND INTERNAL RATE OF RETURN[1]

By F. K. WRIGHT

IN a recent paper on the knotty problem of the relationship between the accounting rate of profit and the internal rate of return, John Kay has elegantly derived some simple equations describing that relationship.[2] He has shown that, over the entire life of an investment (from zero outlay to zero return), a suitably weighted average of the accounting rates of profit is equal to the internal rate of return from the investment.[3] As a special case of this result, the accounting rate of profit when constant over the entire life of the investment must equal the internal rate of return. He has

also shown that, for a firm in steady-state growth, the accounting rate of profit will coincide with the internal rate of return if the firm is growing at its natural rate (i.e. if all profits are continuously reinvested), or if the accountant's valuation of its assets coincides with that of the economist. Where neither of these conditions prevails, the internal rate of return of a steadily growing firm may be expressed as a linear function of the accounting rate of profit, the slope of the line being given by the ratio of the book value of the net assets to the value which an economist would place upon them.[4]

Unfortunately Kay's paper contains some passages which could lead the reader to underestimate the difficulty of applying these results to actual accounting data. Without detracting in any way from the originality and importance of Kay's contribution, the present paper will focus on those passages and on the difficulties which they tend to understate.

The following three passages will engage our attention:

A. '. . . it is possible to deduce a d.c.f. rate of return from a sequence of accounting data without knowledge of either the amount or the scheme of depreciation allowances';[5]

B. the numerical example in which Kay attempts to calculate the d.c.f. yield of U.K. manufacturing industry over a 10-year period;[6]

C. '. . . it follows from the nature of double-entry book-keeping that' there cannot be, 'over a period of years, any systematic over- or understatement of profitability. Distortions in one year will be offset in due course by opposite distortions, so that it is essentially

[1] I am grateful to John Kay for his comments on earlier versions of this paper.

[2] J. A. Kay, 'Accountants, too, could be happy in a Golden Age: the accountant's rate of profit and the internal rate of return', *O.E.P.* xxviii (1976), pp. 447–60.

[3] Ibid., result (iii), p. 452.

[4] Ibid., result (v), p. 455.

[5] Ibid., p. 448.

[6] Ibid., pp. 452–3.

> the timing of changes which is in error. The accountant's rate of profit, measured over a period of years, will be an acceptable indicator of the true rate of return: it is over a single year that it may prove seriously misleading.'[1]

We shall deal with each passage in turn.

Kay has clearly proved that a d.c.f. rate of return can be deduced, without any knowledge of the depreciation charges, from a sequence of accounting data which begins and ends with zero capital stock, so that it covers the entire life of an investment. But the practical usefulness of this result is severely limited by three considerations.

Firstly, interest usually centres on the performance of business firms or industries which are still in operation; only an economic historian is likely to be interested in measuring the rates of return of defunct firms or industries.

But let us suppose, for argument's sake, that a valid figure can be found by Kay's method for an investment which has not yet reached the end of its life. We then encounter the second limiting factor: business firms and industries tend to be rather long-lived investments, yet the internal rate of return is defined as a single figure irrespective of the duration of the investment. One must doubt the relevance, for any contemporary purpose, of a single rate of return which represents the over-all performance to date of a business firm founded in, say, the year 1900.

Thirdly, there is a technical point concerning the weights which Kay's averaging formula assigns to the accounting rates of profit. These will usually be loaded in favour of the early years of the life of an investment. Thus the influence of recent accounting rates of profit on the cumulative weighted average of an old-established firm or industry may be very small, so that the internal rate of return could differ markedly from recent accounting rates of profit. This would further reduce the present-day relevance of such a rate of return.

We turn now to Kay's calculation of a d.c.f. yield for U.K. manufacturing industry during the 1960s. The result is given as 17·12 per cent, which seems to imply a remarkable degree of precision. But it is followed almost immediately by this qualification: 'The discussion above assumes that the economist accepts the accountant's estimate of the initial and terminal capital stock.'[2] In other words, the result is correct if and only if the opening and closing book values happened to coincide with the economic values of the net assets. There is, of course, no warrant for assuming that they did.

Fortunately one of Kay's other results suggests a less misleading way

[1] J. A. Kay, 'Accountants, too, could be happy . . . internal rate of return', *O.E.P.* xxviii (1976), p. 459.

[2] Ibid., pp. 453–4.

of interpreting the accounting data. Inspection of the figures shows that during the ten years in question U.K. manufacturing industry was growing at a fairly steady rate, so that Kay's formula for steady-state growth can reasonably be applied. The annual growth rate was approximately 0·05, and the average profitability 0·17. Substituting these figures in Kay's equation (20), we find that

$$r = 0{\cdot}05 + 0{\cdot}12V/W$$

where r is the d.c.f. rate of return and V/W is the (unknown) ratio of the book value of the industry's net assets to their economic value. Depending on one's subjective probability distribution of the ratio V/W, one obtains a corresponding probability distribution of the values of the d.c.f. rate of return from U.K. manufacturing industry in the 1960s.

Next, we examine the passage in which Kay asserts that, under double-
144 entry book-keeping, systematic over- or understatement of profitability over a period of years cannot occur. We begin by noting what is true.

It does follow from the nature of double-entry book-keeping that, over a period of years, there cannot be any systematic over- or understatement of accounting *profit*. This is so because double-entry book-keeping requires virtually all expenditures to be written off sooner or later. If an item is written off sooner than it should be, it will not be available to be written off at the proper time; if an item is written off too slowly, there will be an excessive amount to be written off in later periods. Thus any profit distortion which may occur will be offset by an equal and opposite distortion in some later period or periods.

It is also true (as Kay has shown) that, over the entire life of an investment, the accounting *rates of profit* must average out (with suitable weights) to the internal rate of return. It follows that any accounting rate of profit which exceeds the internal rate of return must be offset at some stage by a rate of profit which is lower than the internal rate of return, and vice versa. Here, however, the distortions need not be equal and opposite. The weighting of the average permits a few years of low accounting rates of profit early in the life of the investment to offset an indefinitely large number of years of high accounting rates of profit later. Similarly, a few years of high accounting rates of profit early in the life of the investment can compensate for an indefinitely large number of years of lower accounting rates of profit later.

Whilst the nature of double-entry book-keeping ensures that *profits* cannot be misstated in the long run, there is nothing in double-entry book-keeping which automatically corrects distortions in book value. Hence *profitability*, which is profit divided by the book value of assets, can be over- or understated for an indefinitely long period.

The truth of this is easily demonstrated by reference to Kay's analysis of the zero growth case.[1] There he points out that, in a steady state of zero growth, '... $aV = rW$, so that the profits as computed by the accountant are equal to the permanent income of the firm as computed by the economist'. But it also follows that a, the accounting rate of profit, will differ from r, the d.c.f. rate of return, unless $V = W$, i.e. unless the book value of the assets coincides with their economic value. Since V need not equal W, a need not equal r; and this steady state can continue for an indefinitely large number of years.

We must therefore interpret with very great caution Kay's statement that 'the accountant's rate of profit, measured over a period of years, will be an acceptable indicator of the true rate of return'.[2] The number of years required to yield a good indication of the true rate of return may not be much less than the entire life of the investment!

Finally, we consider to what extent any of Kay's broad conclusions may 145
need to be modified in the light of the foregoing discussion. His solution to the problem of regulated utilities[3] still stands, provided that the uniform rate of accounting profit has been maintained from the very inception of the utility company. The apparently analogous argument concerning non-competitive government contracts is on weaker ground, since such contracts are seldom awarded to newly established companies. By the time a company receives such a contract, it is likely to have a substantial stock of assets, the book value of which may differ appreciably from its economic value.

Kay's calculation of a d.c.f. rate of return for U.K. manufacturing industry is only as sound as the accounting valuations on which it is based. In order to determine the magnitude and direction of the error in those valuations, we should need to know the proportion of depreciable assets, the depreciation methods which were being followed, and the time shape of the net cash inflows associated with those assets—precisely the kind of information with which Kay had hoped to be able to dispense.

This means that there is, except in special circumstances, no short cut which will enable us quickly and easily to translate an accounting rate of profit into the equivalent internal rate of return. We cannot avoid detailed and tedious investigations based on a knowledge of, or assumptions about, the pattern of quasi-rents and the depreciation methods in use—investigations like that of Harcourt.[4] Alas, we have not escaped from Harcourt's

[1] J. A. Kay, 'Accountants, too, could be happy . . . internal rate of return', *O.E.P.* xxviii (1976), p. 456. I am grateful to Kay for suggesting the use of this formula to demonstrate my point.

[2] Ibid., p. 459.

[3] Ibid., p. 450.

[4] G. C. Harcourt, 'The accountant in a Golden Age', *O.E.P.* xvii (1965), pp. 66–80. Since it is now clear that this paper has not been superseded by Kay's work, it may be useful to

discouraging conclusion, that he who 'compares rates of profit of different industries, or of the same industry in different countries, and draws inferences from their magnitudes as to the relative profitability of investments in different uses or countries, does so at his own peril'.[1]

University of Melbourne

comment on Kay's critical remarks concerning this paper. In two places Kay hints that Harcourt may have been guilty of lack of care in failing to distinguish between continuous compounding and yearly compounding. Since Harcourt consistently used discrete annual variables and yearly compounding, this distinction simply did not arise in his work and so could not possibly have been mishandled by him.

[1] Ibid., p. 80.

ACCOUNTING RATE OF PROFIT AND INTERNAL RATE OF RETURN; A REPLY

By J. A. KAY

THERE is no disagreement between Professor Wright and myself over the results which characterize the relationship between the accounting rate of profit and the internal rate of return. But while I chose to emphasize the possibility of exploiting them, Professor Wright, as befits an accountant, chooses to emphasize the difficulties. I take the opportunity to offer a simple guide to what can be done; all references are to my 1976 paper.

The most favourable case is the one in which accounting data is available for the whole life of a project, or firm. It is impossible to overstate profitability permanently, just as it is impossible to overstate profits permanently (though one can do either for quite a long time). And if the available accounting data is complete, the internal rate of return is equal to the weighted average accounting rate of profit (p. 452), and very probably a simple average will do: there is a criterion which allows this to be checked (p. 454).

The least favourable case is that in which the accounting data relates only to a single year. If we are dealing with a single project, this situation is hopeless, unless there is some special reason for believing that the accounting rate of return is constant, as there is in the government contract or regulated utility examples. For a continuing firm, however, one might hold one's breath and hope that the assumption that the firm was in balanced growth was not too bad. If so, estimate n, the growth rate, and W/V, the ratio of the economic value of assets to their book value, and apply the formula $(n-a)/(n-r) = W/V$ (p. 455).

Professor Wright emphasizes the intermediate case, where there is an incomplete sequence of accounting information, and this is clearly a common one in practice. In these instances, it is necessary to take some account of what happens in the periods before and after those to which the accounting data relate. This is best done by regarding initial assets as an input into the project and terminal assets as an output from the project (or firm). But how should these assets be valued? In my illustrative example (pp. 452–3) I simply accepted the accounting valuations for this purpose, but Professor Wright is justified in criticizing this assumption. It would be better to use an economic valuation, W, and I indicated that a correction on this account was required, but not what it was. Suppose we have estimates of the economic value of assets at the beginning and end of the period, which show initial assets understated by c_0 and terminal assets by c_z. Then theorem (iii), p. 452, now becomes

(iii′) *If the value of capital employed is discounted at a or r, the weighted average ARP, corrected for errors in initial and final asset valuations, is equal to the IRR.* More formally, if

$$a = \frac{-c_0 + \int_0^z a(t)v(t)\mathrm{e}^{-at}\,\mathrm{d}t + c_z\,\mathrm{e}^{-az}}{\int_0^z v(t)\mathrm{e}^{-at}\,\mathrm{d}t}$$

then
$$W_z\,\mathrm{e}^{-az} + \int_0^z f(t)\mathrm{e}^{-at}\,\mathrm{d}t = \int_0^z g(t)\mathrm{e}^{-at}\,\mathrm{d}t + W_0$$

while relation (8), p. 453, now becomes

148
$$a\sum_{t=0}^{n} \frac{v_t}{(1+b)^t} = -c_0 + \sum_{t=0}^{n} \frac{\pi_t}{(1+b)^t} + c_z(1+b)^n.$$

Proofs of these results follow the same lines as the proofs in my 1976 paper.

As a rule, it will be worth checking to see whether the estimated rate of return is sensitive to these corrections. If the available data covers a substantial part of the life of a project, or a firm, then it will not be. But if the result is sensitive, it will be necessary to prepare estimates of the economic value of assets at the beginning and end of the period under examination. Detailed and tedious investigations of the depreciation methods in use are unlikely to help much, though examination of patterns of quasi-rents probably will. More useful sources may be current price estimates of capital stock prepared for national accounts or 'inflation accounting'. But it is obvious that if we wish to estimate a rate of return over a finite period we need some sort of valuation of what is needed at the beginning and what is left at the end: and given intermediate accounting data we can make estimates of the IRR as accurate as the reliability of these valuations allows.

Professor Wright is correct to stress the care which is needed in making use of accounting data in economics. But much existing literature suggests—wrongly—that the task is hopeless, and it will be unfortunate if his comments serve to confirm that impression.

St. John's College,
Oxford

On the Use of the Accounting Rate of Return in Empirical Research

Geoffrey Whittington*

Introduction

Accountants are acutely aware that, despite the proliferation of Accounting Standards, published financial statements contain a good deal of subjective judgment and variety of practice, which make them not strictly comparable between the same company for different years (time series analysis) or between different companies for the same year (cross-sectional analysis). Furthermore, the recent debate on accounting in a period of rapid inflation has served to emphasise that accounting measures of value and income are very different from those of the economist, and a series of academic papers, Harcourt [1965] and Solomon [1966] being seminal works, has demonstrated that there can be important divergences between the Accounting Rate of Return (ARR)[1] and the Internal Rate of Return (IRR) on investment, the latter being the more relevant return for the appraisal of economic performance. In these circumstances, it is not surprising that many accountants are sceptical of the value of using the ARR, calculated from published accounts, in empirical research, particularly in economics,[2] but also in the area of accounting and finance.

In this paper, we shall be concerned with the measurement of economic performance *ex post*, i.e. with the comparison of the observed ARR for a year, or the average for a number of years, with the IRR. The latter is defined as that rate of discount which will give a zero initial Net Present Value of the lifetime cash flows of a project or (in the case of the whole firm) a group of projects. The calculation of an *ex post* IRR for comparison with an ARR calculated from financial reports has a serious practical drawback in the case of a continuing firm: IRR requires estimates of all future cash flows, which will be extremely subjective in a world of uncertainty. It is this practical obstacle to calculating IRR or any other measure of economic income (explored comprehensively by Kaldor [1955], pp. 62–64), which makes ARR, despite its possible deficiencies, a popular practical alternative for appraising the *ex post* profitability of companies, e.g. in monopoly investigations. In the literature investigating the relationship between ARR and IRR (e.g. the papers by Harcourt and Solomon) it is customary to make 'golden age' assumptions of complete certainty about the future, so that *ex ante* and *ex post* IRRs are identical (expectations are always fulfilled). It might reasonably be argued that this biases the case against ARR, since we are comparing a practical measure (ARR) with a theoretical ideal which is impractical (IRR under conditions of certainty). It should also be noted that the IRR is not always an ideal measure of economic performance even under conditions of certainty, e.g. the IRR assumption of constant discount rate throughout the lifetime of the investment may be inappropriate when interest rates change through time, and maximising a rate of return, such as IRR, is identically equivalent to maximising the absolute amount of profit only when the amount of capital investment is assumed to be fixed. However, in the subsequent argument, we shall accept the framework which is conventional in the current literature and compare ARR with an unambiguous IRR, calculated under conditions of certainty, which is assumed to be an ideal measure of economic performance.

The purpose of this paper is not to deny the justification for scepticism about some uses of ARR but to define those uses in which the deficiencies of ARR are relatively unimportant and

*This paper is part of a programme of research supported by the Esmée Fairbairn Charitable Trust. Helpful comments on an earlier draft were received from Krish Bhaskar, Susan Dev, Harold Edey, John Forker, John Kay, Geoff Meeks, and Richard Morris.

[1] Sometimes referred to as the Book Yield.

[2] A comprehensive survey of the possible mis-use of book yields (in practice, such as monopoly policy, as well as in empirical research) was provided by R. C. Morris [1971].

to identify the specific sources of deficiencies in ARR, so that they can be corrected or allowed for in uses in which they are potentially important. Section II is devoted to the first task, of suggesting uses in which ARR, with all its deficiencies, may be of some relevance. Although this section is couched in terms of using ARR as a proxy for IRR, it is, in fact, a general statement about the use of proxy variables, which may be of some use in other accounting applications. Section III concentrates on the second task of identifying the sources of its deficiencies, particularly in circumstances in which ARR is used as a proxy for IRR. Both of these tasks are important, because the ARR is widely available in published financial statements and it is therefore widely used. Although the user of ARR in Harcourt's words 'does so at his own peril', it seems likely that the absence of better information will force
150 him to continue to use ARR, and it is better to define the nature of the peril and draw up safety rules, rather than to forbid the use of ARR.

Circumstances in which Accounting Rate of Return may be a satisfactory measure

The most obvious type of situation in which the use of Accounting Rate of Return is legitimate is the tautological one in which the relevant variable *is* ARR rather than IRR or some other variable which has ideal theoretical properties. Although the possibility of such a situation is obvious, it may be less obvious that it is likely to occur very often. In reality, because, as emphasised above, ARR is so readily available, whereas information with more desirable theoretical properties is not, ARR (or its components, accounting profit and book value of assets) may often be the relevant variable in explaining how people actually behave. If the object of an empirical study is positive (i.e. explaining actual behaviour) rather than normative (i.e. defining optimal behaviour) ARR may be superior to IRR or other measures merely because, in a world of uncertainty and imperfect information, it is the rule of thumb to which decision-makers cling.

A good example of the use of ARR in this way is by Myron J. Gordon in his well-known share valuation model (M. J. Gordon [1962]), in which the ARR is used as a variable which explains share valuation, on the grounds that investors will use it in their projection of future earnings and dividends. Another example is its use by Singh [1971 and 1975] to explain the incidence of take overs: it is a plausible hypothesis to suggest that companies with low ARRs have a relatively high probability of being taken over, because their management is perceived as being inefficient (albeit on the basis of a fallible rule of thumb) by shareholders and bidders. The ARR is the relevant variable to use in testing this hypothesis.[3] An application in the broader area of the economics of the firm, which is quite common (e.g. Lewellen [1968] and Lewellen and Huntsman [1970] using US data, and Cosh [1975] and Meeks and Whittington [1975] using UK data) is as a factor determining the pay of top managers. Many other applications can be found.

A related application in which ARR is used as an explanatory variable is in the area of forecasting. If forecasting is done on the basis of a properly specified behavioural model which makes use of ARR, this is merely an extension into the future of the type of positive model described in the previous paragraph. Examples of such work are Weaver and Hall's [1971] model for predicting share prices (in which the use of ARR is suggested, but not tested), and Jones, Tweedie and Whittington's [1976] model for selecting high-yielding shares. In the case of naive forecasting, the sole justification for including any explanatory variable, such as ARR, is that it has predictive power, and it is not necessary to specify the detailed underlying causal relationships. An example of such an exercise (which does not make use of ARR, although it might well have done so) is Coen, Gomme and Kendall (1969).[4]

In addition to the cases in which ARR is the variable which the model requires, there may also be circumstances in which ARR is a suitable proxy for IRR. There are three main sets of extenuating circumstances which can eliminate, or at least reduce, the errors arising from using ARR as a proxy for IRR:

(1) *Unsystematic Error*

If we wish to use ARR as a substitute for IRR, or some other index of economic effectiveness, de-

[3]It does not, however, follow that normative inferences can necessarily be derived from the results, e.g. we can say that the hypothesis does not hold (as is, in fact, the case), using ARR, but we cannot necessarily infer that this implies that 'inefficient' companies do not suffer a high incidence of takeover. The latter statement depends on the extent to which ARR reflects IRR or some other 'economic' measure.

[4]This should not be taken to imply that naive forecasting is itself a particularly satisfactory procedure: there must always be some scepticism as to the future stability of a relationship which has no clear theoretical justification. See, for example, the critical discussion at the end of the paper by Coen, Gomme and Kendall.

viations between ARR and the true measure are misleading only if they lead to a systematic bias. For example, if we are concerned with the influence of firm size on profitability, we would probably wish ideally to regress IRR on a size measure. In practice, IRR is not available, so we may wish to use ARR as a proxy.[5] In such a case, the substitution of ARR will be misleading only if the difference between ARR and IRR is systematically correlated with the explanatory variable. For example, if the effect of accounting practices is such that ARR typically exceeds IRR for firms above a certain size and this excess tends to increase consistently with firm size, the apparent relative profitability (measured as ARR) of large firms will be overstated, and the regression coefficient of Profitability on Size will be biased upwards by the substitution of ARR for IRR. If, on the other hand, the difference between ARR and IRR is uncorrelated with size, the regression coefficient will be unbiased, although random variations between ARR and IRR may add to the degree of stochastic 'noise' in the estimation process, reducing the degree of statistical accuracy of the estimates.[6]

More formally, we may state the argument, in terms of the above example, as follows:

We assume that ARR and IRR are linearly related, with a stochastic disturbance term:

$$A_i = c + d.I_i + \mu_i \qquad (1)$$

where
A is ARR
I is IRR
μ is a stochastic error term with zero mean, and cov $(\mu_i I_i) = 0$
i refers to the ith firm
c, d are parameters

We wish to estimate the relationship between IRR and Size, which is of the form:

$$I_i = \alpha + \beta.S_i + \epsilon_i \qquad (2)$$

where
S is Size
ϵ_i is a stochastic error term with zero mean, and cov $\epsilon_i S_i = 0$
α, β are parameters

If we instead use ARR as an observable proxy for IRR, we have:

$$A_i = a + b.S_i + e_i \qquad (3)$$

which, substituting (1) above, is equivalent to:

$$(c + d.I_i + \mu_i) = a + b.S_i + e_i \qquad (4)$$

If we make the following assumptions:

(i) $\quad$ cov $(e_i S_i) = 0$

(ii) $\quad$ cov $(\mu_i S_i) = 0$

(iii) $\quad c = 0$

(iv) $\quad d = 1$

(4) now becomes:

$$I_i = a + b.S_i + (e_i - \mu_i) \qquad (5)$$

Now b is an unbiased estimator of β and a of α, since the error term is a random variable (the sum of two random variables) and is independent of S_i.[7] Obviously, (5) may have a higher residual variance than if we were able directly to test the fundamental relationship (2) (i.e. it is possible that Var $(e_i - \mu_i) >$ Var ϵ_i) but this does not bias the resulting parameter estimate, although it does prevent us from putting a precise confidence interval about the estimate unless we can somehow deduce the properties of μ_i.[8]

It is important to emphasise the fact that random errors need not bias results. Many accountants resort instinctively to arguments of an anecdotal nature, referring to individual observations (... a firm I know of valued its stock in such and such a fashion ... how would that affect your statistical analysis?). Such arguments need be taken seriously only if they indicate a systematic bias in the relationships being examined: otherwise they are merely partial explanations of why we

[5]This has been done by a number of investigations such as Steckler [1963] in the USA and Samuels and Smythe [1965] and Singh and Whittington [1968] in the UK.

[6]In fact, it is possible to think of plausible reasons why the error introduced by using ARR should be correlated with Size, particularly as Size will often be the denominator of ARR, but this is outside the scope of the present paper. The problem would be avoided if Size were measured in terms of Sales, or some other variable not contained in ARR. The regression of Profitability on Size is only one of many possible applications in which ARR may be used as a proxy for IRR. It is chosen here as an illustration because of its simplicity and its popularity in empirical research.
There is, in addition, the familiar 'errors in variables' problem if the measurement of Size is subject to error. For the purposes of this section of the paper, it is assumed that Size (or whatever other explanatory variable is used) is not subject to error.

[7]Assuming that S_i is not itself subject to error. If this assumption does not hold b will be biased downwards.

[8]The simplest assumption is $\mu_i = 0$ for all i: this is a convenient assumption, since $(e_i - \mu_i)$ now becomes e_i. Note that $\mu_i \neq 0$ does not necessarily mean that the variance of the true residual, $(e_i - \mu_i)$ in (5), is greater than the variance of the observed residual, e_i in (3), as cov $(e_i \mu_i)$ is not necessarily $\leqslant$ zero.

need an error term, i.e. why the observed relationship between the dependent variable and the explanatory variables is not exact.

(2) *ARR as a Comparative Measure*

It is apparent from the above discussion of the relationship between profitability and size that, for some purposes, we do not require that ARR be equal to IRR even on average. For example, if we are comparing Profitability and Size across firms, provided that *deviations* of ARR *from its average* are equal to deviations of IRR from its average, ARR will be a perfect surrogate for IRR in a cross-sectional comparison.[9] If there are random divergences between the two sets of deviations from average (as described above) the use of ARR as a surrogate will still yield an unbiased estimate of the effects of Size on IRR, provided that there is, on average, a one-for-one correspondence between the two sets of deviations.[10]

More formally, this can be stated, in terms of our earlier example, as follows. If we are interested only in the coefficient β, then the estimate of this in (5) is unaffected even if $c \neq 0$, i.e. if there is a non-zero constant term in the relationship between ARR and IRR. The effect of such a constant term is merely to bias the constant term in (5) as an estimate of α. We now have:

$$I_i = (a - c) + b \, . \, S_i + (e_i - \mu_i) \qquad (6)$$

Furthermore, for many purposes, we do not even require a one-for-one correspondence: this is necessary for the use of ARR to give an estimate in terms of *units* of IRR, but we may be interested only in the *direction* of the effect. In the latter case, it is sufficient that ARR is correlated with IRR (provided, of course, that the residual is independent of the explanatory variable used in the analysis). For example, in terms of our Profitability-Size example, we may wish to know whether 'true' profitability (IRR) increases with Size but we may not be interested in the exact extent of the relationship (i.e. the percentage points increase in IRR for a £1 million increase in the Size measure). In such a case ARR is an adequate substitute for IRR for the purpose in hand provided (a) that it is correlated with IRR,[11] and (b) that the variance of ARR which is unexplained by IRR is uncorrelated with the explanatory variable used in the analysis (in our example, Size).

Again, this proposition can be more formally stated, within the framework of our chosen example, as follows. If $d \neq 1$ (in (1)) but also $d \neq 0$, we can still deduce the sign of β (in (2)) from the sign of b (in (3)). Substituting our new assumption about the value of y, equation (6) now becomes:

$$I_i = \frac{(a - c)}{d} + \frac{b}{d} \, . \, S_i + \frac{(e_i - \mu_i)}{d} \qquad (7)$$

b is still an unbiased estimator of β. Unfortunately, we are unlikely to know the precise value of d, which would enable us to derive b, but we may be able to make an assumption as to the sign of d. In this case, we can deduce the sign of b, but not its precise value, e.g. if $d > 0$ and $b/d > 0$, then $b > 0$.

(3) *Adjustments to Remove the Effect of Errors in Accounting Data*

There are certain situations in which accounting data are subject to obvious biases. One example is where one company takes over another company of comparable size: in such a situation the subsequent accounting rate of return will be affected crucially by the accounting practices employed to describe the take over, e.g. whether a 'purchase' or 'pooling' approach is adopted to the acquired firm.[12] When such events can be detected, the empirical research worker can attempt to deal with them by appropriate adjustments to the ARR data.[13] If such adjustments are not possible, it may be appropriate to apply the draconian measure of omitting entirely those observations which are affected by mergers and take overs, provided that this does not lead to an important bias in the sample selection process.

An alternative method of adjustment is possible when the sources of bias in ARR are known. In such a case, the sources of bias can be explicitly included in the analysis, so that the variations

---

[9] The same would be true of a time-series comparison, although serial correlation of errors may be a serious problem in such a case.

[10] This is a consequence of the fact that a regression coefficient measures the relationship between deviations from the individual averages of a pair of variables.

[11] As shown later the correlation may be positive or negative, although, in the latter case, we must reverse the sign of the coefficient estimated using ARR, to assess the effect on IRR.

[12] For an excellent critique of US practice in this respect, see Reinhardt [1972], pp. 9–15.

[13] An interesting example is Meeks [1977], a study of post-merger performance, in which post-merger ARR is related to an estimate of the pre-merger ARR which is a weighted average of the ARRs of the parties to the merger.

in ARR which they cause can be attributed to them rather than to the other explanatory variables. For example, growth of assets is a well-known potential source of bias in ARR. In a period of inflation, the higher the recent rate of growth, the higher the relative valuation in the denominator of ARR and the higher the relative valuation upon which the depreciation charge is based, in calculating the numerator.[14] These two biases reinforce one another, one decreasing the numerator (profit) and the other increasing the denominator (capital employed). Thus, other things being equal, rapidly growing companies will tend to have a lower ARR because of the measurement problem, not because their IRR is relatively low. By introducing recent growth as an explanatory variable, we might hope to attribute at least some of this effect[15] to its true source. An example of this is Whittington [1972], a cross-sectional analysis which attempts to relate future profitability (measured as ARR) to various sources of finance. Past growth and past profitability (ARR) are also included as explanatory variables, partly because of their possible influence on the measurement of future profitability in terms of ARR as well as because of their possible causal influence on true profitability (IRR). Obviously, in such an analysis, it is impossible to estimate the extent to which the apparent influence of past ARR and growth is due to real causal factors, rather than measurement bias, but at least it can be hoped that they capture most of the measurement bias, leaving the estimates of the influence of different sources relatively free of such bias.

Deficiencies of ARR as a proxy for IRR

In this section we are concerned with the known sources of discrepancy between ARR and IRR, i.e. with the factors determining the parameters of equation (1).

The two pioneering papers, by Harcourt [1965] and Solomon [1966],[16] calculated the divergences between ARR and IRR both for individual projects and for balanced stocks of projects on alternative assumptions about depreciation policy, asset life, and growth of asset stock. In addition, Harcourt investigated alternative quasi-rent patterns to the 'one-hoss shay' rectangular pattern, and Solomon investigated the effect of price level changes. They found important discrepancies between ARR and IRR due to the fact that the accountant's measure of depreciation does not necessarily follow the pattern of economic depreciation implied by IRR (valuing the asset as the net present value of its future receipts, discounted at the IRR). They both concluded that ARR is not an accurate measure of IRR and, furthermore, failed to find a systematic pattern in the discrepancy which might have allowed a correction to be made.

From the point of view of empirical work of a statistical nature, the conclusions of Solomon and Harcourt are not as depressing as their authors found them. Their discovery of an arbitrary and apparently unsystematic discrepancy between ARR and IRR explains the need for an error term in equation (1). We would prefer this term to be as small as possible, but it need not bias our estimates of the coefficients. These authors were, of course, worried about the use of ARR as a proxy for IRR in a wide range of applications such as the regulation of public utility prices (Solomon) or the comparison of the performance of a particular industry over specific periods of time (Harcourt): in such cases, it might not be sufficient to be right 'on average'.

Later work by Livingstone and Salamon [1970], Solomon [1971], Stauffer [1971], Bhaskar [1972] and Gordon [1974] extended the earlier work, but the only important generalisation was that the IRR and ARR are equal for a firm in steady state growth at a rate g which equals the IRR (a 'golden rule' situation).[17] However, Gordon (analytically) and Bhaskar (by deterministic simulation) show that the discrepancies between ARR and IRR are minimised if the accountant chooses a depreciation method which approximates the economic depreciation implicit in IRR.

The paper by Bhaskar also contains an interesting probabilistic simulation exercise, in which alternative sets of data are generated from a common basic model (a small firm with a balanced stock of 'one-hoss shay' assets) by making the

[14]Reducing-balance depreciation can create a similar bias even in the absence of inflation.

[15]This statement is put in a relatively weak form because we need to know the precise functional form which the bias takes in order to eliminate it completely; the bias is not necessarily a simple linear function of growth measured over an arbitrarily chosen period. Furthermore, when growth is itself measured in terms of assets or profits reported in company accounts, it may be subject to some of the same measurement errors as ARR.

[16]Solomon published some of his results in 1961 as testimony to the Federal Power Commission. See Solomon [1971].

[17]Another result of this work was to reveal that ARR should be measured net of depreciation in order to approximate IRR best.

quasi-rents and asset lives vary in a stochastic manner. A cross-sectional regression of the same form as equation (1) was estimated across the resulting data, and it was found that the constant term was always negative ($c < 0$) and the slope coefficient (d) greater than unity. In terms of the earlier analysis, this would imply that, in using ARR as a surrogate for IRR in empirical work, we can deduce the direction of the influence of the explanatory variable on IRR but not its extent. However, this result may be sensitive to the assumptions of the common underlying model, such as no growth and a constant expected value of quasi-rents.

A recent paper by Kay [1976] has provided a much more general analysis of the relationship between ARR[18] and IRR. By dealing with continuous time, rather than discrete time, Kay is able to use more powerful analytical techniques,
154 and obtains a number of useful generalisations:[19]

(i) If ARR on a project is constant over the project's life, it is equal to IRR.

Apart from the consequence for empirical work that stability of ARR over time suggests that it is a reasonably good proxy for IRR, this has a particularly interesting implication for government regulation of prices: when government regulation is based on the achievement of a constant ARR, this will also lead to the achievement of an IRR identical with that ARR.

(ii) Every sequence of ARRs defines a valuation function under which the present value of the cash flows of the project is zero.

In other words, if the cash flows of a project (both inflows and outflows) are discounted back to its starting point, using the ARR obtaining in each period as the discount rate for that period, the same result would be obtained by discounting at the constant IRR throughout the life of the project. The case of constant ARR ((i) above) is a special case of this general relationship. Where ARR is not constant, the problem becomes one of finding an appropriate averaging device which will yield IRR, or a close approximation to it. It transpires that the simple unweighted average ARR of a project is not a good device for this purpose. Intuition would suggest that this is because a simple average gives the same weight to later ARRs (which occur further in the future and are therefore less valuable) as earlier ARRs (which occur sooner and are therefore more valuable). That this is, in fact, the deficiency in simple averaging of ARRs is confirmed by Kay's third generalisation:

(iii) If the value of capital employed is discounted at IRR, the weighted average ARR is equal to IRR.

In other words, periodic ARRs are averaged, using as weights the average book values of assets employed for the appropriate periods, and discounted back to the start of the project at IRR. Since IRR in these circumstances is equal to the resulting weighted average ARR, Kay is able to propose a method of adjusting a series of observed ARRs and book values to yield IRR. In the example which he chooses, that of an aggregate of continuing companies (in fact, all of the larger companies in UK manufacturing industry), he has to accept the accountant's book values of initial and terminal values as being equivalent to the economist's values (present values of future flows, discounted at IRR), and this is a general restriction of the usefulness of his method in empirical studies of continuing companies.[20] Obviously, in estimating the IRR of an individual project, with limited life, from observed lifetime accounting data, the Kay method does not suffer from this restriction and is very powerful, as it does not depend upon any particular depreciation scheme being used by the accountant.

Further analysis of the Kay adjustment reveals that it is not likely to be of much importance when there is no time trend in ARR. When ARR declines with time, a simple average ARR will be below IRR, and, conversely, when ARR rises through time, its simple average will be above IRR. This follows intuitively from the fact that the adjustment is essentially a weighting process, the weighting declining with time: e.g. if ARR does not vary systematically through time, the weighted average is not likely to differ greatly from a simple average. The latter result is of importance for empirical work which studies whole firms which are aggregations of different projects and which are therefore likely to exhibit more stable rates of return than individual projects. One special case of aggregation, which had been explored

[18] Measured net of depreciation.

[19] Not all of these claim to be original, some having been derived by earlier writers, such as Vatter [1966].

[20] It might be argued that Current Cost Accounting could improve the applicability of his methods, since CCA balance sheet values might be better surrogates for economic value than are the historic cost values used at present.

by earlier writers, is steady-state growth, for which Kay derives his next generalisation:

(iv) For a firm in steady-state growth at rate n, the ARR is constant and the book value of capital grows at n.

For a continuing firm, constancy of ARR does not (as for a finite project) necessarily imply that ARR = IRR, unless the accountant's initial and terminal values for the observed period coincide with those of the economist. However, on the 'golden rule' path, where n = IRR, we have the situation described earlier, in which ARR = IRR, because the growth of the discrepancy between the accountant's book value and economic value (which takes place at rate n) is exactly offset by the effect of discounting (at IRR = n). The general steady-state relationship between the ARR (a), IRR (r), growth rate (n), economist's value of the firm (W) and book value (V) is contained in Kay's fifth generalisation:

(v) For a firm in steady-state growth relationship $(n - a)/(n - r) = W/V$ holds.

On the plausible (but not inevitable) assumption that $r \geqslant n$ (IRR exceeds growth rate) and that $W \geqslant V$ (the accountant values assets at less than the economist's value, because of the doctrine of conservatism), then $a \geqslant r$, i.e. the ARR will be greater than IRR. The nearer are the two sets of values (W and V) then the nearer are the two rate of return measures.

Kay goes on to derive propositions about management policies based upon accountants' profit measures. These are interesting but do not have an immediate bearing on the matter in hand: the use of ARR as a proxy for IRR in empirical studies. For our present purposes, it is sufficient to summarise Kay's results as follows:

(1) There is a general analytical relationship between ARR and IRR. IRR can be derived as an appropriately weighted average of ARRs.

(2) For an individual project, this weighted average may be calculated exactly, but for a continuing firm, errors may remain because of the discrepancy between accounting and economic values of assets at the beginning and the end of the period.

(3) If a simple unweighted average of a project's ARR is taken, this will be a good proxy for IRR when there is no time trend in ARR, and a perfect one when ARR is constant. When ARR declines through time, the simple average will under-estimate IRR; when ARR rises, the simple average will over-estimate IRR.

(4) In the case of a firm in balanced growth, ARR = IRR where the growth rate = ARR (and therefore = IRR). In cases where the rate of growth is less than IRR, it is reasonable to assume that ARR $\geqslant$ IRR, because of the accountant's conservative tendency to undervalue assets.

(5) We might reasonably expect that for a firm as opposed to a project, the process of aggregating a number of projects of different ages, length of life, etc., would lead to relative stability of ARR and thus to relatively small divergences between average ARR and IRR. We might also expect that the process of averaging over a longer period of years will diminish the effect of the discrepancies between the economist's and the accountant's valuations of opening and closing assets. Unless these discrepancies grow proportionately with time, their importance will be reduced because they will be quantitatively smaller relative to the flows, as the period for measuring the flows increases. 155

Conclusion

We have argued (in Section II) that there are circumstances in which ARR might actually be preferable to IRR in empirical research, because of its ability to explain actual behaviour. It was also argued that, in cases in which IRR is the ideal variable which is required, ARR can serve as an unbiased proxy, provided that certain statistical independence conditions are fulfilled. Furthermore, it was argued that, in the latter context, statistical biases might be eliminated by appropriate construction of the model or adjustments to the data.

We next (in Section III) surveyed the considerable literature on the relationship between ARR and IRR. It is clear that there can be considerable divergences between the two measures and that any correspondence between them in practice is likely to be a statistical average relationship rather than an exact one. However, it is also clear that the two measures do have an analytical relationship to one another and that, in certain circumstances, there can be an exact correspondence. In empirical work, we shall have more confidence in using ARR as a proxy for IRR when we have a large number of observations (to minimise the effects of random variations), a long observation period for measuring ARR (to average out the inevitable arbitrary year-to-year fluctuations resulting from accounting measurement), a large aggregate of projects (such as a whole firm) over which ARR is measured (to average out the peculiarities of individual projects), no obvious trend in ARR, and similar rates of growth. We should beware of making comparisons across small numbers of observations (such as comparing a pair of companies), measuring ARR for short periods (such as a single year) or single projects, or across firms with widely divergent rates of growth, and should avoid using unweighted average ARR when there is a clear time trend in the ratio. We should also beware of comparisons across companies with characteristics such as vastly different rates of growth, or belonging to different industries (with assets of different length of life, etc.) which are likely to lead to different degrees of discrepancy between the accountant's book value of assets and economic value.[21] However, we should also be aware that such factors will not necessarily invalidate an empirical study, if the discrepancies between IRR and ARR are not correlated with the explanatory variables used in the study.

References

Bhaskar, K. N., 'Rates of Return under Uncertainty', *Accounting and Business Research*, No. 9, Winter 1972, pp. 40–52.

Coen, P. J., Gomme, E. D. and Kendall, M. G., 'Lagged Relationships in Economic Forecasting', *Journal of the Royal Statistical Society*, Series A, Vol. 132, Part 1, 1969, pp. 133–163.

Cosh, A., 'The Remuneration of Chief Executives in the United Kingdom', *Economic Journal*, Vol. 85, March 1975, pp. 75–94.

Gordon, L. A., 'Accounting Rate of Return vs. Economic Rate of Return', *Journal of Business Finance and Accounting*, Vol. 1, No. 3, Autumn 1974, pp. 343–356.

Gordon, M. J., *The Investment, Financing and Valuation of the Corporation*, Irwin, 1962.

Harcourt, G. C., 'The Accountant in a Golden Age', *Oxford Economic Papers*, Vol. 17, No. 1, March 1965, pp. 66–80.

[21] In this context it should be remembered that the valuation of stocks and work-in-progress is potentially an important source of such discrepancies: the existing literature tends to concentrate on the problems raised by the accounting valuation of fixed assets.

Jones, C. J., Tweedie, D. P. and Whittington, G., 'The Regression Portfolio: A Statistical Investigation of a Relative Decline Model', *Journal of Business Finance and Accounting*, Vol. 3, No. 2, 1976, pp. 71–92.

Kay, J. A., 'Accountants, too, could be happy in a Golden Age: The Accountant's Rate of Profit and the Internal Rate of Return', *Oxford Economic Papers*, Vol. 28, No. 3, Nov. 1976, pp. 447–460.

Kaldor, N., *An Expenditure Tax*, Unwin, 1955, Appendix to Chapter 1.

Lewellen, W. G., *Executive Compensation in Large Industrial Corporations*, New York, 1968.

Lewellen, W. G. and Huntsman, B., 'Managerial Pay and Corporate Performance', *American Economic Review*, 60, Sept. 1970, pp. 710–720.

Livingstone, J. L. and Salamon, G. L., 'Relationship between the Accounting and the Internal Rate of Return Measures: a Synthesis and an Analysis', *Journal of Accounting Research*, Vol. 8, Autumn 1970, pp. 199–216.

Meeks, G., *Disappointing Marriage: A Study of the Gains from Merger*, Cambridge University Press, 1977.

Morris, R. C., *The Book Yield as a Performance Evaluator*. Unpublished paper read to the Southern Accounting Group, Cardiff, Autumn 1971.

Reinhardt, U. E., *Mergers and Consolidations: A Corporate-Finance Approach*, General Learning Press, 1972.

Samuels, J. M. and Smythe, D. J., 'Profits, Variability of Profits and Firm Size', *Economica*, May 1969.

Singh, A. and Whittington, G., *Growth, Profitability and Valuation*, Cambridge University Press, 1968.

Singh, A., *Take-overs, Their Relevance to the Stock Market and the Theory of the Firm*, Cambridge University Press, London, 1971.

Singh, A., 'Take-overs, "Natural Selection" and the Theory of the Firm', *Economic Journal*, Vol. 85, Sept. 1975, pp. 497–515.

Solomon, Ezra, 'Return on Investment: the Relation of Book Yields to True Yield', in *Research in Accounting Measurement*, ed. R. K. Jaedicke, Y. Ijiri, and O. Nielsen, American Accounting Association, 1966.

Solomon, Ezra, 'Return on Investment: The Continuing Confusion Among Disparate Measures', pp. 164–176 of R. R. Sterling and W. F. Bentz (eds.) *Accounting in Perspective*, South-Western Publishing Co., Cincinnati, 1971.

Stauffer, T. R., 'The Measurement of Corporate Rates of Return: A Generalised Formation', *Bell Journal of Economics and Management Science*, Autumn 1971, pp. 434–469.

Weaver, D. and Hall, M. G., 'Evaluation of Ordinary Shares Using a Computer', *Journal of the Institute of Actuaries*, Vol. 93, 1967.

Steckler, H. O., *Profitability and Size of Firm*, Berkeley, 1963.

Vatter, W. J., 'Income Models, Book Yield and Rate of Return', *Accounting Review*, Vol. 41, 1966, pp. 681–698.

Whittington, G., 'The Profitability of Retained Earnings', *The Review of Economics and Statistics*, Vol. LIV, No. 2, May 1972, pp. 152–160.

AUTHOR'S NOTE (1986)

Following the publication of this paper, correspondence with Professor Skerratt revealed a degree of sloppiness in the econometric argument of pp. 203 - 4 of the paper. The main results stated in the paper do hold, but the distinction between the population models (equations (1) to (7)) and estimates of those models is not clearly made. Also there is an error on p. 204 in that it is b/d in equation (7) (not b), which is equivalent to β.

The following note represents our mutually agreed view of how the exposition of pp. 203 - 4 should have been expressed.

ON THE USE OF THE ACCOUNTING RATE OF RETURN IN EMPIRICAL RESEARCH : A CORRECTION

by L.C.L. SKERRATT, UNIVERSITY OF DURHAM

and G. WHITTINGTON, UNIVERSITY OF BRISTOL

Whittington (1979) in equations (1) through (7) discusses the extent to which ARR can proxy for IRR. Although the thrust of the argument is not in doubt, the logic of the exposition requires clarification, since there is some confusion between the true (population) parameters of an economic model and the regression sample estimates of those true parameters. The revised exposition is as follows:

Suppose that equations (1) and (2) are the true unobservable relationships between A, I and S.

$$A_i = c + d.I_i + \mu_i \qquad (1)$$

$$I_i = \alpha + \beta.S_i + \varepsilon_i \qquad (2)$$

where

A is ARR
I is IRR
S is size

μ_i and ε_i are random errors.

If I cannot be easily measured, then A may be used in specifying the relationship between return and size, as in equation (3).

$$A_i = a + b\,S_i + e_i \qquad (3)$$

It can easily be shown that for c = o and d = 1, b is identical to β, the coefficient on size in the equation of theoretical interest.

PROOF:

From equations (1) and (3)

$$c + dI_i + \mu_i = a + b\,S_i + e_i$$

$$I_i = a + b\,S_i + (e_i - \mu_i) \qquad (4)$$

Taking expectations of (2) and (4)

$$\alpha + \beta E(S_i) = a + bE(S_i) \tag{5}$$

Since the parameters α, β, a and b are independent of $E(S_i)$, then equation (5) requires

$$a = \alpha \tag{6}$$

$$b = \beta \tag{7}$$

Consequently, unbiased estimates of the parameters of equation (3) will provide unbiased estimates of the parameters of equation (2).

However, nothing comes without cost and there is a drawback of estimating equation (3) rather than equation (2). From equations (2), (4), (6) and (7) it follows that

$$e_i = \varepsilon_i + \mu_i \tag{8}$$

In the likely case of zero covariance between μ_i and ε_i (the error with which ARR proxies IRR is independent of the error with which size can explain IRR) then $Var(e_i) > Var(\varepsilon_i)$. This means that the precision with which b can be estimated from equation (3) is likely to be less than estimating directly from equation (2). Consequently, the chances of a type II error are increased.

The above approach can also be employed to analyse the cases of $c \neq o$ and $d \neq o$ (p. 204 of the original paper). In the former, then equation (6) needs to be revised,

$$a = \alpha + c \tag{6a}$$

but equation (7) still holds.

Therefore, equation (3) will still capture the influence of size on IRR.

When, in addition, $d \neq o$, i.e. there is a scaling problem in calculating a proxy for IRR, then

$$a = \alpha + c \tag{6b}$$

$$b = \beta.d \tag{7a}$$

That is, the sign of β can be inferred from b if the sign of d is known. However, from equations (2), (4), (6b) and (7a), it follows that

$$e_i = d\,\varepsilon_i + \mu_i \tag{8a}$$

and, consequently, the precision of the estimate of b is reduced.

ESTIMATING THE INTERNAL RATE OF RETURN FROM ACCOUNTING DATA—A NOTE

By A. W. STARK

Introduction

KAY,[1] in a recent paper in this journal, questioned the predominant view concerning the adequacy of the accounting rate of return as a proxy for the true economic rate of return. Indeed he suggested that—

> "... under quite plausible circumstances a simple average accountant's rate of return will be a good estimator of the true rate of return".

and also

> "The accountant's rate of profit, measured over a period of years, will be an acceptable indicator of the true rate of return: it is over a single year that it may prove seriously misleading".

These conclusions were drawn from a model of the firm that did not explicitly include working capital requirements, loan financing and taxes. However, to illustrate his results, Kay used as input data the financial performance of a sample of British manufacturing industry and then estimated the sample pre-tax d.c.f. yield for the ten-year period 1960–69. His example therefore includes periodic working capital requirements, loan financing and taxes. One purpose of this reply is to show that the extension of Kay's model, to the more complicated world of his example, was only one of a whole multitude of such possible extensions; in Section 1 below an appropriate extension is derived and in Section 2 the results are applied to Kay's data to produce a revised estimate of the true rate of return. The main conclusion drawn is that it is *not*, in general, the accountant's rate of profit that helps us to estimate the true rate of return.

The third section of the paper discusses Wright's[2] comments on the validity of Kay's work, and is therefore, concerned with the use of accounting valuations as estimates of their true economic counterparts. This discussion represents a second purpose of the paper and is intended to indicate situations, if any, in which it is appropriate to use the algorithms developed in the following section.

Section 1

This section extends Kay's basic framework to more complicated models of the firm, explicitly dealing with working capital requirements, loan

[1] J. A. Kay, 'Accountants, too, could be happy in a Golden Age: the accountant's rate of profit and the internal rate of return', O.E.P. xxviii (1976), pp. 447–60.

[2] F. K. Wright, 'Accounting rate of profit and internal rate of return', O.E.P. xxx (1978), pp. 464–468.

financing, and taxes. In general results are not proved in full since they follow the style of proof illustrated in Kay's original paper.

Firstly, let us define the following symbols:

$f(t)$ = rate of generation of pre-depreciation profits. (This is not the definition used by Kay i.e. rate of generation of cash flows, but it would appear from Kay's work that he does not distinguish between the two.[3])
$g(t)$ = rate of (fixed) capital expenditure
$d(t)$ = rate of depreciation
$p(t)$ = rate of expenditure on working capital requirements.[4]
$l(t)$ = rate of loan financing
$i(t)$ = rate of interest expenses
$c(t)$ = rate of taxation expense

Consider first the case in which the firm incurs both fixed and working capital investment. In this situation the IRR is defined by the value of r that 161
satisfies:

$$w(0)+\int_0^t g(x)e^{-rx} = \int_0^t (f(x)-p(x))e^{-rx}\,dx + w(t)e^{-rt} \tag{1}$$

where $w(t)$ is the present value of the subsequent cash flows of the unit under consideration. If we further define

$$v(t)=\int_0^t (g(x)-d(x)+p(x))\,dx \tag{2}$$

and
$$f(t)=a(t)v(t)+d(t) \tag{3}$$

then, making one important assumption, highlighted at the end of this section, a solution value for r will be given by:

$$a=\frac{\int_0^t a(x)v(x)e^{-ax}\,dx}{\int_0^t v(x)e^{-ax}} \tag{4}$$

This result is analagous to Kay's result (iii). In accounting terms $v(t)$ is equal to the net book value (NBV) of fixed assets plus working capital, and $a(t)$ is the profit after depreciation divided by the book value of fixed assets plus working capital.

If we extend to the case of loan financing, redefining $v(t)$ and

$$a(t) \quad \text{by} \quad v(t)=\int_0^t (g(x)-d(x)+p(x)-l(x))\,dx \tag{5}$$

[3] For confirmation of this point, see Kay p. 449 op. cit.
[4] Working capital is defined to be the sum of stocks and debtors less creditors.

and
$$f(t) = a(t)v(t) + d(t) + i(t) \tag{6}$$

and r, the IRR by:

$$w(0) + \int_0^t (g(x) - l(x))e^{-rx}\,dx = \int_0^t (f(x) - p(x) - i(x))e^{-rx}\,dx + w(t)e^{-rt} \tag{7}$$

then a, as defined symbolically by equation (4), but using the new definitions for $a(t)$ and $v(t)$, will be a solution for r in equation (7). Notice that in the definition of $a(t)$ the interest element is represented by interest *paid* rather than *charged*. Also $v(t)$ is equal to the NBV of fixed assets plus working capital less loan finance, a definition not identical to owners' equity. Therefore, the rate of profit does not have a direct correspondence with that of the accountant given that the latter would have used different definitions for
162 both profit and capital. It should be emphasised that in this case a constitutes an estimate of the pre-tax rate of return and thus the formula for its derivation can be related directly to the method of estimation used in Kay's work.

Extending the analysis to the case of taxation, if, $a(t)$, satisfies,

$$f(t) = a(t)v(t) + d(t) + i(t) + c(t) \tag{8}$$

and using the previous definition of $v(t)$, the IRR, r is now defined by:

$$w(0) + \int_0^t (g(x) - l(x))e^{-rx}\,dx = \int_0^t (f(x) - p(x) - i(x) - c(x))e^{-rx}\,dx + w(t)e^{-rt} \tag{9}$$

and a solution of r is again given by a, as defined by equation (4), using the appropriate definitions of $a(t)$ and $v(t)$. Analogous to the case of loan financing and associated interest payments, the definition of $a(t)$ uses a *cash flow* definition rather than an accruals definition for the effects of taxation. The definition of $v(t)$ is as mentioned above. As such, $a(t)$ again departs from the accountant's rate of profit.

As mentioned earlier (and by Kay and Wright), these results, depend upon the crucial assumption, that the accountant's valuation $v(t)$ is equal to $w(t)$. This assumption, and its implications, are discussed more fully in Section 3.

Section 2

This section provides an estimate[5] of the true pre-tax d.c.f. yield, using the above results, and a comparison with Kay's estimate is made. To operationalise the algorithm given by equation (4), it must be converted into its discrete time analog. Following Kay's example it is necessary to compute

[5] The data used in deriving this estimate is based on the same sample as that used by Kay op. cit.

the value of b given by:

$$\log(1+b)\sum_{x=0}^{t}\frac{v_x}{(1+b)^x}=\sum_{x=0}^{t}\frac{\Pi_x}{(1+b)^x} \tag{10}$$

where a_x and Π_x are the discrete time analogs of $a(x)$ and $a(x)v(x)$. Again following Kay's example v_x is defined as the average of opening and closing values for the period considered. Inspection of Kay's table 1 shows that he was interested in estimating the pre-tax true rate of return. Such an estimate requires a definition of v_x given by the average of the opening and closing balances of fixed assets (NBV) plus working capital less outstanding loans and overdrafts. Essentially this is equal to shareholders' interest plus minority interests plus the sum of the various tax accounts (i.e. including deferred taxation) plus any dividend liability less any holdings of cash. This includes preference shares as a part of shareholders' interest. This differs from Kay's
definition because he defines v_x by the average of the opening and closing 163
balances of shareholders' interest plus minority interests less preference shares and goodwill. Principally the differences amount to Kay's inclusion of the sum of the various tax accounts, dividend liability and cash. Furthermore, in defining Π_x he accepts interest *charged* as an appropriate proxy for interest *paid*. There is however, no alternative in this respect given the level of disclosure for the sample used.

Using the definitions given above, Table 1 can be derived.

Equation (10), and the above data yield an estimate of the true pre-tax rate of return of 15.0%, compared with Kay's estimate of 17.12%. To estimate the post-tax rate of return it would be necessary to alter the definition of Π_x by taking into account the need to subtract tax *paid* (rather than tax charged). This adjustment gives an estimate of 8.9% for the post-tax rate of return.

TABLE 1
The accountant's data

Year	(£m) v_x	(£m) Π_x	(%) a_x
1961	10,648	1,452	13.64
1962	11,236	1,403	12.48
1963	11,703	1,592	13.60
1964	12,251	1,853	15.13
1965	13,074	1,909	14.60
1966	13,681	1,725	12.61
1967	13,776	1,980	14.37
1968	14,093	2,283	16.20
1969	14,764	2,235	15.14

Source: Business Monitor M3

Section 3

In replying to Kay's original paper, Wright criticised the assumption of equality of $v(t)$, the accounting valuation, and $w(t)$, the economic valuation. Typical of his comments was—

> "Kay's calculation of a d.c.f. rate of return for U.K. manufacturing industry is only as sound as the accounting valuations on which it is based.

As mentioned earlier, Kay had recognised the problem himself. In his reply[6] he argued that any different estimates can easily be incorporated into the algorithm given by equation (6). Indeed he states that if

$$a = \frac{-C_0 + \int_0^t a(x)v(x)e^{-ax}\,dx + C_t e^{-at}}{\int_0^t v(x)e^{-ax}\,dx} \qquad (13)$$

then a will be equal to the IRR where C_0 and C_t are the differences between the alternative valuation method used and the accountant's valuation.

This formula is indeed correct, given the provisos contained earlier in this paper concerning the definitions of terms used. But perhaps the most important point to emphasise is that if alternative estimates of $w(0)$ and $w(t)$, are available they will yield direct IRR values. In these circumstances, there is no need to use the algorithm represented by equation (13). In general, the relevant cash flows can be derived from published accounts[7] and are therefore, derivable from the data given for the sample used in the example above.[8] The only assumption required is that the reduction in the number of firms in the sample is due to intra-sample mergers—an assumption which as with Kay's work, underlies the application of the algorithm in the above example. Indeed, even if we do not have alternative estimates we could still perform a direct IRR calculation. Therefore, the main value of the above algorithms would lie in the time saved, if any, in the preparation of the required input data compared with the time consumed in deriving the appropriate stream of cash flows.

To summarise, it is entirely possible to derive the appropriate cash flow measures, $(f(t)-p(t))$, $i(t)$, $c(t)$, $g(t)$ and $l(t)$ at the level of the individual firm, and at any aggregate level, as long as the amount of disclosure of accounting data is the same at the aggregate level as at the individual level. There *are* problems of disclosure e.g. "profit" on redemption of loans,

[6] J. A. Kay, 'Accounting rate of profit and internal rate of return, a reply', O.E.P. 30 (1978) pp. 469–470.

[7] For a discussion of the differences between accruals based flows and cash flows, see G. H. Lawson and A. W. Stark, 'The concept of profit for fund-raising', Accounting and Business Research, Winter 1975.

[8] For an example of the results of such a derivation, see G. H. Lawson and A. W. Stark, 'Equity values and inflation: dividends and debt financing', Lloyd's Bank Review, January 1981.

treatment of minority interests, profits from associated companies, all of which are examples of the general problem of not being able to "wash out" the effect of the accruals principle and hence not being able to derive the pure cash flow stream. However, examination of the formulae developed, and the mathematical relationships used in deriving them, illustrate that this problem also affects the algorithms developed. Hence the problem is common to both techniques.

Conclusion

This paper has demonstrated an extension of Kay's simple model to the more complicated world of working capital requirements, loan financing and taxation. It has been shown that the accountant's rate of profit, even if measured over a number of years, is not necessarily an acceptable indicator of the true rate of return. A number of ratios can be derived from accounting data which will fulfil such a purpose given certain important assumptions concerning the values of the initial and terminal stock. This assumption is, on the other hand, also common to any direct calculation of the IRR. It has also been pointed out that in the case of the individual firm, and at the level of aggregation of the sample used by Business Monitor M3, it is possible, subject to some limitations on disclosure, to derive the appropriate cash flow series, and that the limitations of disclosure also pose a threat to the validity of the algorithms developed. Thus perhaps we can say that the accountant too will not be happy in a golden age until such time as he is satisfied with the use of his data rather than the use of his definitions.

University of Manchester

THE ACCOUNTING REVIEW
Vol. LVII, No. 2
April 1982

166

Cash Recovery Rates and Measures of Firm Profitability

Gerald L. Salamon

ABSTRACT: Previous analytical work has shown that a firm's cash recovery rate (the ratio of cash recovery during a period to gross investments outstanding during the period) is related to the internal rate of return of firm projects in the event that the firm reinvests all of its cash flows. This paper extends the previous analytical work by establishing a link between a firm's cash recovery rate and the internal rate of return of firm projects in circumstances when the firm does not reinvest all of its cash flows. Additionally, this paper applies the extended model to a group of firms in order to obtain estimates of their internal rates of return. Work of this kind would seem to be of particular interest to economic researchers who are interested in theoretically defensible empirical measures of firm profitability.

INTRODUCTION

ACCOUNTING has a long-standing tradition of responding to the information demands of parties that are interested in firm performance. Economic researchers and regulatory agencies often require a measure of firm profitability to test their theories or make meaningful regulatory decisions. Until recently, these parties have been in a very unenviable position. Such parties, if they were to do any work, were forced to use an accounting rate of return as their measure of firm profitability, and accounting rates of return are known to be theoretically deficient measures of firm profitability. For example, the literature of economics, finance, and accounting contains many analytic illustrations of discrepancies between an accounting-based rate of return and a firm's discounted cash-flow rate of return (e.g., Harcourt [1965], Solomon [1966], Livingstone and Salamon [1970], and Stauffer [1971]). This literature suggests that it is quite hazardous to assume that a ranking of firms by their accounting rates of return is equivalent to a ranking by their discounted cash-flow rates of return.[1] Recent work by Ijiri [1978; 1979; 1980] has provided potential relief to those users of accounting data who have

[1] A work which claims that accounting rates of return can be relied upon as meaningful estimates of a discounted cash-flow rate of return or that these rates can be easily adjusted to obtain such estimates is that of Kay [1976]. However, as pointed out by Wright [1978, p. 466] the relationship between a firm's accounting rate of return and its discounted cash-flow rate of return as developed by Kay requires a knowledge of the ratio of the book value of a firm's net assets to their economic value. Since this ratio is unknown and since this ratio would be influenced by the accounting methods used by the firm, it seems that Kay's claims are unfounded. Fortunately, Ijiri's work points the way toward obtaining meaningful estimates of a firm's discounted cash-flow rate of return without relying on the accounting rate of return.

The comments of David Burgstahler, William R. Kinney, Jr., and the participants of the University of Iowa and Purdue University Accounting Workshops on earlier versions of this paper are gratefully acknowledged.

Gerald L. Salamon is Professor of Accounting, University of Iowa.

Manuscript received January 1981.
Revision received May 1981.
Accepted July 1981.

had to use profitability measures that were known to be deficient.

Ijiri has advocated the preparation of financial reports based upon cash-flow data in order to make the reports more consistent with capital budgeting decision criteria and to make the content of the reports less influenced by the accounting-method choices of the firm. Another important feature of the cash-flow-based financial reports is that they emphasize the calculation of the firm's cash recovery rate (the ratio of cash recovery during a period to gross investments outstanding during the period).[2] The firm's cash recovery rate is important, because Ijiri has shown that under certain conditions a firm's cash recovery rate converges to a constant which is related to the firm's internal or discounted cash-flow rate of return (hereafter, referred to as IRR).[3] This means that if the specified conditions are met, then an estimate of the firm's IRR can be obtained from knowledge of its cash recovery rate. Ijiri has demonstrated the practical usefulness of his ideas by calculating estimates of the IRR for several different actual firms. Ijiri's work is potentially quite important to those parties that require theoretically defensible empirical measures of firm profitability.

When Ijiri established the theoretical (i.e., analytical) link between a firm's cash recovery rate and its IRR, he assumed that the firm reinvested all of its cash flows. In fact, most firms do not reinvest all of their cash flows. Furthermore, if a firm did reinvest all of its cash flows Ijiri's analysis would be unnecessary since prior analytical work has shown that in such circumstances the firm's accounting rate of return is equal to the IRR of firm projects.[4]

This paper examines the link between a firm's cash recovery rate and its IRR when the firm does not reinvest all of its cash flows. The model developed in this paper also extends the prior work of Ijiri by examining the impact of inflation on the relationship between the firm's cash recovery rate and its IRR. While Ijiri's model is shown to be a special case of the one developed here, it is important to note that within the present model there is still a link between the firm's cash recovery rate and its IRR which is largely independent of accounting methods and which can be utilized to obtain empirical estimates of the firm's IRR. This fact, which is important to economic researchers and others interested in measures of firm profitability, is emphasized by re-estimating the IRR of the 20 firms 167
previously examined by Ijiri [1980]. The importance to economic researchers of Ijiri's IRR estimation procedures and the extension of those procedures which are described in this paper are evaluated by comparing firm profit performance

[2] Cash recoveries are calculated as the sum of Funds from Operations, Proceeds From Disposal of Long-Term Assets, Interest Expense, and the decrease in Current Assets (if it occurs). Gross investments are calculated as the average of beginning and ending Total Assets (gross). See Ijiri [1978, pp. 345–347; 1980, pp. 55–56].

[3] Earlier work by Stauffer also showed that the firm's cash recovery rate converged to a constant when all cash flows were reinvested [1971, p. 451]. However, Stauffer's main concern was evaluating the cash recovery rate as an estimate of the firm's discounted-cash-flow rate of return and he found the cash recovery rate a deficient estimate [pp. 439–40, 454]. Stauffer did not address the issue of whether it would be more practical to adjust the cash recovery rate to find an estimate of the firm's discounted-cash-flow rate of return than it would be to adjust its accounting rate of return.

[4] When the firm reinvests all of its cash flows, then its growth rate in gross investment approaches the IRR of firm projects (see Livingstone and Salamon [1970] and Ijiri [1979, p. 265]. For this case, Livingstone and Salamon [1970], Solomon [1966], and Stauffer [1971] show that a firm's accounting rate of return also approaches the IRR of firm projects. Thus, for the case in which the firm reinvests all of its cash flows a firm's accounting rate of return would be a good estimate of the IRR of firm projects; therefore, Ijiri's procedures would be unnecessary.

as measured by the IRR estimates to the profit performance as measured by the rate-of-return measure most frequently used in economic studies—the firm's accounting rate of return. Finally, some preliminary information that may aid future researchers in their choice of a profitability measure is provided by comparing the profit performance of firms as measured by six different empirical measures of the IRR.

The model that links a firm's cash recovery rate and its IRR when the firm does not reinvest all of its cash flows is developed in the next section.

168 *Formulation of the Model*

The model used in this paper is one that has the same structure as one developed earlier by Salamon [1973]. The model assumes that the firm is a collection of projects that have the same useful life, same cash-flow pattern, and same IRR. The collection is assembled by having the firm acquire a project at the end of each year. The project acquired by the firm in any year is different from the projects acquired in other years only with respect to scale. In particular, the model assumes that the firm has a constant rate of growth in real gross investment. Thus, if this growth rate is positive, the project acquired by the firm in the current year is larger than the projects acquired in prior years. The cash inflows (outflows) generated (required) by firm projects occur only at discrete points of time which are one year apart. The point of time at which the firm acquires its first project is designated as the end of year zero. The firm operates in an environment in which there is a constant rate of change in the level of all prices. Thus, the model examines the impact of constant changes in the general price level but ignores those cases where specific prices change at different rates and those cases where the rate of change is different in different years.

The analytical development of the model begins with the following definitions:

p' = the annual rate of change in all prices ($p' > -1$),
g' = the annual rate of growth in real gross investment ($g' > -1$),
r' = the real IRR of all firm projects ($r' > -1$),
n = useful life of all firm projects, and
C_i^j = the real cash flow (i.e., it is measured in terms of the price level which prevailed at the end of year zero) of the project acquired by a firm at the end of the year j, i years after the project's purchase (i.e., the cash is received by the firm at the end of year $i+j$) where $i=0, 1, 2, \ldots, n$ and $j=0, 1, 2, \ldots$. It is assumed that C_0^j is negative, C_n^j is positive, and C_i^j is nonnegative for $0<i<n$ and all j. The absolute value of C_0^j is the amount of real gross investment made by the firm at the end of year j.

For notational convenience and compactness, I define:

$$p = 1 + p',$$
$$g = 1 + g', \text{ and}$$
$$r = 1 + r'.$$

The rate of growth is real gross investment of g' per year and the rate of change in all prices of p' per year are incorporated into the model by defining the nominal amount of dollars which must be paid by the firm to acquire a project at the end of year j as $C_0^0 p^j g^j$. Since the project acquired by the firm at the end of year j is assumed to have the same real IRR as the first project acquired by the firm, the nominal cash flows of the project acquired by the firm at the end of year j are found by multiplying the appropriate nominal cash flows of the first project by the factor $p^j g^j$. Thus, the nominal cash flows of the project acquired at the end of year j can be represented as

$$(n+1)\text{-tuple } (C_0^0 p^j g^j,\ C_1^0 p^{j+1} g^j,\ C_2^0 p^{j+2} g^j, \ldots, C_n^0 p^{j+n} g^j).$$

It is assumed that all projects have the same real IRR, r'. Thus,

$$\sum_{i=0}^{n} (C_i^0 p^{j+i} g^j) p^{-i} r^{-i} = p^j g^j \sum_{i=0}^{n} C_i^0 r^{-i} = 0 \quad (1)$$

Equation (1) says that the present value of the price-level-adjusted cash flows of the project acquired at the end of year j (for any j) is a multiple of the present value of the price-level-adjusted cash flows of the project acquired at the end of year zero. Furthermore, the present value of all projects is equal to zero if the interest rate is r'.

Salamon [1973] used the above structure to develop a model of the relationship between the firm's IRR and the IRR of the firm's projects. In this paper, this structure is used to develop a model of the relationship between the firm's cash recovery rate and its IRR. This development begins by determining expressions for gross investment at the beginning of year $t(I_t)$ and for cash recoveries during year $t(R_t)$ for years $t \geq n$.

Under the conditions of the model, it can be shown that:

$$I_n = -C_0^0[1 + pg + (pg)^2 + \ldots + (pg)^{n-1}] = -C_0^0 \sum_{i=0}^{n-1} (pg)^i$$

If we define

$$S_{n-1} = \sum_{i=0}^{n-1} (pg)^i,$$

then

$$(pg)S_{n-1} = \sum_{i=0}^{n} (pg)^i.$$

Subtraction yields $(1-pg)S_{n-1} = 1-(pg)^n$ so that $S_{n-1} = (1-p^n g^n)/(1-pg)$. Therefore,

$$I_n = -C_0^0(1 - p^n g^n)/(1 - pg)$$

Furthermore, for any year $n+j (j \geq 0)$:

$$I_{n+j} = p^j g^j I_n.$$

Under the conditions of the model, it can also be shown that

$$\begin{aligned} R_n &= C_n^0 p^n + C_{n-1}^0 p^n g + C_{n-2}^0 p^n g^2 + \ldots + C_1^0 p^n g^{n-1} \\ &= p^n g^n [C_n^0 g^{-n} + C_{n-1}^0 g^{-n+1} + C_{n-2}^0 g^{-n+2} + \ldots + C_1^0 g^{-1}] \\ &= p^n g^n \sum_{i=0}^{n} C_i^0 g^{-i}. \end{aligned}$$

Furthermore, for any year $n+j (j \geq 0)$:

$$R_{n+j} = p^j g^j R_n.$$

Therefore, for any year $n+j (j \geq 0)$ the firm's cash recovery rate is a constant (ρ), which is given by:

$$\rho = \frac{R_{n+j}}{I_{n+j}} = \frac{R_n}{I_n} = \frac{(1 - pg) p^n g^n \sum_{i=1}^{n} C_i^0 g^{-i}}{(1 - p^n g^n)(-C_0^0)}$$

However, from Equation (1) we have that:

$$\sum_{i=0}^{n} C_i^0 r^{-i} = 0$$

so that

$$-C_0^0 = \sum_{i=1}^{n} C_i^0 r^{-i}.$$

Therefore, for $(n+j)(j \geq 0)$:

$$\rho = \frac{(1 - pg)p^n g^n \sum_{i=1}^{n} C_i^0 g^{-i}}{(1 - p^n g^n) \sum_{i=1}^{n} C_i^0 r^{-i}} \tag{2}$$

Equation (2) suggests that the firm's cash recovery rate is a function of p', g', n, r' and of the real cash inflows of the first project acquired by the firm. In other words, if we were to try to use Equation (2) to estimate a firm's IRR we would
170 have to have knowledge of the cash-flow pattern of the firm's projects as well as knowledge of p', g' n, and ρ.

Some relationships between the current model and the one developed by Ijiri can now be examined. If $g' = r'$ and $p' = 0$, then Equation (2) collapses into (recall that $p = 1 + p'$ and that $r = 1 + r'$):

$$\begin{aligned}\rho &= \frac{(1 - r)r^n}{(1 - r)^n} \\ &= \frac{-r'(1 + r')^n}{1 - (1 + r')^n} \\ &= r'/[1 - (1 + r')^{-n}] \qquad (3)\end{aligned}$$

which is what Ijiri terms the "capital recovery factor" [1979, p. 259]. In other words, in this case, the firm's cash recovery rate is simply the reciprocal of the present value of an ordinary annuity of \$1 for n years at an interest rate of r'. This means that the procedures which Ijiri followed for estimating an IRR would be appropriate if $g' = r'$ and $p' = 0$. In this special case, then, the firm's IRR could be estimated without specific knowledge of the cash-flow pattern of the firm's projects.

If $g' = r'$ but $p' \neq 0$, then Equation (2) collapses into:

$$\rho = \frac{(1 - pr)p^n r^n}{1 - p^n r^n}.$$

The right-hand side of this equation can be interpreted as the capital recovery factor associated with an interest rate of $r' + p' + r'p'$ (i.e., $(1 + r')(1 + p') - 1$) which is a nominal IRR rather than a common-dollar or real IRR. Thus, if a firm's growth rate were equal to the IRR of its projects, then the procedures followed by Ijiri would lead to an estimation of a nominal rather than a real IRR.

As mentioned above, Equation (2) requires specific knowledge of project cash flows in order to estimate a firm's IRR from knowledge of its cash recovery rate. A cash-flow pattern parameter (b) is now introduced in order to simplify the analytical model for purposes of empirical application. The cash-flow pattern parameter b is such that:

$$C_{j+1}^0 = b^j C_1^0 \quad \text{for } j = 0, 1, \ldots, n-1.$$

Thus, if $b = 1$ the real cash flows of the firm's projects are level, and if $b < 1 (> 1)$ the real cash flows of the firm's projects are declining (increasing). This means that:

$$\begin{aligned}\rho &= \frac{(1 - pg)p^n g^n \sum_{i=1}^{n} C_1^0 g^{-i} b^{i-1}}{(1 - p^n g^n) \sum_{i=1}^{n} C_1^0 r^{-i} b^{i-1}} \\ &= \left[\frac{(1 - pg)p^n g^n}{1 - p^n g^n}\right] \frac{\sum_{i=1}^{n} g^{-i} b^{i-1}}{\sum_{i=1}^{n} r^{-i} b^{i-1}}.\end{aligned}$$

The n_{th} order sums in the above expression can be simplified by using a technique similar to that used in the earlier derivation of the expression for I_n. This simplification leads to:

TABLE 1
FIRM-SPECIFIC PARAMETERS AND ESTIMATED RATES OF RETURN

					Internal Rates of Return					
					Useful Life = 20 years			*Useful Life = Estimated Life*		
						Cash Flow Pattern			*Cash Flow Pattern*	
Firm	*Estimated Useful Life (Years)*	*Real Growth Rate*	*Average Cash Recovery Rate 1972–1978*	*Average Accounting Rate of Return 1972–1978*	*Ijiri IRR(1)*	*Level (b = 1) IRR(2)*	*Declining (b = .8) IRR(3)*	*Ijiri IRR(4)*	*Level (b = 1) IRR(5)*	*Declining (b = .8) IRR(6)*
Alcoa	20.26	1.7%	8.4%	4.7%	5.6%	1.3%	0.9%	5.6%	1.4%	1.0%
American Brands	15.47	3.0	10.5	6.1	8.4	3.8	5.0	6.5	2.3	1.8
American Can	18.98	1.4	8.0	4.9	5.0	0.8	0.1	4.5	0.4	−0.5
Bethlehem Steel	24.75	0.3	6.9	3.1	3.3	−0.8	−2.0	4.6	0.4	0.6
Chrysler	26.21	4.0	7.7	1.2	4.5	0.7	−2.6	6.0	2.1	−0.7
DuPont	13.79	2.4	11.2	8.5	9.3	4.5	7.3	6.5	2.2	2.1
Esmark	18.04	1.9	11.2	4.8	9.3	4.4	7.8	8.7	4.0	6.4
General Electric	13.61	4.9	10.5	7.6	8.4	4.1	3.3	5.3	1.3	−0.9
General Foods	20.86	4.6	11.1	7.4	9.2	4.7	4.9	9.3	4.9	5.3
General Motors	19.02	3.0	14.3	10.4	13.1	7.6	14.1	12.8	7.5	13.4
Goodyear	18.87	4.4	8.0	4.4	5.0	1.1	−2.2	4.5	0.8	−2.7
Gulf	18.94	2.7	11.1	6.5	9.2	4.4	6.7	8.8	4.2	6.0
IBM	8.74	9.5	18.9	14.1	18.2	12.8	16.7	11.8	7.4	6.6
Int'l Harvester	23.22	1.2	8.2	4.3	5.3	1.0	0.8	6.1	1.7	2.6
Int'l Paper	21.75	3.4	11.3	7.1	9.4	4.7	6.5	9.8	5.0	7.4
RCA	8.76	5.5	13.5	4.8	12.1	7.3	9.5	3.5	−0.3	−2.3
Texaco	24.34	4.3	10.0	6.7	7.8	3.5	2.6	8.6	4.3	4.3
Untd Tech	15.69	6.4	9.0	5.7	6.4	2.6	−1.2	4.4	0.8	−3.2
U.S. Steel	31.62	−0.1	6.2	4.5	2.1	−1.8	−3.6	4.7	0.4	1.6
Westinghouse	19.29	3.1	7.1	4.8	3.6	−0.2	−3.5	3.3	−0.4	−3.9

Source: The firms and their average cash recovery rates over 1972–1978 are taken from Ijiri [1980, p. 56, Fig. II]. All other information is calculated per explanations in the text.

$$\rho = \left[\frac{(1 - pg)p^n g^n}{1 - p^n g^n}\right]\left[\frac{g^n - b^n}{g^n(g - b)}\right] \times \left[\frac{r^n(r - b)}{r^n - b^n}\right]. \tag{4}$$

The three separate terms within square brackets on the right-hand side of Equation (4) indicate that a firm's cash recovery rate is a function of (1) the relation between the inflation rate and the real growth rate in gross investment, (2) the relation between the growth rate in gross investment and the cash-flow pattern of firm projects, and (3) the relation between the cash-flow pattern of firm projects and the IRR of the firm. Additionally, the cash recovery rate is dependent on the useful life of firm projects.

In the next section of the paper, an application of this model to a group of firms is described.

Application of the Model: Background

Ijiri [1980] calculated the cash recovery rates of 20 firms for each of the years 1972–1978. The average of these annual recovery rates for each firm was then set equal to the capital recovery factor (as given in Equation (3)), and an estimate of the firm's IRR was derived assuming that each firm had projects with a useful life of 20 years. The firms, their average cash recovery rate, and their IRR as calculated by Ijiri (IRR(1)) from Equation (3) are reproduced along with other information in Table 1.[5] The basis for the other information in Table 1 is described below.

[5] In the model, which is discrete, the cash recovery rate is calculated by using gross investment at the beginning of the year, while in the empirical section the cash recovery rate is calculated by using average gross investment since for actual firms cash flows are approximately continuous. This is the procedure followed by Ijiri and

Under the assumed conditions of the current model, the average cash recovery rate for each firm should have been set equal to the right-hand side of Equation (4) rather than Equation (3). If this is done, estimates of p', g', and b (in addition to n) are needed before the resulting equation can be solved for each firm's IRR (r'). The overall inflation rate (p') and each firm's growth rate (g') should be estimated over reasonably long periods of time since the model developed in this paper is applicable only to a firm that has existed for at least as long as the useful life of its projects. The annual rate of change in prices was estimated by the
172 rate of change in the Consumer Price Index from 1959 to 1978 as reported in *Survey of Current Business: Business Statistics, 1979*. The annual rate of growth in real gross investment for each firm was based upon the change in the price-level-adjusted gross assets of the firm from 1959 to 1978. The information on the gross assets of each firm was obtained from COMPUSTAT tapes. In particular, the estimates of $p'(\hat{p}')$ and $g'(\hat{g}')$ were found as follows:

$$\hat{p}' = 1/19 \ln (\mathrm{CPI}_{78}/\mathrm{CPI}_{59}) = .042$$

$$\hat{g}' = 1/19 \ln \left(\frac{\mathrm{GA}_{78}}{\mathrm{CPI}_{78}} \Big/ \frac{\mathrm{GA}_{59}}{\mathrm{CPI}_{59}} \right)$$

where

CPI_{78} = the consumer price index at 12/31/78

CPI_{59} = the consumer price index at 12/31/59

GA_{78} = the gross assets of the firm on 12/31/78

GA_{59} = the gross assets of the firm on 12/31/59

The project cash-flow pattern parameter (b) is not so easily handled since there is very little publicly available information about the "typical" cash-flow pattern of the projects of actual firms. In order to determine how dependent the IRR estimation procedure is on this parameter, two different values for each firm have been examined: $b=1$ (level cash flows) and $b=.8$ (declining cash flows). This tactic, of course, only scratches the surface of this question since it may be true that different firms (or industries) would have projects with different typical cash flow patterns. Additional research on this issue is needed to refine the estimates of each firm's IRR.

The question of whether it is appropriate to use a single useful life for the projects of all firms also needs to be given consideration. An examination of an annuity present value table (which gives the reciprocals of the capital recovery factor of Equation (3)) reveals that firms with useful lives of less than 20 years will have their IRRs over-estimated and those with useful lives of greater than 20 will have their IRRs underestimated when all firms are assumed to have the same useful life of 20 years. Consequently, it may be appropriate to obtain an independent estimate of the useful life of the projects of each firm. A rough estimate of the useful life of firm projects was obtained for each firm by dividing the average of its gross plant for the year by its depreciation expense for the year (per COMPUSTAT tapes) for each year 1972 through 1978. The average of these annual estimates was used as the estimate ($\hat{n}$) of the life of each firm's projects (n).

The decisions made regarding the cash-flow pattern parameter and the treatment of the useful life of firm projects means that four different estimates of IRR are obtained for each firm by solving

---

allows the results of this paper to be compared with his. For purposes of consistency in the empirical section, growth rates and inflation rates are also estimated by assuming continuous rather than discrete compounding.

Equation (4). Table 1 displays the firms, the firm-specific parameters, the average accounting rate of return during the years 1972–1978, and the four IRRs based upon Equation (4). Table 1 also displays two different measures of IRR based upon Ijiri's procedures (i.e., by solving Equation (3)). One estimate assumes that all firms have projects with a composite useful life of 20 years (as did the original work of Ijiri), and the other estimate relies on the firm-specific estimate of project lives which was described earlier. When comparing the IRR estimates made by Ijiri to those IRR estimates based upon the model embodied in Equation (4), it is important to remember that Ijiri's estimates are nominal while those obtained by solving Equation (4) are real. Consequently, it is not surprising that Table 1 indicates that the IRR estimates associated with Equation (4) are uniformly lower than those of Ijiri given the inflation rate which existed in the economy over the relevant estimation period.[6]

Application of the Model: Analysis of Results

The levels of the profitability measures depicted in Table 1 are not nearly so important as is their degree of similarity or dissimilarity. Two questions are of interest:

1. How similar (dissimilar) are the accounting rate of return and the six IRR estimates?
2. How similar (dissimilar) are the IRR estimates of Ijiri and the IRR estimates based upon the model developed in this paper?

Analyzing the data associated with the first question will provide some preliminary evidence on whether results of prior economic studies that used an accounting rate of return as the measure of firm profitability would remain the same if the research was repeated using any of the IRR estimates which are given in Table 1. Analyzing the data associated with the second question will provide some information to guide future researchers when they are chosing a measure of firm profitability. Table 2 provides evidence on both of these questions.

The correlation coefficients given in the last line of Panel A of Table 2 indicate that there is a strong association between the accounting rate of return and each of the IRR estimates. However, the last line of Panel B of Table 2 indicates that, as a minimum, 30 percent of the variation in the accounting rate of return is explained by factors other than the IRR of firm projects (as measured by IRR(1) through IRR(6)). This level of unexplained variation suggests that more valid and powerful tests of economic hypotheses would result if profitability were measured by an IRR estimate rather than by the accounting rate of return. Thus, it may be appropriate for economists to repeat some of their prior studies that utilized accounting rates of return as the measure of a firm's rate of profit performance. Some preliminary guidance about which IRR estimate should be used as the profitability measure in these replications can be gained by further analysis of the information in Table 2.

If researchers are willing to view the firm as a composite project and assume that the projects of all firms have a common cash-flow pattern (either all level or all declining), then Table 2 suggests that the choice of which IRR estimate to use is most sensitive to the researchers' beliefs about project lives. All of the IRR estimates which assume a constant life of

[6] A reviewer of this paper has pointed out that Ijiri's estimates can easily be converted from nominal rate to reasonably accurate real rates by subtracting .042 from the nominal rates.

TABLE 2

PEARSON CORRELATION COEFFICIENTS AND PROPORTIONS OF UNEXPLAINED VARIANCE

A. Pearson Correlation Coefficients (C)

	Internal Rates of Return						*Average Accounting Rate of Return 1972–1978*
	Useful life = 20 years			*Useful Life = Estimated Life*			
		Cash Flow Pattern			*Cash Flow Pattern*		
	Ijiri	*Level (b = 1)*	*Declining (b = .8)*	*Ijiri*	*Level (b = 1)*	*Declining (b = .8)*	
	IRR(1)	*IRR(2)*	*IRR(3)*	*IRR(4)*	*IRR(5)*	*IRR(6)*	*ARR*
IRR(1)	1.000						
IRR(2)	.998	1.000					
IRR(3)	.968	.949	1.000				
IRR(4)	.717	.695	.776	1.000			
IRR(5)	.741	.725	.767	.996	1.000		
IRR(6)	.583	.543	.708	.942	.907	1.000	
ARR	.837	.836	.809	.715	.735	.587	1.000

B. Proportions of Unexplained Variance $(1 - C^2)$

	Internal Rates of Return						*Average Accounting Rate of Return 1972–1978*
	Useful life = 20 years			*Useful Life = Estimated Life*			
		Cash Flow Pattern			*Cash Flow Pattern*		
	Ijiri	*Level (b = 1)*	*Declining (b = .8)*	*Ijiri*	*Level (b = 1)*	*Declining (b = .8)*	
	IRR(1)	*IRR(2)*	*IRR(3)*	*IRR(4)*	*IRR(5)*	*IRR(6)*	*ARR*
IRR(1)	1.000						
IRR(2)	.004	.000					
IRR(3)	.063	.099	.000				
IRR(4)	.486	.517	.413	.000			
IRR(5)	.451	.474	.414	.008	.000		
IRR(6)	.660	.705	.499	.113	.177	.000	
ARR	.299	.301	.346	.489	.460	.655	1.000

20 years (IRR(1), IRR(2), and IRR(3) in Table 2) are very highly correlated, and all of the IRR estimates which rely on a firm-specific estimate of project life (IRR(4), IRR(5), IRR(6) in Table 2) are also highly correlated. Furthermore, the level of association between pairs of IRR measures that differ only on the useful life assumption (i.e., IRR(1)–IRR(4), IRR(2)–IRR(5), IRR(3)–IRR(6)) is much lower. This suggests that an assumption that all firms have projects with the same composite life reflects an inappropriate pattern of rate-of-return differences among firms if, as is probable, firms are composed of projects with different composite lives.

An examination of Table 2 for those

pairs of internal rates of return that differ only as to the level of the cash flow pattern parameter (i.e., IRR (2) and IRR(3) or IRR(5) and IRR(6)) suggests that a ranking of a set of firms by their IRRs would be largely unaffected by whether the IRR was calculated assuming level cash flows or declining cash flows. For example, the correlation coefficient of IRR(2), which assumes the firm is composed of projects whose cash flows are level, and IRR(3), which assumes the firm is composed of projects whose cash flows are declining, is .968. This suggests that the results of future empirical work on firm profitability may be insensitive to the level of the estimate of the cash-flow pattern parameter as long as it can be assumed that the cash-flow pattern parameters of the projects of all firms are about the same. This very preliminary observation is comforting because the cash-flow pattern parameter is a nuisance parameter in empirical work given the absence of information on typical cash-flow patterns for projects. The assumption that different firms have projects with similar cash-flow patterns may not be inappropriate given the widespread use of accelerated depreciation for tax purposes and the sometimes expressed concern of management for liquidity[7] (i.e., typical cash-flow patterns are likely to be declining). However, it is also true that the particular rate of decline may differ systematically across firms. Thus, future research on cash flow patterns is appropriate and would enhance our ability to obtain refined estimates of a firm's IRR from knowledge of its cash recovery rate.

Conclusions and Suggestions for Future Research

In the late 1960s and early 1970s, a literature developed which addressed the relationship between a firm's accounting rate of return and its IRR. The goal of that research was to specify the relationship between the firm's accounting rate of return and its IRR so that interested parties could adjust the known accounting rate of return to obtain an estimate of the unknown IRR. This research was abandoned because the relationship between the accounting rate of return and the IRR depended on so many factors that an adjustment of the accounting rate of return of a real firm was simply not a practical procedure for finding an estimate of its IRR. In retrospect, it is obvious that the complexity of the relationship between a firm's accounting rate of return and its IRR is due to the fact that the firm's accounting rate of return is influenced by so many factors besides the profit rate of firm projects. Ijiri has shown that if a measure of a firm's IRR is desired it can be obtained by analyzing a model of the relationship between the IRR and the firm's cash recovery rate rather than by analyzing a model of the relationship between the IRR and the firm's accounting rate of return.

This paper has extended the work of Ijiri by building a model of the relationship between a firm's cash recovery rate and its IRR when the firm operates in an inflationary environment and does not reinvest all of its cash flows. This paper has shown that an evaluation of firms by their accounting rates of return is different than an evaluation by any of the IRRs which were calculated. This finding has strong implications for the results of prior studies of firm profitability that have relied on accounting rates of return. This paper has demonstrated that estimated IRRs are sensitive to the assump-

[7] The popularity of the payback method in practice suggests that managers are concerned with liquidity as well as profitability. The payback method has a tendency to favor projects with cash flows that are large in the project's initial years.

tions that researchers must make about the useful life of firm projects. In addition, the results reported in this paper suggest that research on the cash-flow pattern of firm projects is needed if refined IRR estimates are to be obtained.

The analytical model described in this paper made several assumptions about the firm and its environment. The model assumed that the firm invested in projects that had the same useful lives, cash-flow patterns, and IRRs. It is, of course, true that firms invest in a variety of projects with different lives, cash-flow patterns, and IRRs. Ijiri [1979, p. 261] has observed, however, that if the mix of
176 such projects is reasonably stable over time then the firm may be thought of as a composite project with a given life and cash-flow pattern. The stable project mix assumption may be a reasonable one for large, mature firms since for such firms the impact of new ventures would seem to be relatively small in many cases.

The model also assumed that investment growth rates and inflation rates[8] were constant. The impact of relaxing either or both of these assumptions on the results of this paper is unclear. One possible avenue for future research would be to determine the impact of cyclical investment expenditures on the relationship between cash recovery rates and internal rates of return (perhaps via a simulation).[9]

It is clear that additional work is needed on the relationship between a firm's cash recovery rate and its internal rate of return in environments more complex than that considered in this paper. However, it is also clear that we are closer than ever before to having an empirical measure of the profit performances of firms which is directly linked to a discounted cash-flow rate of return. This should be welcome news to economists and other parties who are interested in a theoretically more defensible measure of firm profitability than the accounting rate or return.

[8] The model assumes an environment of certainty. The model thus avoids addressing any issues associated with differences between actual and expected inflation rates.

[9] Livingstone [1969] incorporated a cyclical investment function for firms in a study of the tax allocation issue.

REFERENCES

Harcourt, G. C., "The Accountant in a Golden Age," *Oxford Economic Papers* (March 1965), pp. 66–80.

Ijiri, Y., "Cash-Flow Accounting and Its Structure," *Journal of Accounting, Auditing, and Finance* (Summer 1978) pp. 331–348.

———, "Convergence of Cash Recovery Rate," *Quantitative Planning and Control*, Edited by Y. Ijiri and A. Whinston (New York: Academic Press, Inc., 1979), pp. 259–267.

———, "Recovery Rate and Cash Flow Accounting," *Financial Executive* (March 1980) pp. 54–60.

Kay, J. A., "Accountants, Too, Could be Happy in a Golden Age: The Accountants Rate of Profit and The Internal Rate of Return," *Oxford Economic Papers* (November 1976) pp. 447–460.

Livingstone, J. L., "Accelerated Depreciation, Tax Allocation, and Cyclical Asset Expenditures of Large Manufacturing Companies," *Journal of Accounting Research* (Autumn 1969) pp. 245–256.

———, and G. L. Salamon, "Relationship between the Accounting and the Internal Rate of Return Measures: A Synthesis and an Analysis," *Journal of Accounting Research* (Autumn 1970), pp. 199–216.

Salamon, G. L., "Models of the Relationship Between the Accounting and Internal Rate of Return: An Examination of the Methodology," *Journal of Accounting Research* (Autumn 1973) pp. 296–303.

Solomon, E., "Return on Investment: The Relation of Book-Yield to True Yield," *Research in Accounting Measurement*, Edited by R. K. Jaedicke, Y. Ijiri, and O. Nielsen (Menasha, Wisconsin: American Accounting Association, 1966) pp. 232–244.

Stauffer, T. R., "The Measurement of Corporate Rates of Return: A Generalized Formulation," *The Bell Journal of Economics and Management Science* (Autumn 1971) pp. 434–469.

Wright, F. K., "Accounting Rate of Profit and Internal Rate of Return," *Oxford Economic Papers* (November 1978) pp. 464–468.

SOME FORMAL CONNECTIONS BETWEEN ECONOMIC VALUES AND YIELDS AND ACCOUNTING NUMBERS

K.V. Peasnell*

Introduction

Textbooks and articles too numerous to mention caution against attempting to derive the economic value of a firm or investment by means of discounting future accounting profit numbers. Similarly, accountants and economists have long recognised the dangers of imputing economic significance to accounting profit rates. The conventional wisdom is summed up in the following recent statement by Appleyard (1980, p.543): "Indeed, it is well known that (conventionally measured) accounting income cannot be related to a firm's capital stock in a simple way". The purpose of the present article is to show how both a firm's economic value and its economic yield can be derived from accounting numbers in a very simple fashion.

Many of the following results have appeared previously in the literature, but they are scattered over different books and journals, and over long periods of time, and have been derived from different models employing different assumptions, and with varying degrees of rigour. Scarce wonder, then, that even careful researchers, such as Appleyard, should often overlook them. Of course, it is widely recognised (e.g. see Bierman and Schmidt, 1980, ch.21, or Brealey and Myers, 1981, ch.12), that when economic depreciation methods are used to compute accounting income then the discounted present value of the resultant income stream is equal to the sum of discounted cash flows. But it is less generally appreciated that this is a special case, that there are an *infinite* number of income measures, employing any kind of depreciation methods one cares to select, which can be discounted (after simple adjustment) to provide an economic value of magnitude equal to that obtained by discounting cash flows.

The results reported here are of general applicability. The most important assumption employed is the conventional one that cash flows (and hence accounting incomes) occur at the end of each period; but a "period" can in theory be made as long or as short as one desires – a year, a week, an hour. Far from being restrictive, it is of almost general applicability. No assumptions are made about whether one is valuing the firm as a whole, an identifiable project, or the incremental effect of a particular course of action. The general level of prices is assumed to remain constant throughout – but this is merely for expositional convenience.

**The author is Wolfson Professor of Accounting and Finance at the University of Lancaster. An earlier version of this paper was presented at the Northern Accounting Group, Birmingham University, on the 24th September 1981; thanks are due to the discussant Tony Appleyard and to the participants for their helpful comments. The paper has also benefited from the constructive criticisms of Tony Steele, Charles Ward, Ivey Papps and Bill Fung. (Paper received June 1981, revised March 1982)*

The Equation of Value

Consider the conventional neoclassical economic approach to asset valuation. A forecast is made of future benefits resulting from ownership of the asset, "dividends" (net of new capital) over the "planning horizon" (or project life, if shorter); these dividends are discounted at rate(s) appropriate to their futurity and riskiness. In conventional algebraic form, asset value is

$$V_o = \sum_{t=1}^{N} v_t C_t + v_N R_N \quad \ldots\ldots \quad (1)$$

where C_t is the dividend expected in period t; v_t is the present value of £1 to be received t periods hence,

178 $$v_t = \frac{1}{(1+i_1)\ (1+i_2)\ .\ .\ .\ (1+i_t)}, \quad \ldots\ldots \quad (2)$$

and i_1, i_2, ..., are the one-period opportunity cost rates|specified at t=o.[1] R_N is either the liquidating receipt or a valuation at horizon date N of the capital stock, depending on the circumstances.

The economic valuation model represented by equation (1) is based on a theory of human action: acquire the asset if the value of holding is greater than its sacrifice value (C_o). The excess net present value (NPV) is the measure of the net benefit of ownership:

$$NPV = V_o - C_o = \sum_{t=1}^{N} v_t C_t + v_N R_N - C_o \quad \ldots\ldots \quad (3)$$

C_o is the buying or selling price of the firm as a whole, or its constituent assets, depending on the circumstances.

Accounting profit is defined for the purposes of this paper as follows:

Accounting Identity 1. Accounting profit is equal to net dividends (C_t) paid plus the change in the net book value of the firm's assets ($A_t - A_{t-1}$) during the period:

$$P_t \equiv C_t + (A_t - A_{t-1}) \quad \ldots\ldots \quad (4)$$

Notice that in this definition accounting profit is of the all-inclusive or "clean surplus" variety: all prior-year adjustments, extraordinary items and asset re-valution surpluses are passed through the profit and loss account. Hence, here all Current Cost Accounting (ACC) holding gains and losses are deemed to affect the (accounting) value of the enterprise and must be included in profit.

The following points concerning the Equation of Value and the Accounting Identity are worth noting before proceeding:

(i) The Equation of Value is cast in the form of the expected dividend-capitalisation model, but it is of much wider applicability than this implies.[2] In addition to valuing (all or some of) the firm's equity shares, obviously the model can be adapted to the valuation of all the firm's securities (by defining dividends to include interest payments and discounting at the weighted cost of capital or all-equity rate). Less obviously, the model can be used in the valuation of individual projects of the firm: here C_t is the net cash flow from the project, i.e. the payout the (shareholder-wealth-maximising) management *could* make to owners. (This is nothing other than the irrelevance of dividends separation theorem of Modigliani and Miller in unconventional guise.)

(ii) The variables C_t, P_t ($t=1, 2, \ldots, N$) and R_N will be most commonly employed as ex ante magnitudes (i.e. projections) and can be thought of as mathematical expectations of underlying random variables. However, on occasion it might be useful to work with ex post values; in other words, to compute the lifetime accounting earnings and the hindsight present 179
value (or realised internal rate of return) in order to see in retrospect how well the firm or project performed (e.g. as in Hansen, 1977). The propositions which follow hold for both ex ante and ex post appraisals.

(iii) No restriction is placed on the sign or magnitude of NPV in equation (3), except that NPV $\geqslant$ o is implied in decisions to buy or continue holding an asset; strict equality (i.e. NPV = o) is neither required nor ruled out. Of course, in an ex ante asset choice setting, if NPV $\neq$ o then there are difficulties in viewing the discount rates i_t as equilibrium rates or equation (1) as an equilibrium capital asset pricing model. However, this is a cloud which hangs over all the capital budgeting literature at present, as Findlay and Williams (1979) point out. The present paper is "traditional" in the sense that no assumptions concerning the existence or absence of (partial or general) equilibrium – or associated institutional considerations such as transaction costs, arbitrage opportunities and heterogeneity of expectations – are embodied in the fundamental valuation model.

(iv) The analysis is a conventional, purely static, one, in the sense that no allowance is made for the possibility of discount rates changing at a later date. Similarly, all specific price changes are as envisaged at t=o.

(v) The accounting profit identity (4) is defined to be consistent with the measure of cash flow payoff C_t employed in the fundamental equation of value (1). If the objective is to value the equity shares of the firm, the C_t will be the dividends (per share), and profit (per share) will be the profit attributable to equity shareholders, i.e. after deduction of interest and tax. On the other hand, if the decision is whether or not to accept a project, and the valuation is to be made on the basis of operating cash flows, profit can be defined in like fashion; profit and related assets are specified as project-generated increments to the firm's total profits and book assets.

Armed with the definition of accounting profit it is a simple matter to spell out the relationship between net present value and accounting profits in completely general form.

Theorem 1. Suppose accounting profit P_t is defined according to Accounting Identity 1.

Then

$$NPV = \sum_{t=1}^{N} v_t (P_t - i_t A_{t-1}) + (E_N - E_o) \quad \ldots (5)$$

where

$$E_N = v_N (R_N - A_N) \quad \ldots (6)$$

180 $$E_o = C_o - A_o \quad \ldots (7)$$

In other words, NPV is equal to the sum of discounted excess income plus the difference of discounted accounting capital valuation errors.

Proof. Rearrange equation (3) so that cash-flow is written as a function of profit plus the change in book value.

$$C_t = P_t + A_{t-1} - A_t \quad \ldots (8)$$

and substitute into equation (3):

$$NPV = \sum_{t=1}^{N} v_t (P_t + A_{t-1} - A_t) + v_N R_N - C_o$$

$$= \sum_{t=1}^{N} v_t P_t + \sum_{t=1}^{N} v_t A_{t-1} - \sum_{t=1}^{N} v_t A_t + v_N R_N - C_o$$

$$= \sum_{t=1}^{N} v_t P_t + \sum_{t=1}^{N} v_t A_{t-1} - \sum_{t=o}^{N-1} v_t A_t + v_N (R_N - A_N) - (C_o - A_o)$$

$$= \sum_{t=1}^{N} v_t P_t + \sum_{t=1}^{N} (v_t - v_{t-1}) A_{t-1} + (E_N - E_o) .$$

As $v_t - v_{t-1} = -i_t v_t$,

$$NPV = \sum_{t=1}^{N} v_t (P_t - i_t A_{t-1}) + (E_N - E_o) \quad \ldots (9)$$

The proof is complete.

Comparing equations (3) and (5), it can be seen that a discounted cash flow stream has been replaced by a special kind of discounted incomes stream (plus a valuation error term). Income is defined not as conventional accounting profit but as the excess of accounting profit over (a measure of) the opportunity cost of capital invested in the business.

The error term $E_N - E_o$ in (5) warrants comment. It is a "plug", in the sense that without the term the relationship between accounting profits and economic value will not hold; but it is not just a number designed to force the relationship to hold. The error is the difference between two valuations at two (and only two) points in time. One can go further. Only when the valuation employs a limited time slice of the life history of the asset will either error arise at all. In a capital budgeting exercise, there will be no opening valuation error (i.e. $E_o = o$) because C_o, the initial project outlay, will be recorded in the opening balance sheet; similarly, at the end of the project's life the book value of project assets will be written down to scrap value (i.e. $A_N = R_N$). See Peasnell (1981).[3]

A special result suggests itself immediately:

Corollary 1. Let $E_N = E_o$. 181

Then

$$NPV = \sum_{t=1}^{N} v_t (P_t - i_t A_{t-1}) \quad \ldots \ldots \quad (10)$$

The proof is trivial.

NPV is now a function of excess incomes alone. Notice that the requirement that $E_N = E_o$ is a weaker one than the requirement that there be no valuation differences, i.e. that $A_N = R_N$ and $A_o = C_o$. All that is necessary is that the valuation errors grow over the complete planning horizon at the (geometric) mean rate of discount: intermediate patterns of valuation errors are of no consequence.

The excess-income variable shown on the right-hand-side of equation (9) entered the management accounting literature as "residual income"; i.e. Tomkins (1973). But it has been widely argued there that residual income can be dis counted to a present value as in equation (10) only if "economic depreciation" is employed. However, examination of equation (10) indicates that no such restriction is necessary; *any* depreciation method will do.

It has long been known, of course, that when assets are recorded in the books at "economic value" (in other words, depreciated by the appropriate "economic" method) then the resultant income numbers can be discounted *without adjustment* to arrive at the theoretically correct present value. See for example Lee (1980) or Revsine (1973) for simple mathematical and numerical demonstrations of this point. There are a number of possibilities the most important of which are summarised in the following result.

Corollary 2. Let book value be equal to the discounted present value of cash flows. In other words, let

$$A_t = \sum_{j=t+1}^{N} (v_j / v_t) C_j + (v_N / v_t) A_N \quad \ldots \ldots \quad (11)$$

(i) Then NPV = $P_o = A_o - C_o$ and $P_t = i_t A_{t-1}$ for all t=1,2, . . . , N.

(ii)Let $C_1 = P_1$, $C_2 = P_2, \ldots, C_n = P_N$. Given that i_t can be defined over all possible future periods, then

$$V_o = \sum_{t=1}^{\infty} v_t P_t \qquad (12)$$

(iii) Let $i_1 = i_2 = \ldots = i_N = r$ where r is the Internal Rate of Return (IRR), i.e. is a rate which ensures that NPV = 0. Then

$$P_o = A_o - C_o = 0 \text{ and } P_t = rA_{t-1} \text{ for all } t=1, \ldots, N.$$

Proof. The proof of (i) is in two parts. Equations (11) and (1) together imply that $A_o = V_o$. This is a necessary condition for NPV = $P_o = A_o - C_o$ to hold. A sufficient condition is that $E_N = 0$ and $P_t = i_t A_{t-1}$ for all t . $E_N = 0$ by

assumption. Recall the definition of P_o given in Identity 1:

$$P_t \equiv C_t + (A_t - A_{t-1}) \qquad (4)$$

Given equation (11), A_t can be written as

$$A_t = A_{t-1}(1+i_t) - C_t$$

which when substituted into (4) yields

$$P_t = i_t A_{t-1}$$

as required. Part (iii) of the corollary follows immediately.

Proof of part (ii) is a very simple matter. By hypothesis $C_t = P_t$ for all t . So equation (1) can be rewritten immediately as

$$V_o = \sum_{t=1}^{N} v_t P_t + v_N A_N \qquad (1a)$$

Substituting the accounting value formula equation (11) hypothesised in the corollary up to a more distant horizon M-N periods hence (M>N), and substituting again for P_t, yields.

$$V_o = \sum_{t=1}^{M} v_t P_t + v_M A_M \qquad (1b)$$

and when $M \to \infty$, (1b) becomes

$$V_o = \sum_{t=1}^{\infty} v_t P_t$$

as required. Q.E.D.

The same result can be recovered from equation (5), which is to be expected given that (5) was derived from (1). The proof is not therefore given.

The central result of this section of the paper is given in Theorem 1. *Any* measure of profit consistent with Accounting Identity 1 can be incorporated in an economic valuation model. All the conventional "economic income" results can be recovered as special cases. The importance of beginning and ending accounting valuations and the nature of the errors they can induce is clearly brought out in the theorem.

Accounting Rates of Return

Accounting rates of return define a discount function which can be used, formally speaking, in the same fashion as the IRR. This little appreciated result is shown below.

Accounting Identity 2. Let accounting profit P_t be defined according to Accounting Identity 1. The accounting rate of return (ARR) of a period is equal to the ratio of the accounting profit of the period to the book value of assets at the beginning of the period:

183

$$a_t \equiv \frac{P_t}{A_{t-1}} \quad \ldots \ldots \quad (13)$$

There are other definitions of ARR, of course, but this one is of central importance to the following result.

Theorem 2. Let ARR be defined according to Accounting Identity 2. Suppose there are no opening or closing accounting valuation errors; in other words, let $A_0 = C_0$ and $A_N = R_N$. Let

$$v_t^* = \frac{1}{(1+a_1)\ (1+a_2) \ldots (1+a_t)} \quad \ldots \ldots \quad (14)$$

define an accounting discount function. Then the present value of cash flows C_t (t=1, . . . , N) and R_N discounted at the ARRs (that is to say, "priced" at v_t^*) is exactly equal to the initial sacrifice value of the capital stock ($V_0 = C_0$):

$$C_0 = \sum_{t=1}^{N} v_t^*\ C_t + v_N^*\ R_N \quad \ldots \ldots \quad (15)$$

Proof. We proceed by the method of induction. Suppose N=1. By hypothesis v_t^* is a discount function, so we can interpret a_1 as a rate at which funds A_0 can be "invested" (in an accounting sense) to "yield" $A_0\ (1+a_1)$. More precisely, Accounting Identity 1 can be rearranged to yield

$$A_0 + P_1 \equiv C_1 + A_1 \quad \ldots \ldots \quad (16)$$

and from Accounting Identity 2 profit can be written as

$$P_1 \equiv a_1\ A_0$$

and substituted into (16):

$$A_0\ (1+a_1) \equiv C_1 + A_1.$$

Hence, $A_0 = v_1^* C_1 + v_1^* A_1$, as required. Next, assume that Theorem 2 is true for N-1 (N>2). Therefore by hypothesis we know that the following is true:

$$C_0 = \sum_{t=1}^{N-1} v_t^* \; C_t + v_{N-1}^* \; A_{N-1} \quad \ldots\ldots\ldots\ldots\ldots\ldots\ldots (17)$$

Proceeding as before,

$$A_{N-1} + P_N \equiv C_N + R_N ,$$

$$A_{N-1} \, (1+a_N) \equiv C_N + R_N ,$$

so

$$A_{N-1} = (v_N^*/v_{N-1}^*) \, (C_N + R_N) .$$

Substituting into equation (17) yields equation (15). Q.E.D.

184

Substantially the same result is obtained by Kay (1976) using a continuous-time framework and the integral calculus.

It is widely presumed in the accounting and economics literatures that, for the most part in practice, ARRs are artifacts without economic significance. From a formal point of view, of course, Theorem 2 shows that ARRs are the direct accounting analogues of market rates of interest. In a centrally planned economy ARRs can be used in the same way that interest rates are used in a market economy. In a sense, this is the function ARRs often serve at present in the internal management control systems of large divisionalised companies operating in capitalist economies. In which case the v* function can be viewed as "accounting prices"; the ARRs influence and determine the economic actions of subordinates in "accounting markets" because the ARRs are principals of direct interest to the actors rather than surrogates of "true yields" or unobserved market rates.

Viewed from a more conventional angle, it is clear that ARRs can be of direct economic interest when asset stocks are priced at current market prices. The most straightforward case is where profit is defined in Accounting Identity 1 as net dividends plus the change in net resale values of assets. Profit, here, is measured from the base-line of the revenue foregone by not selling the asset at the beginning of the period, the firm having left open the possibility of selling at the end instead. So ARR here has a clear action-meaning. See Chambers (1966) for elaboration. When book values of assets are shown at second-hand replacement cost the action-meaning is not so obvious, but has been articulated at some length by Bell and Johnson (1979).

The surrogate properties of the ARR function v* have received a great deal of attention in the literature. See Harcourt (1965), Solomon and Laya (1966) and Stauffer (1971) for examples of the difficulties researchers have encountered in using ARRs as surrogates of IRR. Theorem 2 immediately suggests a special result (which arises again in a different form in the next section) that is entirely independent of the basis of accounting asset valuation:

Corollary 3. Suppose there are no opening and closing valuation errors and ARR is defined as in Accounting Identity 2. Let $a_1 = a_2 = \ldots = a_N = a$ (a constant). Then the constant ARR is equal to the IRR.

Proof. The IRR is defined as a constant rate of discount such that $V_0 = C_0$. Given the hypothesis concerning v^*, equation (15) then defines such a rate. Q.E.D.

Of course, it cannot generally be assumed that ARR remains constant through time. Equation (15) suggests no generally applicable function of the ARRs which can be used to estimate IRR. But two special results are worth noting. For convenience where appropriate in the remainder of this paper IRR is written as r.

Corollary 4. Suppose $C_1 = C_2 = \ldots = C_N = 0$. Then one plus the IRR is 185
equal to the geometric mean of the compounded return obtained by investing at the IRRs; in other words,

$$1+r = \left\{ \prod_{t=1}^{N} (1 + a_t) \right\}^{1/N} \qquad (18)$$

Proof. An immediate consequence of the hypothesis and Corollary 3 is

$$v_N = \frac{1}{(1+r)^N} = \frac{1}{(1+a_1)\,(1+a_2)\,\ldots\,(1+a_N)}.$$

The N-th root of the reciprocal gives the desired result.

Corollary 5. Suppose $C_1 = C_2 = \ldots = C_N = C \neq 0$. Suppose R_N is finite for all N and $v_t^* N = 0$ in the limit $N \rightarrow \infty$.

$$r = \frac{1}{\sum_{t=1}^{\infty} v_t^*} \qquad (19)$$

Proof. From equation (15) we can write

$$\sum_{t=1}^{N} v_t^* \; C_t + v_N^* \; R_N = \sum_{t=1}^{N} v^t \; C_t + v^N \; R_N$$

where $v = (1+r)^{-1}$. As by hypothesis $C_1 = C_2 = \ldots = C_N = C$, this can be re-written

$$C\sum_{t=1}^{N} v_t^* + v_N^* \; R_N = C(1-v^N)\,/\,r + v^N \; R_N.$$

When $N \rightarrow \infty$, $v_N^* \; R_N = v^N \; R_N = 0$. Thus

$$\sum_{t=1}^{\infty} v_t^* = \frac{1}{r}$$

thereby proving the theorem.

Deriving Economic Yields

The IRR can be derived from an ARR time-series by a somewhat different route.

Theorem 3. Let ARR be defined according to Accounting Identity 2 and the IRR discount function be written $v = (1+r)^{-1}$. Then the IRR is equal to a linear weighted sum of ARRs plus a proportion of the accounting valuation error:

$$r = \sum_{t=1}^{N} w_t a_t + E \quad \text{.......... (20)}$$

where

$$w_t = \frac{v^{t-1} A_{t-1}}{\sum_{j=o}^{N-1} v^j A_j} \quad \text{.......... (21)}$$

$$\sum_{t=1}^{N} w_t = 1 \quad \text{.......... (22)}$$

$$E = \frac{E_N - E_o}{\sum_{j=1}^{N} v^j A_{j-1}} \quad \text{.......... (23)}$$

Proof. We proceed by using the result in Theorem 1. Set $v_t = v^t$ and $i_t = r$ for all t and NPV = 0:

$$NPV = \sum_{t=1}^{N} v^t (P_t - rA_{t-1}) + (E_N - E_o) = 0.$$

Rearranging,

$$r = \frac{\sum_{t=1}^{N} v^t P_t}{\sum_{t=1}^{N} v^t A_{t-1}} + \frac{E_N - E_o}{\sum_{t=1}^{N} v^t A_{t-1}}$$

and noting that $P_t = a_t A_{t-1}$, we obtain

$$r = \frac{\sum_{t=1}^{N} a_t (v^t A_{t-1})}{\sum_{t=1}^{N} v^t A_{t-1}} + \frac{E_N - E_o}{\sum_{t=1}^{N} v^t A_{t-1}}$$

Equations (20) – (23) follow immediately

In the special case where the accounting valuation errors are offsetting, $E_N = E_o$, then IRR is a straightforward linear weighted sum of ARRs:

$$r = \sum_{t=1}^{N} w_t \; a_t \quad \ldots\ldots (20a)$$

187

Then the IRR can be obtained from a time-series of ARRs by solving r in (20a), noting that r also appears in the right-hand of (21), through v in w_t (hence the solution must be obtained by numerical methods).

Theorem 3 suggests an alternative proof of Corollary 3. The proof is as follows. Suppose $a_1 = a_2 = \ldots = a_N = a$ (a constant), as is hypothesised in the corollary. Then substitution into (20a) yields

$$r = \sum_{t=1}^{N} w_t \; a$$

$$= a \sum_{t=1}^{N} w_t$$

$$= a$$

because $\Sigma\, w_t = 1$. Thus IRR equals the constant ARR, as required.

The IRR is defined to be constant throughout the investment holding period whereas ARRs can and do vary through time. Perhaps the most obvious way of utilising a time-series of ARRs in practice is to take a simple arithmetic average of them and to treat the result as a proxy for the (constant) IRR. The following result provides sufficient conditions for such an average to give an accurate estimate of the IRR.

Corollary 6. Let $E_N = E_o$. Suppose the book value of the firm's assets grows through time at a constant rate equal to the IRR. Then the IRR is equal to the mean ARR; in other words,

$$r = \frac{1}{N} \sum_{t=1}^{N} a_t \quad \ldots\ldots (24)$$

Proof. Let g be the constant rate of growth in book value. Then $A_t = A_o (1+g)^t$ for t=1, . . ., N. Therefore the weight w_t in (21) can be written as

$$w_t = \frac{v^{t-1}\ A_o (1+g)^{t-1}}{\sum_{j=0}^{N-1} v^j\ A_o\ (1+g)^j}$$

$$= \frac{\{(1+g)\ /\ (1+r)\}^t}{\sum_{j=1}^{N} \{(1+g) / (1+r)\}^j} \qquad (25)$$

But if g=r, then (25) reduces to $w_t = \frac{1}{N}$ for all t. Substitution in (20a) completes the proof.

It is interesting to compare the result in Corollary 6 with that in Corollary 4. In Corollary 6, given a constant book growth rate equal to the IRR, the IRR is equal to the arithmetic mean of the ARRs. In Corollary 4, given that the liquidating payoff is the only non-zero cash flow, one plus the IRR is equal to the geometric mean of one plus the ARRs. In this context, an extension of Corollary 4 is worth noting.

Corollary 7. Let $E_N = E_o$. Suppose $C_1 = C_2 = \ldots = C_N = 0$.
Let

$$\dot{r} = \log_e (1+r)$$

and

$$\dot{a} = \log_e (1+a_t)$$

be the continuously compounded IRR and the continuously compounded ARR in period t, respectively. Then the continuous IRR is equal to the arithmetic mean of the continuous ARRs; in other words,

$$\dot{r} = \frac{1}{N} \sum_{t=1}^{N} \dot{a}_t \qquad (26)$$

Proof. Follows immediately from Corollary 4.

Of course, the requirement that there be only one cash flow, the final one, makes Corollary 7 of limited practical value. Corollary 6 is a different kettle of fish. But the requirement that not only must book value grow at a rate that is (completely) constant through time but be (exactly) equal to the IRR, is restrictive. It would be helpful to have some indication about which ARRs to pay the most attention to when the growth rate is not equal to the IRR. This is provided by the next result.

Corollary 8. Let $E_N = E_o$. Suppose the book value of the firm's assets grows at a constant rate. Then if the constant rate of growth is less than the IRR, the IRR is more closely related to earlier ARRs than to later ones; conversely, if the constant growth rate is more than the IRR, the IRR is more closely related to later ARRs than to earlier ones.

Proof. Using eqution (25), the ratio of successive period's weights is

$$\frac{w_{t+1}}{w_t} = \frac{1+g}{1+r} \quad \ldots\ldots\ldots\ldots\ldots\ldots\ldots\ldots\ldots\ldots (27)$$

So, when $g<r$ then $w_{t+1}/w_t<1$, implying that the weights decrease from period 189
to period. This would result in successive ARRS being less heavily weighted with the passage of time. On the other hand, if $g>r$ then $w_{t+1}/w_t>1$ and the weights increase through time resulting in increasing influence of later ARRs. Q.E.D.

Unfortunately, there is no way of putting these results to simple, practical use. Ideally, one would like to know when a simple average of ARRs, $\frac{1}{N}\Sigma a_t$, is likely to yield an underestimate or overestimate of IRR. Of course, it is easy enough to determine whether or not book values are growing at a (roughly) constant rate; the difficulty resides in not knowing whether or not the growth rate thus measured is greater than, equal to, or less than the IRR.

Equation (20a) provides an elegant and simple link between accounting and economic measures of return. The IRR is shown to be a linear sum of ARRs. But sight should not be lost of the fact that the general relationship is given by equation (20) and this shows that there is a valuation error term which needs to be kept firmly in mind. The error term has been the subject of an exchange between Wright (1978) and Kay (1978). The following results provide some insights into the nature of the problem.

Corollary 9. Let the book value of the firm's assets grow at a constant rate. Suppose the ratio of the book value of the assets to their market value is constant through time. Then the accounting error is constant for all $N \geq 1$ and is of amount

$$E = \left[\frac{C_o - A_o}{A_o}\right](g-r) \quad \ldots\ldots\ldots\ldots\ldots\ldots\ldots\ldots\ldots (28)$$

Further, when the asset growth rate is zero the IRR is proportional to a linear weighted sum of ARRs:

$$r = (A_o / C_o) \sum_{t=1}^{N} w_t \, a_t \quad \ldots\ldots\ldots\ldots\ldots\ldots\ldots\ldots (29)$$

Proof. Consider equations (6), (7) and (23). By hypothesis the ratio of book value to market value is a constant and can be written as:

$$C_o/A_o = R_N/A_N = \lambda .$$

Hence market values can be written as proportional to book values:

$$C_o = \lambda A_o \text{ and } R_N = \lambda A_N .$$

Thus,

$$E_N - E_o = v^N (R_N - A_N) - (C_o - A_o)$$

$$= (\lambda - 1)(v^N A_N - A_o)$$

190 $$= (\lambda - 1) A_o [\{(1+g)/(1+r)\}^N - 1] \quad \ldots\ldots\ldots\ldots (30)$$

given that $A_N = A_o (1+g)^N$ by assumption. Now consider the denominator of equation (23):

$$\sum_{j=1}^{N} v^j A_{j-1} = \sum_{j=1}^{N} v^j A_o (1+g)^{j-1}$$

$$= A_o \left[\frac{\{(1+g)/(1+r)\}^N - 1}{g-r} \right] \quad \ldots\ldots\ldots\ldots (31)$$

Substituting (30) and (31) back into (23) yields

$$E = (\lambda - 1)(g-r)$$

$$= \left[\frac{C_o - A_o}{A_o} \right] (g-r)$$

as required. The second part of the corollary is obtained by setting g=o in equation (28), substituting the resultant expression for E back into (20) and rearranging terms. Q.E.D.

Corollary 10. Let the book value of the firm's assets grow at a constant rate. Suppose the difference between the book value of the assets and their market value is constant through time.

(i) Suppose the growth rate is less than the IRR. Then in the limit $N \to \infty$ the accounting error is constant,

$$E = \left[\frac{C_o - A_o}{A_o} \right] (g-r) \quad \ldots\ldots\ldots\ldots (32)$$

and the IRR is proportional to a linear weighted sum of ARRs:

$$r = (A_o / C_o) \sum_{t=1}^{N} w_t a_t \quad \ldots\ldots\ldots\ldots\ldots\ldots \quad (33)$$

(ii) Suppose the growth rate is greater than or equal to the IRR. Then in the limit $N \to \infty$ the accounting error disappears, i.e.

$$E = 0 \quad \ldots\ldots\ldots\ldots\ldots\ldots\ldots\ldots\ldots\ldots \quad (34)$$

Proof. Consider equation (23). By hypothesis the numerator is

$$E_N - E_o = v^N (R_N \quad A_N) - (C_o - A_o)$$

$$= (v^N - 1)(C_o - A_o) \quad \ldots\ldots\ldots\ldots\ldots\ldots \quad (35)$$

191

The denominator of (23) can be written as in equation (31). Substituting (35) and (31) into (23) yields

$$E = \left[\frac{C_o - A_o}{A_o}\right]\left[\frac{(1+r)^{-N} - 1}{\{(1+g)/(1+r)\}^N - 1}\right](g - r) \quad \ldots\ldots\ldots \quad (36)$$

As $N \to \infty$ $(1+r)^{-N} \to 0$. If $g < r$, $\{(1+g)/(1+r)\}^N \to 0$ as $N \to \infty$.
As E is exactly equal to equation (28) in Corollary 9, equation (33) follows immediately. This proves part (i) of the corollary.

Turning to part (ii), if $g > r$, then $\{(1+g)/(1+r)\}^N \to \infty$ as $N \to \infty$. Hence $E = 0$ as $N \to \infty$, as required. Next, rewrite equation (36) as

$$E = \frac{f(g)}{h(g)}$$

where

$$f(g) = \left[\frac{C_o - A_o}{A_o}\right]\{(1+r)^{-N} - 1\} \quad (g+r)$$

and

$$h(g) = \{(1+g)/(1+r)\}^N - 1.$$

When $g = r$, then $f(g) = h(g) = 0$; in which case $E = f(g) / h(g) = 0/0$ which is undefined. However, provided the first derivative of $h(g)$ with respect to g (i.e. $h'(g)$) is non-zero, the limiting value of E when g approaches r can be obtained from l'Hospital's Rule:

$$\lim_{g \to r} \frac{f(g)}{h(g)} = \lim_{g \to r} \frac{f'(g)}{h'(g)}$$

$$= \lim_{g \to r} \left[\frac{\{(C_o - A_o) / A_o\} \; \{(1+r)^{-N} - 1\}}{N(1+g)^{N-1} / (1+r)^N} \right]$$

$$= \left[\frac{C_o - A_o}{A_o} \right] \left[\frac{1}{N} (1+g) \; \{(1+r)^{-N} - 1\} \right]$$

Hence $E \to O$ as $N \to \infty$.Q.E.D.

Corollary 9 is true for all values of N whereas Corollary 10 is a special result that holds only for very long periods of time (as $N \to \infty$).

192 **A Numerical Example**

A lot of attention has been devoted to the error terms in equations (5) and (20), and properly so. However, sight should not be lost of the fact that these errors do not arise in one very important application area, the appraisal of corporate projects (e.g. decisions to buy or replace capital assets). Moreover, this is an area where the use of accounting numbers (alongside, in competition with, even to the exclusion of the economic measures) has persisted to an extent which has both surprised and frustrated many financial theorists. Brealey and Myers (1981, pp.248-249) offer the following explanation:

> "Much of the pressure for good book earnings comes from the top management. Chief executives have good reasons to shoot for good short-run earnings. Probably their bonus depends on it. The market watches current earnings per share (partly because it isn't allowed to look over top management's shoulder at the 5-year plan). Is it surprising that top management does not always jump happily into high-NPV projects that will depress next year's earnings per share?"

Their solution is to urge businessmen to pay less attention to accounting messages.

An additional explanation for the importance which firms seem to attach to accounting profits might be that executives at all levels are simply more familiar with them, given that accounting earnings figures are used for a variety of purposes within and without enterprises. The "functional fixation" aspect of the problem needs to be reckoned with. To the extent that cash-flow capital budgeting measures appear to managers to be incapable of being arithmetically reconciled with the now familiar accounting measures, then there is a danger that they will not receive the attention they deserve. In these circumstances, there is a lot to be said for presenting the project data in a manner such that the arithmetical connections with accounting profits is made obvious.[4]

How this might be done can best be seen via a numerical example. A firm is contemplating buying a machine for an initial outlay of £10,000. The projected cash flow benefits to the firm are a level £2,296 each year for six years. Investors in the company expect to earn 8 per cent each year. The project is acceptable, because it has a positive NPV (=£614); also the project offers the prospect of a yield greater than the opportunity cost of capital (IRR = 10% > 8%).

Consider the impact the project is expected to have on accounting earnings of the firm. Depreciation is calculated on a straight-line basis assuming zero scrap value. Historical cost (HC) profit is therefore a level £2296–1667 = £629 per year. Replacement prices of the asset are expected to grow at 4 per cent per annum. CCA operating profits and revaluation surpluses can be computed for the project along the lines now required of British companies according to SSAP 16 (ASC, 1980). It is assumed that for CCA purposes assets are also depreciated straight-line over 6 years.

All three ways of assessing the project's worth – economic value and yield, HC profits, CCA profits and surplus – can be reconciled in one schedule for 193
presentation to management. Such a schedule, based on the data of the example, is set out in Table 1.

A number of features of the table are worthy of attention. Managers can see at a glance how the project affects reported income over the years. The "adjusted income" figures show whether or not enough profits are generated to cover costs of capital, taking one year with another.[5] If adjusted income is positive every year then the project is attractive – it must have a positive NPV. This is a useful property of adjusted income. Adjusted income is arguably a more intuitively understandable concept than is NPV.

The table shows the time-pattern of accounting profit rates. The weights indicate the overall importance to be attached to one accounting rate compared to another. For example, the year six HCA rate is six times as large as the comparable year one rate, but its overall importance (in terms of "impact" on IRR) is but a tenth of year one's. Also, everything can be viewed the other way round: IRR can be thought of – explained to managers – as a weighted average of accounting rates. In this context, it is helpful to bear in mind that IRR must fall somewhere within the range of accounting rates, i.e. it is at least as large as the smallest and no greater than the largest accounting rate (Peasnell 1982). In this particular example, one can see at a glance from the CCA rates that the IRR must be somewhere between 9.62% and 13.21%; the HCA rates are less informative, for the possible spread is 6.29%–37.78%.[6]

The example is a simple one. But the approach can be applied to much more complicated situations. In the present example, the differences between the cash flows and the profit numbers are associated with the machine. However, no new principles are involved if complications such as taxation, changes in working capital (inventory buildups and run downs, debtors, creditors, accruals), and geared financing are introduced. In all cases, excess income figures can be computed and used as substitutes for cash flows: they can be used even in the calculation of betas (Peasnell, 1981).

TABLE 1

EXAMPLE OF PROJECTED CASH FLOWS AND ACCOUNTING RESULTS

Cash Flow Results	YEARLY PAYOFFS							NPV	
	0	1	2	3	4	5	6	8%	IRR
	–10,000	2,296	2,296	2,296	2,296	2,296	2,296	614	10%
Historical Cost Profit Results									
Profit before depreciation		2,296	2,296	2,296	2,296	2,296	2,296		
less: depreciation		1,667	1,667	1,667	1,667	1,667	1,667		
Net profit		629	629	629	629	629	629		
less: cost of (HCA) capital 8%		800	667	533	400	267	133		
Adjusted income		(171)	(38)	96	229	362	496	614	
HCA rate of profit		6.29%	7.55%	9.44%	12.58%	18.88%	37.78%		10%
Weights for averaging profit rates		.332	.251	.183	.125	.075	.034		
Current Cost Profit Results									
Profit on historical cost basis		629	629	629	629	629	629		
less: depreciation adjustment		67	136	208	283	361	442		
Current cost profit		562	493	421	346	268	187		
add: increase in current costreserve		400	348	289	225	156	81		
Total gains		962	841	710	571	424	268		
less: cost of (CCA) capital 8%		800	693	577	450	312	162		
Adjusted income		162	148	133	121	112	106	614	
CCA rate of profit		9.62%	9.78%	9.85%	10.15%	10.87%	13.21%		10%
Weights for averaging profit rates		.288	.227	.251	.121	.077	.036		

In working with CCA data it is essential to define profits not as current cost profit but as total gains; in other words, movements on current cost reserve must be added to current cost profit to arrive at total gains or "business income" (as Edwards and Bell label it). Complications such as "monetary working capital" and "gearing" adjustments present no difficulties. The former is a deduction and the latter an addition in arriving at current cost profit; they are respectively added to and deducted from revaluation surpluses in the computation of movements on current cost reserve. Both adjustments net out in the business income figure.

Concluding Remarks

This paper pulls together into a common analytical framework a number of results concerning the mathematical connections between the conventional economic concepts of value and yield and accounting models of profit and return. The results are presented in a formal theorem-and-proof format, not 195
because the difficulty of the mathematics involved is sufficiently great as to justify such a treatment (the contrary is the case), but in order to emphasise the analytical character of the relationships. More conventional presentations, emphasising particular economic concepts and accounting principles, tend to obscure the important fact that the relationships are essentially formal or mathematical in character. It is to be hoped that one benefit of a formal treatment of the subject will be to dispel the idea, commonplace in the literature, that only a limited class of models of accounting profit and value are "admissible" in the sense of being consistent with (i.e. discountable to) conventional economic value and providing reliable proxies for IRR.

Of greater practical importance is the opportunity which widespread knowledge of these formal connections makes possible for tidying up corporate financial planning. It is a simple matter to tie together financial statement projections and economic measures of value. There is reason to hope that doing so might reduce functional fixation with accounting numbers.

Examination of Corollary 1 reveals that any all-inclusive measure of profit (suitably adjusted) can be discounted back to economic value. Hence the choice of profit concept must depend on other factors. For example, the choice could depend on the predictive value of the profit time-series, or on the indications which the accounting signals provide of the firm's adaptive capacity. Theorem 1 pinpoints the impact that opening and closing differences between the accounting and economic asset valuations can have on the model. The extent of these are dependent on (a) choice of accounting models and (b) the decision problem to hand. In capital budgeting the errors are of no importance at all.

Results are presented indicating the mathematical connections between accounting and economic yields. Again, the relationships hold regardless of the profit construct employed. Whether or not accounting yields have any economic significance outside of this mathematical relationship with the IRR depends on the accounting model involved. Notwithstanding the suggestion of Brief et al. (1980) to the contrary, it is difficult to assign economic significance to accounting yields except either (a) as surrogate measures of IRR or (b) when they are defined in terms of entry-or exit-market process. But this is another story.

NOTES

[1] Alternatively, if C_t is the certainty-equivalent of the expected dividend, rather than expected value, then i_t is the one-period riskless rate of interest.

[2] The expected dividend-capitalisation model is shown by Garman & Ohlson (1980) to be a specialisation of a wider class of valuation models. The requirements for it to serve as an equilibrium capital asset pricing model are: (a) that future dividends be sufficient to specify alternative future states of nature; (b) that the covariation between the random element in dividend growth and economy-wide variables, conditional on previous period's dividends, is a constant.

[3] For earlier derivations of this result see Edwards and Bell (1961) and Edwards (1978, 1980). The idea of deducting a cost of capital charge from profit has a long pedigree; for an exhaustive review of the very early literature see Wells (1978).

[4] A stronger case can be made for using accounting profits data if profits and book values are based on exit-prices of the resources employed on the project. See Peasnell (1981).

[5] Caution needs to be exercised in interpreting the capital charges, because interest is charged on accountants' valuations of capital stock. Only if assets are valued at exit-prices can the charges be given an ambiguous opportunity cost interpretation (Peasnell, 1981, p.65).

[6] No claim is made here that, in general, CCA rates display less variation than do HCA ones.

REFERENCES

Accounting Standards Committee (1980), *Statement of Standard Accounting Practice No. 16: Current Cost Accounting.*

Appleyard, A.R. (1980), "Takeovers: Accounting Policy, Financial Policy and the Case Against Accounting Measures of Performance", *Journal of Business Finance and Accounting* (Winter 1980), pp.541-554.

Bell, P.W. and L.T. Johnson (1979), "Current Value Accounting and the Simple Production Case: Edbejo and Other Companies in the Taxi Business", in R.R. Sterling and A.L. Thomas (eds.), *Accounting for a Simplified Firm Owning Depreciable Assets* (Scholars Book Co., 1979), pp.95-130.

Bierman, H. and S. Smidt (1980), *The Capital Budgeting Decision*, 5th edn. (Macmillan).

Brealey, R. and S. Myers (1981), *Principles of Corporate Finance,* (McGraw-Hill).

Brief, R.P., B. Merino and J. Weiss (1980), "Cumulative Financial Statements", *Accounting Review* (July 1980), pp.480-490.

Chambers, R.J. (1966), *Accounting, Evaluation and Economic Behavior* (Prentice-Hall, 1969).

Edwards, E.O. and P.W. Bell (1961), *The Theory and Measurement of Business Income* (University of California Press, 1961).

Edwards, E.O. (1978), "The Primacy of Accounting Income in Decisions on Expansion: An Exercise in Arithmetic", in C. van Dam (ed.), *Trends in Managerial and Financial Accounting* (Martinus Nijhoff, 1978), pp.45-62.

——— (1980), "The Fundamental Character of Excess Income", *Accounting and Business Research* (Autumn 1980), pp.375-384.

Findlay, M.C. and E.E. Willaims (1979), "Owners' Surplus, the Marginal Efficiency of Capital and Market Equilibrium", *Journal of Business Finance and Accounting* (Spring 1979), pp.17-36.

Garman, M.B. and J.A. Ohlson, "Information and the Sequential Valuation of Assets in Arbitrage-Free Economies", *Journal of Accounting Research* (Autumn 1980), pp. 420-440.

Hansen, P. (1977), "The Accounting Theory of Profit: An Analysis Based on Material from Practice", in W.T. Baxter and S. Davidson (eds.), *Studies in Accounting*, 3rd edn. (Institute of Chartered Accountants in England and Wales), pp.156-167.

Harcourt, G.C. (1965), "The Accountant in a Golden Age", *Oxford Economic Papers* (1965), reprinted in R.H. Parker and G.C. Harcourt (eds.), *Readings in the Concept and Measurement of Income* (Cambridge University Press, 1969), pp.310-325. 197

Kay, J.A. (1976), "Accountants, Too, Could be Happy in a Golden Age: The Accountant's Rate of Profit and the Internal Rate of Return", *Oxford Economic Papers* (November 1976), pp.447-460.

——— (1978), "Accounting Rate of Profit and Internal Rate of Return: A Reply", *Oxford Economic Papers* (November 1978), pp.469-470.

Lee, T.A. (1980), *Income and Value Measurement: Theory and Practice*, 2nd edn. (Thos. Nelson, 1981).

Peasnell, K.V. (1981), "On Capital Budgeting and Income Measurement", *Abacus*, (June 1981), pp.52-67.

——— (1982), "Estimating the Internal Rate of Return from Accounting Profit Rates," *Invesment Analyst* (April 1982), pp.26-31.

Revsine, L. (1973), *Replacement Cost Accounting* (Prentice-Hall, 1973).

Solomon, E. and J.C. Layà (1966), "Measurement of Company Profitability: Some Systematic Errors in the Accounting Rate of Return", in A.A. Robichek (ed.), *Financial Research and Its Implications for Management Decisions* (Wiley, 1966).

Stauffer, T.R. (1971), "The Measurement of Corporate Rates of Return: A Generalised Formulation", *Bell Journal of Economics and Management Science* (Autumn 1971), pp.434-469.

Tomkins, C. (1973), *Financial Planning in Divisionalised Companies* (Accountancy Age Books).

Wells, M.C. (1978), *Accounting for Common Costs* (University of Illinois, 1978).

Wright, F.K. (1978), "Accounting Rate of Profit and Internal Rate of Return", *Oxford Economic Papers* (November 1978), pp.464-468.

Journal of Business Finance & Accounting, 12(3), Autumn 1985, 0306 686X $2.50

LIMITATIONS OF USING THE CASH RECOVERY RATE TO ESTIMATE THE IRR: A NOTE

R.P. Brief*

A recent paper by Luckett (1984) reviewed the 25 or so years of writing on the problem of using the accounting rate of return (ARR) to estimate the internal rate of return (IRR). His conclusions were 'not heartening for researchers' (p. 229). All of the estimation methods discussed to date, with one possible exception, have important practical limitations.

The exception is a method, first devised by Ijiri (1978) and then elaborated 199
on by Salamon (1982), which derives the estimate of the IRR from the cash recovery rate (CRR) and other information about the firm. Although Luckett did not actually analyze this method in his survey, he commented that this new approach to the problem (hereafter, the CRR method) 'potentially brings some hope'(p. 229).

This conjecture about the potential of the CRR method, which at least partly reflects Salamon's optimistic conclusion (1982, p. 302), is too sanguine. The CRR method is based on a restrictive set of assumptions which limit its practical usefulness. The purpose of this note is to review these assumptions and their implications in order to explain the limitations of the CRR method.

ASSUMPTIONS UNDERLYING THE CRR METHOD

The CRR method (Salamon, 1982) is based on a model which has the same structure as one developed by Salamon in 1973. It assumes that a firm is a collection of projects that differ only in scale. Every project has the same life of n years, cash flow profile and IRR; and cash flows in any year during the life of a project are assumed to be related to cash flows in the first year by a cash flow profile parameter, b.

The initial project is acquired in year zero which is 'arbitrarily designated' (Salamon, 1973, p. 297). Since a constant growth rate of gross investment, g', and a constant growth rate of prices, p', are assumed, everything in the model is linked to the initial project, i.e., the project acquired in year zero.

* The author is Professor of Business Statistics and Accounting at New York University. (Paper received October 1984)

The critical analytical result is that the cash recovery rate in any year $n+j$, where $j \geqslant 0$, is a constant and a function of five parameters: g', p', b, n and IRR (Salamon, 1982, p. 297). Letting $1+g' = g$, $1+p' = p$ and IRR $+ 1 = r$, Salamon showed that

$$\mathrm{CRR} = \left[\frac{(1-pg)p^n g^n}{1-p^n g^n}\right]\left[\frac{g^n - b^n}{g^n(g-b)}\right]\left[\frac{r^n(r-b)}{r^n - b^n}\right]. \tag{1}$$

Therefore, the IRR is derived by estimating p, g, n, b and CRR and solving equation (1) for r.

The most important implication of the assumptions underlying the derivation of equation (1) is that after period n, cash flows, D_{n+j}, grow indefinitely at a constant rate of growth (Salamon, 1973, p. 298). That is,

$$D_{n+j} = p^j g^j D_n, \text{ where } j = 0, 1, 2, \ldots \tag{2}$$

200

Since equation (2) specifies a firm's future cash flows and since historical cash flows can be calculated, the CRR method, in effect, assumes that the firm's entire stream of cash flows is 'known.' Therefore, as an alternative to the CRR method, the IRR can be determined in the more usual way directly from the firm's cash flows.[1] In comparison to the CRR method, the direct method does not require data about a project's life, n. Nor does it require information about a project's cash flow profile.

The CRR method requires that the estimate of the IRR must be made at least n years after year zero. The year that the initial project is acquired. Therefore, the estimate of the IRR must relate to a multiperiod time horizon that begins no later than n years ago and that ends when the firm winds up. Consequently, since all projects are assumed to be homogenous from year zero until the firm liquidates, the projects before year zero might be different than those after year zero. In this case, the direct IRR calculation gives an average of the IRRs of the different kinds of projects. In comparison, an estimate of the IRR based on equation (1) would relate only to the class of projects acquired after year zero.

LIMITATIONS OF THE CRR METHOD

Information about a firm's past and future cash flows is needed to estimate the IRR, but some researchers have questioned whether such information even exists.

> The economic rate of return is difficult – perhaps impossible – to compute for entire firms. Doing so requires information about both the past and the future which outside observers do not have, if it exists at all (Fisher and McGowan, 1983, pp. 90–91).

Others, like Luckett, point out that estimates of future cash flows are 'highly subjective' (p. 223) and, in the case of a going concern, 'the analysis can only be undertaken if special assumptions are made about the cash flow enabling it to be treated as a perpetuity, and this will limit the analysis in practical cases' (p. 227).

The problem of predicting future cash flows is not dealt with explicitly in the derivation of the CRR method. Instead, the prediction model is embedded in the assumptions underlying the method. These assumptions imply that after year *n* when the steady state is reached, a firm's cash flows will grow indefinitely at a constant annual growth rate of *pg* as equation (2) shows. Since the CRR method was devised as a general method of estimating a firm's IRR, its usefulness depends on whether or not the environment reflects these assumptions thereby giving the prediction model in equation (2) external validity.

This issue of external validity has not been addressed. Until it is the CRR method has no justification. Furthermore, since the growth of firms is variable and difficult to predict, it is not likely that such empirical work, even if undertaken, will conclude that the assumptions underlying the CRR method correspond to the real world. As Malkiel (1963, p. 1027) pointed out there is 'an uncomfortably large degree of indeterminacy' in economic models of this kind. For this reason, the potential of the CRR method is in doubt.

NOTES

1 Stark (1982) pointed out that the method developed by Kay (1976) to estimate the IRR also was an alternative to the direct calculation. Thus, Luckett's suggestion (p. 213, p. 221) that Kay's method can be used in the *absence* of cash flow information is not, strictly speaking, correct. Unless cash flows can be derived from a firm's financial statements, neither Kay's algorithm nor a direct calculation is possible (Stark, 1982, pp. 524–524).

REFERENCES

Fisher, F.M. and J.J. McGowan (1983), 'On the Misuse of Accounting Rates of Return to Infer Monopoly Profits,' *American Economic Review* (March 1983), pp. 82–97.

Ijiri, Y. (1978), 'Cash-Flow Accounting and Its Structure,' *Journal of Accounting, Auditing & Finance* (Summer 1978), pp. 331–348.

Kay, J.M. (1976), 'Accountants, Too, Could be Happy in a Golden Age: The Accountant's Rate of Profit and the Internal Rate of Return,' *Oxford Economic* Papers (November 1976), pp. 447–460.

Luckett, P.F. (1984), 'ARR vs. IRR: A Review and Analysis,' *Journal of Business Finance & Accounting* (Summer 1984), pp. 213–232.

Malkiel, B.G. (1963), 'Equity Yields and Structure of Share Prices,' *American Economic Review* (December 1963), pp. 1004–1031.

Salamon, Gerald L. (1973), 'Models of the Relationship Between the Accounting and Internal Rate of Return,' *Journal of Accounting Research* (Autumn 1973), pp. 296–303.

______ (1982), 'Cash Recovery Rates and Measures of Firm Profitability,' *The Accounting Review* (April 1982), pp. 292–302.

Stark, A.W. (1982), 'Estimating the Internal Rate of Return from Accounting Data – A Note,' *Oxford Economic Papers* (November 1982), pp. 520–525.

Accounting Books Published by Garland

New Books

Ashton, Robert H., ed. *The Evolution of Behavioral Accounting Research: An Overview.* New York, 1984.

Ashton, Robert H., ed. *Some Early Contributions to the Study of Audit Judgment.* New York, 1984.

*Brief, Richard P., ed. *Corporate Financial Reporting and Analysis in the Early 1900s.* New York, 1986.

Brief, Richard P., ed. *Depreciation and Capital Maintenance.* New York, 1984.

*Brief, Richard P., ed. *Estimating the Economic Rate of Return from Accounting Data.* New York, 1986.

Brief, Richard P., ed. *Four Classics on the Theory of Double-Entry Bookkeeping.* New York, 1982.

*Chambers, R. J., and G. W. Dean, eds. *Chambers on Accounting.* New York, 1986.
Volume I: Accounting, Management and Finance.
Volume II: Accounting Practice and Education.
Volume III: Accounting Theory and Research.
Volume IV: Price Variation Accounting.
Volume V: Continuously Contemporary Accounting.

Clarke, F. L. *The Tangled Web of Price Variation Accounting: The Development of Ideas Underlying Professional Prescriptions in Six Countries.* New York, 1982.

Coopers & Lybrand. *The Early History of Coopers & Lybrand.* New York, 1984.

*Included in the Garland series Accounting Thought and Practice Through the Years.

*Craswell, Allen. *Audit Qualifications in Australia 1950 to 1979.* New York, 1986.

Dean, G. W., and M. C. Wells, eds. *The Case for Continuously Contemporary Accounting.* New York, 1984.

Dean, G. W., and M. C. Wells, eds. *Forerunners of Realizable Values Accounting in Financial Reporting.* New York, 1982.

Edey, Harold C. *Accounting Queries.* New York, 1982.

*Edwards, J. R., ed. *Legal Regulation of British Company Accounts 1836–1900.* New York, 1986.

*Edwards, J. R., ed. *Reporting Fixed Assets in Nineteenth-Century Company Accounts.* New York, 1986.

Edwards, J. R., ed. *Studies of Company Records: 1830–1974.* New York, 1984.

Fabricant, Solomon. *Studies in Social and Private Accounting.* New York, 1982.

Gaffikin, Michael, and Michael Aitken, eds. *The Development of Accounting Theory: Significant Contributors to Accounting Thought in the 20th Century.* New York, 1982.

Hawawini, Gabriel A., ed. *Bond Duration and Immunization: Early Developments and Recent Contributions.* New York, 1982.

Hawawini, Gabriel, and Pierre Michel, eds. *European Equity Markets: Risk, Return, and Efficiency.* New York, 1984.

*Hawawini, Gabriel, and Pierre A. Michel. *Mandatory Financial Information and Capital Market Equilibrium in Belgium.* New York, 1986.

*Hawkins, David F. *Corporate Financial Disclosure, 1900–1933: A Study of Management Inertia within a Rapidly Changing Environment.* New York, 1986.

*Johnson, H. Thomas. *A New Approach to Management Accounting History* New York, 1986.

*Kinney, William R., Jr., ed. *Fifty Years of Statistical Auditing.* New York, 1986.

Klemstine, Charles E., and Michael W. Maher. *Management Accounting Research: A Review and Annotated Bibliography.* New York, 1984.

*Lee, T. A., ed. *A Scottish Contribution to Accounting History.* New York, 1986.

*Lee, T. A. *Towards a Theory and Practice of Cash Flow Accounting.* New York, 1986.

Lee, Thomas A., ed. *Transactions of the Chartered Accountants Students' Societies of Edinburgh and Glasgow: A Selection of Writings, 1886–1958.* New York, 1984.

*McKinnon, Jill L. *The Historical Development and Operational Form of Corporate Reporting Regulation in Japan.* New York, 1986.

Nobes, Christopher, ed. *The Development of Double Entry: Selected Essays.* New York, 1984.

*Nobes, Christopher. *Issues in International Accounting.* New York, 1986.

*Parker, Lee D. *Developing Control Concepts in the 20th Century.* New York, 1986.

Parker, R. H. *Papers on Accounting History.* New York, 1984.

*Previts, Gary John, and Alfred R. Roberts, eds. *Federal Securities Law and Accounting 1933–1970; Selected Addresses.* New York, 1986.

*Reid, Jean Margo, ed. *Law and Accounting: Pre-1889 British Legal Cases.* New York, 1986.

Sheldahl, Terry K. *Beta Alpha Psi, from Alpha to Omega: Pursuing a Vision of Professional Education for Accountants, 1919–1945.* New York, 1982.

*Sheldahl, Terry K. *Beta Alpha Psi, from Omega to Zeta Omega: The Making of a Comprehensive Accounting Fraternity, 1946–1984.* New York, 1986.

Solomons, David. *Collected Papers on Accounting and Accounting Education.* New York, 1984.

Sprague, Charles F. *The General Principles of the Science of Accounts and the Accountancy of Investment.* New York, 1984.

Stamp, Edward. *Selected Papers on Accounting, Auditing, and Professional Problems.* New York, 1984.

*Storrar, Colin, ed. *The Accountant's Magazine—An Anthology.* New York, 1986.

Tantral, Panadda. *Accounting Literature in Non-Accounting Journals: An Annotated Bibliography.* New York, 1984.

*Vangermeersch, Richard, ed. *The Contributions of Alexander Hamilton Church to Accounting and Management.* New York, 1986.

*Vangermeersch, Richard, ed. *Financial Accounting Milestones in the Annual Reports of United States Steel Corporation—The First Seven Decades.* New York, 1986.

Whitmore, John. *Factory Accounts.* New York, 1984.

Yamey, Basil S. *Further Essays on the History of Accounting.* New York, 1982.

Zeff, Stephen A., ed. *The Accounting Postulates and Principles Controversy of the 1960s.* New York, 1982.

Zeff, Stephen A., ed. *Accounting Principles Through the Years: The Views of Professional and Academic Leaders 1938–1954.* New York, 1982.

Zeff, Stephen A., and Maurice Moonitz, eds. *Sourcebook on Accounting Principles and Auditing Procedures: 1917–1953 (in two volumes).* New York, 1984.

Reprinted Titles

American Institute of Accountants. *Fiftieth Anniversary Celebration.* Chicago, 1963 (Garland reprint, 1982).

American Institute of Accountants. *Library Catalogue.* New York, 1937 (Garland reprint, 1982).

Arthur Andersen Company. *The First Fifty Years 1913–1963.* Chicago, 1963 (Garland reprint, 1984).

*Bevis, Herman W. *Corporate Financial Reporting in a Competitive Economy.* New York, 1965 (Garland reprint, 1986).

*Bonini, Charles P., Robert K. Jaedicke, and Harvey M. Wagner, eds. *Management Controls: New Directions in Basic Research.* New York, 1964 (Garland reprint, 1986).

Bray, F. Sewell. *Four Essays in Accounting Theory.* London, 1953. *Bound with* Institute of Chartered Accountants in England and Wales and the National Institute of Economic and Social Research. *Some Accounting Terms and Concepts.* Cambridge, 1951 (Garland reprint, 1982).

Brown, R. Gene, and Kenneth S. Johnston. *Paciolo on Accounting.* New York, 1963 (Garland reprint, 1984).

*Carey, John L., and William O. Doherty, eds. *Ethical Standards of the Accounting Profession.* New York, 1966 (Garland reprint, 1986).

Chambers, R. J. *Accounting in Disarray.* Melbourne, 1973 (Garland reprint, 1982).

Cooper, Ernest. *Fifty-seven Years in an Accountant's Office. See* Sir Russell Kettle.

Couchman, Charles B. *The Balance-Sheet.* New York, 1924 (Garland reprint, 1982).

Couper, Charles Tennant. *Report of the Trial . . . Against the Directors and Manager of the City of Glasgow Bank.* Edinburgh, 1879 (Garland reprint, 1984).

Cutforth, Arthur E. *Audits.* London, 1906 (Garland reprint, 1982).

Cutforth, Arthur E. *Methods of Amalgamation.* London, 1926 (Garland reprint, 1982).

Deinzer, Harvey T. *Development of Accounting Thought.* New York, 1965 (Garland reprint, 1984).

De Paula, F.R.M. *The Principles of Auditing.* London, 1915 (Garland reprint, 1984).

Dickerson, R. W. *Accountants and the Law of Negligence.* Toronto, 1966 (Garland reprint, 1982).

Dodson, James. *The Accountant, or, the Method of Bookkeeping Deduced from Clear Principles, and Illustrated by a Variety of Examples.* London, 1750 (Garland reprint, 1984).

Dyer, S. *A Common Sense Method of Double Entry Bookkeeping, on First Principles, as Suggested by De Morgan. Part I, Theoretical.* London, 1897 (Garland reprint, 1984).

*_The Fifth International Congress on Accounting, 1938 {Kongress-Archiv 1938 des V. Internationalen Prüfungs- und Treuhand-Kongresses}_. Berlin, 1938 (Garland reprint, 1986).

Finney, H. A. _Consolidated Statements_. New York, 1922 (Garland reprint, 1982).

Fisher, Irving. _The Rate of Interest_. New York, 1907 (Garland reprint, 1982).

Florence, P. Sargant. _Economics of Fatigue of Unrest and the Efficiency of Labour in English and American Industry_. London, 1923 (Garland reprint, 1984).

Fourth International Congress on Accounting 1933. London, 1933 (Garland reprint, 1982).

Foye, Arthur B. _Haskins & Sells: Our First Seventy-Five Years_. New York, 1970 (Garland reprint, 1984).

Garnsey, Sir Gilbert. _Holding Companies and Their Published Accounts_. London, 1923. _Bound with_ Sir Gilbert Garnsey. _Limitations of a Balance Sheet_. London, 1928 (Garland reprint, 1982).

Garrett, A. A. _The History of the Society of Incorporated Accountants, 1885–1957_. Oxford, 1961 (Garland reprint, 1984).

Gilman, Stephen. _Accounting Concepts of Profit_. New York, 1939 (Garland reprint, 1982).

*Gordon, William. _The Universal Accountant, and Complete Merchant . . ._ [Volume II]. Edinburgh, 1765 (Garland reprint, 1986).

*Green, Wilmer. _History and Survey of Accountancy_. Brooklyn, 1930 (Garland reprint, 1986).

Hamilton, Robert. _An Introduction to Merchandise, Parts IV and V (Italian Bookkeeping and Practical Bookkeeping)_. Edinburgh, 1788 (Garland reprint, 1982).

Hatton, Edward. _The Merchant's Magazine: or, Trades-man's Treasury_. London, 1695 (Garland reprint, 1982).

Hills, George S. _The Law of Accounting and Financial Statements_. Boston, 1957 (Garland reprint, 1982).

*A *History of Cooper Brothers & Co. 1854 to 1954*. London, 1954 (Garland reprint, 1986).

Hofstede, Geert. *The Game of Budget Control*. Assen, 1967 (Garland reprint, 1984).

Howitt, Sir Harold. *The History of The Institute of Chartered Accountants in England and Wales 1880–1965, and of Its Founder Accountancy Bodies 1870–1880*. London, 1966 (Garland reprint, 1984).

Institute of Chartered Accountants in England and Wales and The National Institute of Economic and Social Research. *Some Accounting Terms and Concepts*. *See* F. Sewell Bray.

Institute of Chartered Accountants of Scotland. *History of the Chartered Accountants of Scotland from the Earliest Times to 1954*. Edinburgh, 1954 (Garland reprint, 1984).

International Congress on Accounting 1929. New York, 1930 (Garland reprint, 1982).

*Jaedicke, Robert K., Yuji Ijiri, and Oswald Nielsen, eds. *Research in Accounting Measurement*. American Accounting Association, 1966 (Garland reprint, 1986).

Keats, Charles. *Magnificent Masquerade*. New York, 1964 (Garland reprint, 1982).

Kettle, Sir Russell. *Deloitte & Co. 1845–1956*. Oxford, 1958. *Bound with* Ernest Cooper. *Fifty-seven Years in an Accountant's Office*. London, 1921 (Garland reprint, 1982).

Kitchen, J., and R. H. Parker. *Accounting Thought and Education: Six English Pioneers*. London, 1980 (Garland reprint, 1984).

Lacey, Kenneth. *Profit Measurement and Price Changes*. London, 1952 (Garland reprint, 1982).

Lee, Chauncey. *The American Accomptant*. Lansingburgh, 1797 (Garland reprint, 1982).

Lee, T. A., and R. H. Parker. *The Evolution of Corporate Financial Reporting*. Middlesex, 1979 (Garland reprint, 1984).

*Malcolm, Alexander. *A Treatise of Book-Keeping, or, Merchants Accounts; In* *the Italian Method of Debtor and Creditor; Wherein the Fundamental Principles of That Curious and Approved Method Are Clearly and Fully Explained and Demonstrated . . . To Which Are Added, Instructions for Gentlemen of Land Estates, and Their Stewards or Factors: With Directions Also for Retailers, and Other More Private Persons.* London, 1731 (Garland reprint, 1986).

*Meij, J. L., ed. *Depreciation and Replacement Policy.* Chicago, 1961 (Garland reprint, 1986).

Newlove, George Hills. *Consolidated Balance Sheets.* New York, 1926 (Garland reprint, 1982).

*North, Roger. *The Gentleman Accomptant; or, An Essay to Unfold the Mystery of Accompts; By Way of Debtor and Creditor, Commonly Called Merchants Accompts, and Applying the Same to the Concerns of the Nobility and Gentry of England.* London, 1714 (Garland reprint, 1986).

Pryce-Jones, Janet E., and R. H. Parker. *Accounting in Scotland: A Historical Bibliography.* Edinburgh, 1976 (Garland reprint, 1984).

Robinson, H. W. *A History of Accountants in Ireland.* Dublin, 1964 (Garland reprint, 1984).

Robson, T. B. *Consolidated and Other Group Accounts.* London, 1950 (Garland reprint, 1982).

Rorem, C. Rufus. *Accounting Method.* Chicago, 1928 (Garland reprint, 1982).

*Saliers, Earl A., ed. *Accountants' Handbook.* New York, 1923 (Garland reprint, 1986).

Samuel, Horace B. *Shareholder's Money.* London, 1933 (Garland reprint, 1982).

The Securities and Exchange Commission in the Matter of McKesson & Robbins, Inc. Report on Investigation. Washington, D.C., 1940 (Garland reprint, 1982).

The Securities and Exchange Commission in the Matter of McKesson & Robbins, Inc. Testimony of Expert Witnesses. Washington, D.C., 1939 (Garland reprint, 1982).

*Shaplen, Robert. *Kreuger: Genius and Swindler.* New York, 1960 (Garland reprint, 1986).

Singer, H. W. *Standardized Accountancy in Germany. (With a new appendix.) Cambridge, 1943 (Garland reprint, 1982).*

The Sixth International Congress on Accounting. London, 1952 (Garland reprint, 1984).

*Stewart, Jas. C. (with a new introductory note by T. A. Lee). *Pioneers of a Profession: Chartered Accountants to 1879.* Edinburgh, 1977 (Garland reprint, 1986).

Thompson, Wardbaugh. *The Accomptant's Oracle: or, Key to Science, Being a Compleat Practical System of Book-keeping.* York, 1777 (Garland reprint, 1984).

*Vatter, William J. *Managerial Accounting.* New York, 1950 (Garland reprint, 1986).

*Woolf, Arthur H. *A Short History of Accountants and Accountancy.* London, 1912 (Garland reprint, 1986).

Yamey, B. S., H. C. Edey, and Hugh W. Thomson. *Accounting in England and Scotland: 1543–1800.* London, 1963 (Garland reprint, 1982).